M000113736

The Doctrines of Grace

THE
DOCTRINES
OF
GRACE

REDISCOVERING THE
EVANGELICAL GOSPEL

James Montgomery Boice
Philip Graham Ryken

CROSSWAY BOOKS

A PUBLISHING MINISTRY OF
GOOD NEWS PUBLISHERS
WHEATON, ILLINOIS

Library of Congress Cataloging-in-Publication Data
Boice, James Montgomery, 1938–2000
    The doctrines of grace : rediscovering the evangelical gospel
/ James Montgomery Boice, Philip Graham Ryken.
      p.   cm.
    Includes bibliographical references and index.
    ISBN 13: 978-1-58134-299-4
    ISBN 10: 1-58134-299-3 (HC : alk. paper)
    1. Calvinism. 2. Grace (Theology) I. Ryken, Philip Graham, 1966–
II. Title.
BX9422.3 B65   2002
230'.42—dc21   2001007701

RRDH		16	15	14	13	12	11	10	09	08	07
15	15	15	14	13	12	11	10	9	8	7	6

To HIM who loved us long ago,

Before we came to be,

Who left his throne for earth below

To save a wretch like me:

To HIM who freed us from our sin

By dying on the cross,

To make us whole without, within,

Redeemed from dreadful loss:

All praise to Christ from grateful men

Forevermore. Amen.

Contents

Foreword

I have often wondered how my ministry would change if I were to hear a prognosis from my physician that I had a terminal disease and only months or weeks left to live. Would I retire from active ministry to care solely for my own needs? Would I try to continue ministry with a renewed sense of urgency? Would my messages be more bold?

I don't know the answers to these questions. But I do know what Jim Boice did when the above scenario became real to him. From the day he learned he was dying of cancer to his actual demise, the span of time was a mere six weeks. Forty-two days. The last two of those weeks he was bedridden and extremely weak. While the virulent disease was sapping his strength daily, Dr. Boice called upon a reservoir of strength in his own soul, a strength quickened and sustained by the grace of God, to continue writing hymns and this present volume. He did not live long enough to see this work completed but was encouraged by the assurance that his colleague Dr. Philip Ryken would complete it for him.

As familiar as I am with Jim Boice's style and content, on a first reading I could not detect where Jim's writing ended and Phil's began. Of one thing I was sure: Jim did not write the last chapter. Yet in an earlier draft of chapter 2, in the midst of a treatment of Abraham Kuyper, reference was made to Kuyper's famous Stone Lectures at Princeton University in 1898. This reference was followed by the comment: "We shall return to the subject of these lectures in our final chapter." When I read this comment I wondered to whom the "we" and "our" referred. Was the plural used as a result of editing that occurred after Dr. Boice's death, indicating the joint project with Dr. Ryken? Or was this merely a case of Dr. Boice employing the editorial "we"? In the event, it was not God's will for Jim to pen the chapter promised.

It is no surprise to me that this final work from Jim Boice, who wrote literally scores of books over the course of his ministry, should focus on the doctrines of grace. Here was a man who not only believed in the doctrines of grace but also loved those doctrines and had fire in his bones about propagating them. I knew Jim Boice for more than thirty years and never saw that fire diminish. His soul was held captive by the doctrines of grace. His ministry was an ongoing doxology to the doctrines of grace because they so clearly manifest the God of that grace.

In this book Drs. Boice and Ryken not only provide a lucid and compelling exposition of the doctrines of grace but also provide a historical framework for their development. The book traces the historical impact of these biblical truths. It also makes bare the sad state of affairs that afflicts the church when these doctrines are denied or neglected.

In our day there remain many who still confess their belief in the doctrines of grace in particular and Reformed theology in general. Indeed, I think there are more academic institutions in America today that embrace Reformed theology than at any time in our nation's history. However, there are few that have a zeal and passion to propagate that faith.

James Montgomery Boice was not merely an adherent of Reformed theology or an admirer of the magisterial Reformers; he was himself a Reformer. His ministry at Tenth Presbyterian Church; the Philadelphia Conference on Reformed Theology; his writing ministry; his care for the inner city of Philadelphia; his statesmanship as a national Christian leader—all of these expressions of service flowed out of his love for the Reformed faith.

It is not surprising that the last literary work of James Boice would focus on his first love, the doctrines of grace. This work is not simply a tribute to Dr. Boice and his ministry—it is, at its core, a tribute to the grace of God, to whom belongs all the glory for our redemption. As Dr. Boice now enjoys the felicity of his eternal rest, we are left to work for the recovery of the Reformed faith in our time.

R. C. Sproul
Lent, 2001
Orlando, Florida

Preface

※

James Boice liked to finish what he started, so it is not surprising that in his final months he was working to complete two major projects. One was a book of *Hymns for a Modern Reformation*. The other was the present volume—a biblical, theological, historical, and practical presentation of the doctrines of grace.

When it became apparent that Dr. Boice would be unable to complete either of these projects himself, he entrusted them to colleagues on the staff of Philadelphia's Tenth Presbyterian Church. Dr. Paul Jones had written the music for the hymns, so it was natural for him to prepare the hymnal for publication. Then, during our last staff meeting together at the church before his death in June of 2000, Dr. Boice asked me to finish writing *The Doctrines of Grace*.

Fortunately, the volume was already half written. Not only had Dr. Boice prepared a complete outline for the book and determined the thesis for each chapter, but he had also written a full draft of the five chapters on the Five Points of Calvinism. These chapters form the middle section of the book (chapters 3 through 7). Here my only contributions have been some light stylistic editing and several small additions that integrate this section with the rest of the book.

Dr. Boice and I only had time for one brief discussion about the chapters that remained to be written. However, I was delighted to discover that for each of these chapters he had left behind notes containing ideas that he wanted to emphasize, quotations he hoped to use, books he intended to consult, and so forth. I have used as much of this material as possible, incorporating it into the overall flow of the book.

Chapter 1 is an introduction to the doctrines of grace. The sections entitled "The Doctrines of Grace," "The Five Points of Arminianism," and "The Five Points of Calvinism," are partly adapted from material Dr. Boice prepared for the New Members class at Tenth Church. As indicated in the text itself, "Today's False Gospel" is a summary of his argument in *Whatever Happened to the Gospel of Grace?* which was published by Crossway in 2001.

The main thesis of chapter 2 is the one that Dr. Boice wanted to advance, namely, that Calvinism is good for the church, and that its abandonment generally leads to liberalism. Also, the examples given are the ones that he intended to use: Calvin, Edwards, and Kuyper. In keeping with a suggestion I made to him in an earlier conversation, I have added a section on the Puritans. The closing analysis of current trends in evangelical theology is entirely my own, although I believe it is thoroughly consonant with Dr. Boice's views.

In some ways chapter 8 is the most important chapter in the book. James Boice wanted to portray the kind of Christianity that, in my view, he so ably represented: biblically based, theologically rigorous Calvinism that is also practically minded and kindly hearted. In accordance with the notes that were left for me, the chapter's basic outline comes from Al Martin's booklet *The Practical Implications of Calvinism.* I have done my best to convey what Dr. Boice so earnestly wanted to convey: the warmth and vitality of true Reformed spirituality.

The notes for chapter 9 were less extensive. Dr. Boice planned to draw from Kuyper's *Lectures on Calvinism,* but it was left for me to develop the implications of Reformed theology for church and culture. However, the final appeal to make a personal response to the doctrines of grace comes from Dr. Boice himself.

Readers will find that this is a polemical book. By this I mean that it argues for a theological position—Calvinism as set over against Arminianism. It is our conviction that evangelicalism is in desperate need of the best kind of Calvinism. It was Dr. Boice's intention for this book to mount a vigorous defense of Reformed theology while at the same time maintaining the highest standards of Christian charity. This has also been my intention. Readers will have to judge for themselves how well we have succeeded, which leads me to emphasize that while I wish to give my late colleague full acknowledgment for his part in writing this book, I also accept full responsibility for all of its shortcomings.

Many friends helped to complete this project. Randall Grossman, Michael Horton, Mark Noll, Richard Phillips, Jonathan Rockey, Leland Ryken, and R. C. Sproul reviewed the manuscript and made helpful suggestions for its improvement. Dr. Boice's personal assistant, Mary Beth McGreevy, made corrections for style, and Patricia Russell helped prepare the indexes. I am grateful to the session of Tenth Presbyterian Church for allowing sufficient study time to complete the book during the month prior to my installation as senior minister. I also thank Greg and Mary Berzinsky for providing a place for me to work free from distraction. Finally, here I express publicly what I communicated to James Montgomery Boice privately: thanksgiving to God for the extraordinary privilege of sharing with him in the preaching ministry of Tenth Church and of joining him in the defense of biblical orthodoxy.

Earlier I mentioned that Dr. Boice wrote *Hymns for a Modern Reformation*. Appropriate stanzas from these hymns appear at the beginning of each chapter. The complete hymns have been published by Tenth Presbyterian Church; hymnals and recordings may be ordered through the Alliance of Confessing Evangelicals at www.AllianceNet.org.

Philip Graham Ryken
Memorial Day, 2001
Philadelphia

Part One

The Doctrines of Grace

ONE

Why Evangelicalism
Needs Calvinism

How marvelous, how wise, how great,
How infinite to contemplate:
Jehovah's saving plan.
He saw me in my lost estate
Yet purposed to regenerate
This faithless, fallen man.

The world should realize with increased clearness that Evangelicalism stands or falls with Calvinism."[1] The great Princeton theologian Benjamin Breckinridge Warfield wrote those words a century ago. At the time, Calvinism still had a major influence on evangelicalism, helping to define its theology, shape its spirituality, and clarify its mission. That is no longer as true as it once was. Increasingly Calvinism is defined over against evangelicalism, and while many Calvinists still consider themselves evangelicals, most evangelicals are suspicious of Calvinism.

On a first reading, therefore, Warfield's claim seems excessive, and probably false. One doubts whether it would find widespread acceptance in the contemporary church. What has Calvinism to do with evangelicalism? And why would the vitality of the evangelical church in any way depend on Calvinist theology?

As surprising as it may seem, Warfield's claim is the thesis of this book, namely, that evangelicalism stands or falls with Calvinism. To put this in a slightly less provocative way, evangelicalism needs Calvinism. In order to see why this is so, it helps to remove the labels. By "Evangelicalism," Warfield essentially meant what German Lutherans meant when they first started using the term during the Protestant Reformation: a church founded on the gospel, the good news of salvation through the death and resurrection of Jesus Christ. And when Warfield spoke of "Calvinism," he was referring to the Protestant Reformation, with its insistence on justification by grace alone, through faith alone, because of Christ alone. To put it more simply, evangelicalism stands for the gospel and Calvinism stands for grace. What Warfield was really saying, therefore, is something that every Christian should and must believe: the gospel stands or falls by grace. As Warfield recognized, the gospel is not really the gospel unless it is a gospel of *grace*; in other words, the gospel is only good news if it announces what *God* has done to save sinners. And if that is true, then the gospel stands or falls with the doctrines of grace.

THE DOCTRINES OF GRACE

The doctrines of grace—these words are shorthand for five distinct Bible teachings that were linked together in response to the theology that developed in Holland in the late sixteenth century. This theology was associated with the name of Jacob Arminius (1560–1609). Arminius and his followers stressed the free and therefore self-determining will of man, which led them by a logical process to deny John Calvin's (1509–1564) doctrine of strict predestination, and especially the teaching that Jesus died only for the elect, those whom God had chosen. The Synod of Dort (1618–1619) was called to respond to the theological deviations of the Arminians, and from it came *The Canons of the Synod of Dort*, containing the classical summation of the five doctrines of grace known today as TULIP, or "The Five Points of Calvinism."

TULIP is an acrostic, the letters of which stand for the doctrines that were most in dispute: Total depravity, Unconditional election, Limited atonement, Irresistible grace, and the Perseverance of the saints. These are not the wisest or the most accurate ways of speaking about these doctrines; however, they are the most common way, and the acronym is a convenient handle for remembering them. These doctrines are important because they take confidence away from any spiritual good that might be thought to reside in man and instead anchor it in the will and power of God alone.

Although these doctrines constitute the purest expression of Calvinism, Calvin did not invent them, nor were they characteristic of his thought alone during the Reformation period. These truths are contained in the Old Testament Psalms. They were taught by Jesus, even to his enemies, as recorded in John 6 and 10 and elsewhere. The apostle Paul confirmed them in his letters to the Romans, the Ephesians, and others. Saint Augustine argued for the same truths over against the denials of Pelagius. Martin Luther was in many ways a Calvinist (as, in important respects, Calvin was a Lutheran). So were Ulrich Zwingli and William Tyndale. For this reason, it is perhaps more accurate to describe this theology as "Reformational" rather than "Calvinist." The Puritans were Reformed theologians, too, and it was through their teaching that England and Scotland experienced some of the greatest and most pervasive national revivals the world has ever seen. Among these Puritans were the heirs of the Scottish Reformer John Knox: Thomas Cartwright, Richard Sibbes, John Owen, John Bunyan, Matthew Henry, Thomas Boston, and many others. In America many thousands were influenced by Jonathan Edwards, Cotton Mather, and George Whitefield, all of whom were Calvinists.

In more recent times the modern missionary movement received its direction and initial impetus from those in the Reformed tradition. The list of these pioneers includes such great missionaries as William Carey, John Ryland, Henry Martyn, Robert Moffat, David Livingstone, John G. Paton, and John R. Mott. For all of these men, the doctrines of grace were not merely an appendage to Christian thought; rather, these were the central doctrines that fueled their evangelistic fires and gave form to their preaching of the gospel.

In short, the doctrines known as Calvinism did not emerge late in church history, but find their origins in the teaching of Jesus, which has been preserved throughout the church in many periods, and which has always been characteristic of the church at its greatest periods of faith and expansion. It follows from this that the evangelical church will again see great days when these truths are widely and fearlessly proclaimed. If that is true, then nothing is more needed today than a recovery of precisely these doctrines: total depravity, unconditional election, limited atonement, irresistible grace, and the perseverance of the saints (or, as they are identified in this book, radical depravity, unconditional election, particular redemption, efficacious grace, and persevering grace). These gracious doctrines have been prominent in the minds and hearts of God's people in some of the church's finest hours.

TODAY'S FALSE GOSPEL

Sadly, this is not the church's finest hour. We live in an age of weak theology and casual Christian conduct. Our knowledge is insufficient, our worship is irreverent, and our lives are immoral. Even the evangelical church has succumbed to the spirit of this age. *Whatever Happened to the Gospel of Grace?*—the book that serves as a prologue to the present volume—argued that the evangelical movement has lost its grip on the gospel.[2]

Perhaps the simplest way to say this is that evangelicalism has become *worldly*. This can be demonstrated by comparing it with yesterday's liberalism. What was once said of liberal churches must now be said of evangelical churches: they seek the world's wisdom, believe the world's theology, follow the world's agenda, and adopt the world's methods. According to the standards of worldly *wisdom*, the Bible is unable to meet the demands of life in these postmodern times. By itself, God's Word is insufficient to win people to Christ, promote spiritual growth, provide practical guidance, or transform society. So churches supplement the plain teaching of Scripture with entertainment, group therapy, political activism, signs and wonders—anything that promises to appeal to religious consumers. According to the world's *theology*, sin is merely a dysfunction and salvation means having better self-esteem. When this theology comes to church, it replaces difficult but essential doctrines like the propitiation of God's wrath with practical techniques for self-improvement. The world's *agenda* is personal happiness, so the gospel is presented as a plan for individual fulfillment rather than as a pathway of costly discipleship. The world's *methods* for accomplishing this self-centered agenda are necessarily pragmatic, so evangelical churches are willing to try whatever seems like it might work. This worldliness has produced the "new pragmatism" of evangelicalism.

Another way to explain what is wrong with the evangelical church is to identify major ideas in contemporary thought, and then see whether they have made any inroads into the church. *Whatever Happened to the Gospel of Grace?* identified six major cultural trends: secularism, humanism, relativism, materialism, pragmatism, and anti-intellectualism or "mindlessness." *Secularism* is the view that the universe is all there is; God and eternity are excluded. *Humanism* is the belief that—in the words of the ancient pagan philosophers—"Man is the measure of all things." This inevitably leads to the worship of self. *Relativism* teaches that because there is no God, there are no absolutes; truth is relative. *Materialism* is closely related to secularism. If nothing exists except the here-and-now, then the meaning of life can be found only in personal possessions. *Pragmatism* measures truth by its practical utility. What is right and true is whatever works. *Mindlessness* is the overall "dumbing down" of popular culture, the shrinking of the American mind, which television has done a great deal to accelerate. Most people have short attention spans, especially when it comes to discussing anything worthwhile or important. In the lyrics of one popular entertainer, "I'm not aware of too many things."

These are some of the prevailing trends in American culture at the dawn of the new millennium. If the church has become worldly, then we would expect to find these same attitudes in evangelical churches. And of course that is exactly what we do find. As surprising as it may sound, evangelicalism has become increasingly secular. In an effort to make newcomers feel comfortable, pastors teach as little theology as possible. Worship has become a form of popular entertainment rather than transcendent praise. New church buildings are designed to look more like office parks than houses of worship. All of these trends contribute to the secularization of what once was sacred.

At the same time, evangelical churches have become much more humanistic. This is inevitable: the less we talk about God, the more we talk about ourselves. Sermon content is determined more by the intended audience than by the sacred Scripture. This quickly leads to relativism in thought and conduct. Moral convictions are no longer determined by careful argument on the basis of biblical absolutes; they are uninformed choices based on personal feelings. The church is also materialistic. The evangelical attitude toward money is captured in the title of a book recently edited by Larry Eskridge and Mark Noll: *More Money, More Ministry*.[3] When financial prosperity becomes a significant priority, churches find themselves forced to figure out what works. This quest both derives from and results in the new pragmatism mentioned earlier. Most pastors want their churches to be bigger and better, but even if they are not better, it would be better if they were bigger! Not surprisingly, their parishioners want to be healthier and wealthier, too. Behind all these worldly attitudes there lurks a pervasive mindlessness, an unwillingness to think very seriously about anything, but especially Christian doctrine. Evangelicalism has become a religion of feeling rather than of thinking.

So when we ask the question, "Whatever happened to the gospel of grace?" the answer turns out to be that many evangelical churches have exchanged godliness for worldliness. This happens in too many ways to count, but "The Cambridge Declaration" includes a helpful summary: "As evangelical faith has become secularized, its interests have been blurred with those of the culture. The result is a loss of absolute values, permissive individualism, and a substitution of wholeness for holiness, recovery for repentance, intuition for truth, feeling for belief, chance for providence, and immediate gratification for enduring hope. Christ and his cross have moved from the center of our vision."[4] What happened to the grace of the gospel? It was lost in the church study, when the minister decided to give his people what they wanted rather than what they needed. It was lost in the Christian bookstore, somewhere between the self-help section and the aisle full of Jesus merchandise. And it was lost in our minds and hearts when we decided to accept the world's theology of human achievement, saving room for our own personal contribution to salvation.

What has replaced the gospel of grace is a message that is partially biblical but ultimately self-centered. Like everything else in creation, the human soul abhors a vacuum. When something essential disappears from our theology and our spirituality, something else rushes in to replace it. When God himself disappears, what replaces him is the self. To quote again from "The Cambridge Declaration," "Unwarranted confidence in human ability is a product of the fallen human nature. This false confidence now fills the evangelical world—from the self-esteem gospel to the health and wealth gospel, from those who have transformed the gospel into a product to be sold and sinners into consumers who want to buy, to others who treat Christian faith as being true simply because it works."

One place to observe this misplaced confidence in human ability is in the area of Christian witness, where a self-centered gospel has produced a self-absorbed evangelism. When evangelicals think of evangelism, rather than thinking first of the gospel message they are prone to think of a particular response to that message. This perhaps explains why testimonies of saving faith tend to emphasize personal experience rather than the person and work of Jesus Christ. However, as J. I. Packer warned in his book *Evangelism and the Sovereignty of God,* there is an inherent danger in defining evangelism "in terms of an effect achieved in the lives of others; which amounts to saying that the essence of evangelizing is producing converts."[5] Such an approach inevitably turns evangelism into another form of pragmatism. However, the essence of evangelism does not lie in the results; it rests in the message itself—the good news of salvation in the death and resurrection of Jesus Christ. This is not to say that the gospel message does not demand a response. Of course it does. But that response is not the work of the evangelist; it is the work of God, and this is most clearly understood when the presentation of the gospel is grounded in the doctrines of grace.

It is sometimes thought that the Five Points of Calvinism tend to dull one's passion for sharing the gospel. This view is mistaken, both in its understanding of Calvinism and in its understanding of evangelism. The truth is exactly the opposite, namely, that the doctrines of grace establish the most solid foundation and provide the most enduring motivation for the most effective proclamation of the gospel. As we shall see, only thoroughly biblical convictions about divine election, particular redemption, and irresistible grace give confidence that the gospel has the power actually to accomplish God's saving purpose.

One of the brightest examples of better evangelism through Calvinism was the nineteenth-century preacher Charles Haddon Spurgeon. Spurgeon was one of the greatest evangelists England has ever seen, as well as one of the country's staunchest defenders of the doctrines of grace. He wrote:

> I have my own private opinion that there is no such thing as preaching Christ and him crucified unless we preach what is nowadays called Calvinism. It is a nickname to call it Calvinism; Calvinism is the Gospel and nothing else. I do not believe we can preach the Gospel . . . unless we preach the sovereignty of God in his dispensation of grace; nor unless we exalt the electing, unchangeable, eternal, immutable, conquering love of Jehovah; nor do I think we can preach the Gospel unless we base it upon the special and particular redemption of his elect and chosen people which Christ wrought out upon the cross; nor can I comprehend the Gospel which allows saints to fall away after they are called.[6]

If Spurgeon was right, then Warfield was right, too: evangelicalism stands or falls with Calvinism. Or to restate our thesis, the doctrines of grace preserve the gospel of grace.

THE FIVE POINTS OF ARMINIANISM

The heart of this book is an exposition of the doctrines of grace from Holy Scripture. But before giving a thorough biblical defense of these doctrines, it may prove useful to offer a brief overview summarizing the theological issues at stake whenever we consider God's grace in the gospel.

Although the doctrines of grace have been taught throughout the history of the church, the so-called Five Points of Calvinism were developed in response to the theology of Jacob Arminius. Arminius taught systematic theology at the University of Leyden. In 1610, the year after the professor died, his followers drew up five articles of faith that summarized his understanding of salvation. The Arminians, as they came to be called, presented these doctrines to the state of Holland in the form of a protest (or Remonstrance), arguing that the Dutch confessions should be amended to conform to their views. Here are the five planks of their theological platform:

> *Article I:* That God, by an eternal unchangeable purpose in Jesus Christ his Son, before the foundation of the world, hath determined, out of the fallen, sinful race of men, to save in Christ, for Christ's sake, and through Christ, those who, through the grace of the Holy Ghost, shall believe on this his Son Jesus, and shall persevere in this faith and obedience of faith, through this grace, even to the end. . . .

> *Article II:* That, agreeably thereto, Jesus Christ, the Saviour of the world, died for all men and for every man, so that he has obtained for them all, by his death on the cross, redemption and the forgiveness of sins; yet that no one actually enjoys this forgiveness of sins except the believer. . . .

> *Article III:* That man has not saving grace of himself, nor of the energy of his free will, inasmuch as he, in the state of apostasy and sin, can of and by himself neither think, will, nor do any thing that is truly good (such as saving Faith eminently is); but that it is needful that he be born again of God in Christ, through his Holy Spirit, and renewed in understanding, inclination, or will, and all his powers, in order that he may rightly understand, think, will, and effect what is truly good. . . .

> *Article IV:* That this grace of God is the beginning, continuance, and accomplishment of all good, even to this extent, that the regenerate man himself, without prevenient or assisting, awakening, following and co-operative grace can neither think, will, nor do good, nor withstand any temptations to evil; so that all good deeds or movements, that can be conceived, must be ascribed to the grace of God in Christ. But as respects the mode of the operation of this grace, it is not irresistible. . . .

Article V: That those who are incorporated into Christ by a true faith, and thereby become partakers of his life-giving Spirit, have thereby full power to strive against Satan, sin, the world, and their own flesh, and to win the victory; it being well understood that it is ever through the assisting grace of the Holy Ghost; and that Jesus Christ assists them through his Spirit in all temptations. . . . But whether they are capable, through negligence, of forsaking again the first beginnings of their life in Christ, of again returning to this present evil world, of turning away from the holy doctrine which was delivered them, of losing a good conscience, of becoming devoid of grace, that must be more particularly determined out of the Holy Scripture, before we ourselves can teach it with the full persuasion of our minds.[7]

These articles may be summarized as follows: "I. God elects or reproves on the basis of foreseen faith or unbelief. II. Christ died for all men and for every man, although only believers are saved. III. Man is so depraved that divine grace is necessary unto faith or any good deed. IV. This grace may be resisted. V. Whether all who are truly regenerate will certainly persevere in the faith is a point which needs further investigation."[8]

What these statements hold in common is an uncertainty about, and in some places a resistance to, God's absolute sovereignty in grace. At the heart of the Arminian position lies the insistence that divine sovereignty must somehow be accommodated to human capability. Election and reprobation are not divine decrees; they are based on human choices. The efficacy of the atonement does not rest on Christ's saving work alone but also on the sinner's faith and repentance. Although God's grace is attractive and persuasive, it is not powerful enough to triumph over those who stubbornly resist his love. And whether or not a Christian will persevere to the very end is open to question, because perseverance ultimately depends on the Christian rather than on Christ. Although these are distinct doctrinal issues, they are linked by a common concern to downplay predestination so as to allow human beings to determine their own spiritual destiny.

The Arminian Remonstrance produced a storm of theological

controversy, culminating in the Synod of Dort, an international conference on Reformed doctrine. As the delegates met over the course of seven months, their debates served to clarify the Arminian position. Despite some reassurances to the contrary, the Reformed delegates eventually concluded that Arminianism could not avoid the following theological implications:

1. *Human ability.* Human nature has been damaged by the Fall, but not totally disabled. Even if we are not basically good, at least we are not completely bad. The will is not enslaved to sin, but is capable of believing in Christ, even prior to regeneration (although not entirely apart from God's grace). Thus every sinner retains the ability to choose for or against God, either cooperating with God's Spirit unto salvation or resisting God's grace unto damnation.

2. *Conditional election.* God's choice to save certain individuals was based on foreseen faith, on his ability to know in advance that they would freely believe the gospel. Election is conditional in that it is ultimately determined by individual choice: the only people God has chosen are those whom he already knew would believe. Furthermore, the faith that he foresees is not exclusively a divine gift but partly a human decision. Therefore, the ultimate cause of salvation is not God's choice of the sinner but the sinner's choice of God.

3. *Indefinite atonement.* Christ's work on the Cross makes salvation possible for everyone but not actual for anyone in particular. Although the crucifixion enabled God to grant forgiveness, this is given only on the condition of personal faith. Christ died for each and every person; however, only those who believe will be saved. Thus the atonement only becomes effective if and when someone chooses to accept it.

4. *Resistible grace.* Everyone who hears the gospel is called to faith in Christ, not only outwardly but also inwardly. The Spirit speaks to every heart, doing everything he can to persuade the sinner to trust in Christ. However, sinners are able to resist the Holy Spirit, and they will not be regenerated unless and until they repent. To put this another

way, the Spirit's application of Christ's saving work is contingent on the sinner's prior acceptance of the gospel. The Holy Spirit cannot impart new spiritual life unless the sinner is willing to receive it.

5. *Defectible grace.* Those who believe in Christ and are truly saved nevertheless can fully and finally lose their salvation by falling away from their faith. Eternal life is not secure when a sinner comes to Christ, but depends on the Christian's faithfulness to Christ until death.

There are different versions of Arminian theology, and not all Arminians would agree with all five of the preceding doctrines, at least as they are described here. However, the previous summary expresses what many evangelicals believe today. And what all five of these doctrines share is the insistence that the sovereignty of God's grace must in some way be limited by the freedom of human choice. Regeneration, election, atonement, glorification: the efficacy of these central acts of salvation does not depend on God alone but also on the cooperation of fallen sinners. In their study of *The Five Points of Calvinism,* David Steele and Curtis Thomas conclude that for the Arminian, "Salvation is accomplished through the combined efforts of *God* (who takes the initiative) and *man* (who must respond)—man's response being the determining factor. God has provided salvation for everyone, but His provision becomes effective only for those who, of their own free will, 'choose' to cooperate with Him and accept His offer of grace. At the crucial point, man's will plays a decisive role; thus *man,* not God, determines who will be the recipients of the gift of salvation."[9]

This helps explain why Arminian theologies are so prevalent in contemporary evangelicalism. For Arminianism, human decision making holds a central place in salvation. This results in a theology that is not exclusively God-centered but is distorted in the direction of the self. And of course this is what the spirit of the age demands. In these postmodern and increasingly post-Christian times, people are clamoring for attention. They are looking for spiritual experiences that are secularized, humanized, and relativized. Arminianism supplies exactly what today's evangelicalism demands: a gospel that preserves a determinative role for personal choice.

THE FIVE POINTS OF CALVINISM

By contrast, Calvinism insists that salvation is by grace from beginning to end. Salvation is a gift, in every sense of the word—God's gift for undeserving sinners who cannot be redeemed apart from God's saving grace. The gift is given to those to whom God chooses to give it; and although it is *offered* to everyone, it is not *given* to everyone. When God does choose to grant this gift, however, he effectively places it in the hands of his child; and once it is received, it can never be lost, stolen, or damaged. Truly, it is the gift that keeps on giving!

These gracious principles were defined and defended in *The Canons of the Synod of Dort*. As mentioned previously, an international team of theologians met at Dort to consider the Arminian position. Their deliberations resulted in a series of carefully worded doctrinal propositions that represented a century of mature theological and practical reflection on the great truths of the Reformation. In short, the Synod concluded that the decrees of election and reprobation were based on God's sovereign choice rather than on foreseen faith or unbelief; that although Christ's death was sufficient for all, it was efficient only for the elect; that humanity was totally corrupted by the Fall, and thus unable to choose salvation prior to regeneration; that God's grace is effective to convert the unbeliever; and that God so preserves believers that they can never totally fall from grace. These five basic points can be organized as follows:

1. *Total depravity.* The words "total depravity" are not the best way of speaking about the doctrine of utterly pervasive sin, or man's inability in spiritual things, because they suggest that we are all as bad as we can be and that everyone is equally sinful. That is not true, of course. Some sin more than others and will suffer greater punishment in hell for their sins. As theologian John Gerstner used to say, we are not as bad as we could be, because in each of us there is infinite room for *de*provement!

Rather than signifying that the unregenerate person is wholly evil in everything he does, total depravity teaches that nothing he does is ever completely good. Sin has pervaded every part of our physical, mental, and emotional makeup so that there is nothing about us that remains untouched by sin. In the interests of accuracy, therefore, it is better to speak of *radical* depravity, comprehensive iniquity, or the pervasiveness of sin. Our motives are never entirely pure, and thus to one extent or another all our actions are corrupted by evil desires. This corruption invades every aspect of our being, so that nothing we are or do is completely free from sin.

In this sad and pervasively sinful state we have no inclination to seek God, and therefore *cannot* seek him or even respond to the gospel when it is presented to us. In our unregenerate state, we do not have free will so far as "believing on" or "receiving" Jesus Christ as Savior is concerned. In fact, such is our slavery to sin that we cannot understand our need of Christ until God first gives us spiritual understanding. Even faith must come as a gift, because prior to the regenerating work of the Holy Spirit our depravity renders us impotent to cooperate with God's saving grace.

2. *Unconditional election.* If the condition of the human race is as bad as the biblical doctrine of depravity indicates, then salvation must originate with God. It must be a work of the triune God, accomplished and applied by him without any assistance on our part. Since we are never going to seek him, he is going to have to reach out to us and save us (if, in fact, we are to be saved). And this is what God does. The first step in this reaching out is God's determination to do it, which is what the word *election* refers to. It means that what happens in an individual's salvation is determined by the prior decision of God, who established the decrees of salvation in Christ before the world began. "Unconditional" indicates that this decision is made apart from anything God might foresee in the sinful creature. If election were based on anything that the sinner might be or do, then ultimately salvation would depend on human merit. But in order to prove that salvation is all of grace, election is a loving act of God's sovereign will. Faith in Christ is not the cause of election but one of its results.

3. *Limited atonement.* Of the five doctrines summarized by the TULIP acrostic, the most difficult for most people to understand and accept is limited atonement. Part of the problem is the terminology itself, because here the words really are misleading. "Limited" atonement suggests that somehow the death of Christ did not do all that it could do or ought to do, that it was ineffective in some way. That is not what the doctrine of limited atonement is meant to affirm, however. What Reformed people want to say by these words is that the atonement had a specific object in view, namely, the salvation of those whom the Father had given the Son before the foundation of the world, and that it was effective in saving those persons. Thus it would be better to call this doctrine *definite* atonement, or particular redemption.

Particular redemption signifies that the death of Christ has saving efficacy for the elect, and for the elect only. Christ made satisfaction for sin when he died on the Cross, offering himself as the perfect substitute for God's chosen people. Therefore, according to the plan of salvation, Christ's death atoned for the sins of the elect but not for the sins of those who never come to him in faith.

4. *Irresistible grace.* Somehow the benefits of the atonement must be applied to the elect. This is the work of the Holy Spirit, whose inward operation enables sinners to repent and believe in Christ. In addition to the outward call of the gospel, made to everyone, the Holy Spirit issues an inward call. This inward calling is made only to the elect and inevitably draws them to faith in Christ. Because God is sovereign in their salvation, it is not possible for them permanently or effectively to reject this effectual calling. God's grace is irresistible and invincible; the Spirit never fails to accomplish his saving purpose in the mind, the heart, and the will of God's chosen people. This is how the Westminster Confession of Faith describes the Spirit's gracious, efficacious work: "All those whom God hath predestinated unto life, and those only, he is pleased, in his appointed and accepted time, effectually to call, by his Word and Spirit, out of that state of sin and death in which they are by nature, to grace and salvation by Jesus Christ; enlightening their minds spiritually and savingly to understand the things of God; taking away their heart of stone, and giving

unto them an heart of flesh; renewing their wills, and by his almighty power determining them to that which is good, and effectually drawing them to Jesus Christ; yet so as they come most freely, being made willing by his grace" (Chap. 10, Sec. 1).

5. *The perseverance of the saints.* Sometimes this doctrine is called the doctrine of "eternal security." It has two parts: 1) that God perseveres with his people, and 2) that because God perseveres with his people, they also persevere. The saints are simply the people of God, those whom God considers holy through the work of his Son. The perseverance of the saints really is the *preservation* of the saints, for their perseverance depends on God's preserving grace. It is the faithfulness of Christ, rather than the faithfulness of the Christian, that brings the saints to glory.

Each of these five doctrines makes a unique contribution to our understanding of God's grace. Each can be analyzed separately and also defended separately, as we shall see. However, these five doctrines are logically and theologically interrelated. They all serve to emphasize the grace of God in salvation. Warfield wrote,

Now these Five Points form an organic unity, a single body of truth. They are based on two presuppositions that Scripture abundantly supports. The first presupposition is the complete impotence of man, and the second is God's absolute sovereignty in grace. Everything else follows. The meeting place of these two foundation truths is the heart of the Gospel, for it follows that if man is totally depraved, the grace of God in saving him must of necessity be sovereign. Otherwise, man will inevitably refuse it in his depravity, and will remain unredeemed."[10]

The doctrines of grace stand or fall together, and together they point to one central truth: salvation is all of grace because it is all of God; and because it is all of God, it is all for his glory.

To fully appreciate the glory of God in the doctrines of grace, it helps to recognize the role of each person of the Trinity in the Five

Points of Calvinism. Election is the choice of God the Father. The atonement is the sacrifice of God the Son. The grace that draws us to Christ and enables us to persevere to the very end is the work of God the Holy Spirit. Thus salvation is all God's work from beginning to end—the coordinated work of the triune God—as it must be, if we are to be saved. Consider: if we are actually dead in our sins (radical depravity), then only God could choose us in Christ (unconditional election), only Christ could atone for our sins (particular redemption), and only the Spirit could draw us to Christ (efficacious grace) and preserve us in him (persevering grace). Therefore, all praise and glory belong to God alone: "For from him and through him and to him are all things. To him be the glory forever!" (Rom. 11:36).

TO GOD ALONE BE THE GLORY

Even this brief summary of the doctrines of grace is sufficient to reveal what is at stake in the conflict between Calvinism and Arminianism. Ultimately it is our view of God. Does he dispose everything—including everything that pertains to our salvation—for his own glory, or not? The starting point for any system of doctrine ought to be the greater glory of God. This is why, in and of themselves, the Five Points are not the heart of Calvinism; they simply serve to explain distinctive aspects of Reformed soteriology (i.e., the theology of salvation). However, all five points do *flow* from the heart of Calvinism, which is a passion for God's glory. Each doctrine draws attention away from what human beings can accomplish, in order to declare, "Salvation is of the LORD" (Jonah 2:9, KJV).

With its emphasis on the glory of God in salvation, Calvinism can help evangelicalism mature by restoring a proper view of God's majesty.[11] A large part of the problem in the church today is that our contemplation of God is not sufficiently or properly elevated. As Thomas Schreiner and Bruce Ware write in their book on divine sovereignty:

> Ours is a culture in which the tendency is to exalt what is human and diminish what is divine. Even in evangelical circles, we find increasingly attractive a view of God in which

God is one of us, as it were, a partner in the unfolding drama of life. But lost in much of this contemporary evangelical theology is the full omniscience, omnipotence, splendor, greatness, supremacy, rulership, and unqualified lordship of God. In contrast, the vision of God affirmed in these pages [their book, *Still Sovereign*] is of One who reigns supreme over all, whose purposes are accomplished without fail, and who directs the course of human affairs, including the central drama of saving a people for the honor of his name, all with perfect holiness and matchless grace.[12]

This is one place where the doctrines of grace can help us, because together they show that God really does save sinners. We are dead in our sins, and therefore can do nothing to save ourselves, but together the Father, the Son, and the Holy Spirit have done and will continue to do everything that is necessary for our salvation: choosing, redeeming, calling, and preserving. Thus the one point of Calvinism that the Five Points aim to demonstrate (and which Arminianism tends to deny) is that every aspect of salvation is the absolutely gracious work of the totally sovereign God. To him be the glory forever!

Having a high view of God means something more than giving glory to God, however; it means giving glory to God *alone*. This is the difference between Calvinism and Arminianism. While the former declares that God alone saves sinners, the latter gives the impression that God enables sinners to have some part in saving themselves. Calvinism presents salvation as the work of the triune God—election by the Father, redemption in the Son, calling by the Spirit. Furthermore, each of these saving acts is directed toward the elect, thereby infallibly securing their salvation. By contrast, Arminianism views salvation as something that God makes possible but that man makes actual. This is because the saving acts of God are directed toward *different* persons: the Son's redemption is for humanity in general; the Spirit's calling is only for those who hear the gospel; narrower still, the Father's election is only for those who believe the gospel. Yet in none of these cases (redemption, calling, or election) does God *actually* secure the salvation of even one single sinner![13] The inevitable result is that rather than depending exclusively on divine grace, salvation depends partly on a human response. So although Arminianism is willing to give God the glory, when it comes to salvation, it is unwilling to give him *all* the glory. It divides the glory between heaven and earth, for if what ultimately makes the difference between being saved and being lost is man's ability to choose God, then to just that extent God is robbed of his glory. Yet God himself has said, "I will not yield my glory to another" (Isa. 48:11).

Here many Arminians will wish to demur, protesting that they really *do* want to give God all the glory. And with good reason: every true Christian recoils at the thought of claiming any personal merit, and wants instead to give God all the praise. A striking illustration of this comes from an encounter between Charles Simeon and John Wesley. Simeon preached generally Calvinist doctrine at Cambridge. Wesley, of course, was a famous evangelist well known for his opposition to Calvinism. As Wesley indicates in his journal, the two men met on December 20, 1784. Simeon recorded their conversation, in which he began to question Wesley concerning his theology of salvation:

> "Sir, I understand that you are called an Arminian; and I have been sometimes called a Calvinist; and therefore I suppose we are to draw daggers. But before I consent to begin the combat, with your permission I will ask you a few questions. . . . Pray, Sir, do you feel yourself a depraved creature, so depraved that you would never have thought of turning to God, if God had not first put it into your heart?"
>
> "Yes," says [Wesley], "I do indeed."
>
> "And do you utterly despair of recommending yourself to God by anything you can do; and look for salvation solely through the blood and righteousness of Christ?"
>
> "Yes, solely through Christ."
>
> "But, Sir, supposing you were at first saved by Christ, are you not somehow or other to save yourself afterwards by your own works?"
>
> "No, I must be saved by Christ from first to last."
>
> "Allowing, then, that you were first turned by the grace of God, are you not in some way or other to keep yourself by your own power?"

"No."

"What, then, are you to be upheld every hour and every moment by God, as much as an infant in its mother's arms?"

"Yes, altogether."

"And is all your hope in the grace and mercy of God to preserve you unto His heavenly kingdom?"

"Yes, I have no hope but in Him."

"Then, Sir, with your leave I will put up my dagger again; for this is all my Calvinism; this is my election, my justification by faith, my final perseverance: it is in substance all that I hold, and as I hold it; and therefore, if you please, instead of searching out terms and phrases to be a ground of contention between us, we will cordially unite in those things wherein we agree."[14]

Wesley was hardly a Calvinist, but perhaps it may be said that he was a Calvinist at heart. He instinctively recognized the truth of a principle that he had not yet worked into his theology with complete consistency, namely, that sinners contribute nothing to their own salvation—it is God's work from beginning to end. He knew that in order for the gospel to be a gospel of grace it must be all of grace.

Is there anything that we can contribute to our salvation? Only the sin from which we need to be saved, for we are the objects of divine grace. Yet the constant temptation is to slip the human element back into the equation. Theologians call this "synergism," a term that comes from the Greek words *syn*, meaning "with," and *ergos*, meaning "work." In theology, synergism is the belief that we work together with God to accomplish and apply our salvation. But this is fatal to any sound doctrine of salvation, for it has the inevitable result of increasing the place of man and thus diminishing the glory of God in salvation.

To prove this point, Arthur Custance rehearsed Martin Luther's debate with his friend and protégé Philip Melanchthon. Especially in his later years, Melanchthon argued that even if a sinner cannot contribute anything positive to his salvation, at least he does not resist God's grace when it comes. This "non-resistance" may seem like a very small contribution, certainly too small to make much difference. However, Luther warned that this "very little" was actually more dangerous than the "very much" that the Pelagians demanded when they argued that man was wholly capable of meriting God's grace. What made it dangerous was its subtlety. After all, what was the harm in adding just a little bit of human effort to the work of God? But Luther recognized that this was tantamount to the error of Roman Catholicism, which insisted that the will of man is the decisive factor in salvation. He also recognized that the leaven of synergism eventually works its way through the entire loaf of soteriology.

What was at issue then—and what remains at issue today—was the Reformation principle of *sola gratia,* by grace alone. To add anything at all to God's grace is to destroy its graciousness, its very nature as a gift. This leads Custance to conclude,

> The difference between a monergistic and a synergistic faith, between a *God only* and a *God and* Gospel, is nothing less than the difference between the Gospel of our Lord and Savior Jesus Christ on the one hand, and all other religious systems of belief . . . on the other. There are basically only two alternatives. If man contributes any essential part towards his salvation, he effectively becomes his own savior. . . .
>
> There is here a clear point of demarcation. It is all of God or it is not good news at all. If man is free to resist, God is not free to act, for He is bound by man's freedom. If God is to be free to act, man must be bound by the will of God. . . . But in a fallen world, God's grace must be irresistible or man's will can remain forever opposed to God, and the will of the creature overrides the will of the Creator.
>
> In truth there is no "Gospel" that is not entirely rooted in the sovereignty of God's grace in salvation, which is the sum and substance of Calvinism. . . . The crucial issue is the sovereignty of God's grace. . . .
>
> The only defense against Synergism is an unqualified Calvinism ascribing all the glory to God by insisting upon the total spiritual impotence of man, an Election based solely upon the good pleasure of God, an Atonement intended only

for the elect though sufficient for all men, a grace that can neither be resisted nor earned, and a security for the believer that
is as permanent as God Himself.[15]

In other words, the only defense against a doctrine of salvation
that exalts humanity—and thus the only hope for evangelicalism—is
a thoroughgoing Calvinism. To receive the grace of the gospel as God's
grace, we must recover the doctrines of grace.

TWO

What Calvinism Does
in History

We face death for God each day;
What can pluck us from his way?
Let God's people ever say,
Nothing. Hallelujah!

The real question, of course, is whether or not the doctrines of grace are taught in the Bible. If they are biblical doctrines, then they ought to be defended and applied; otherwise, they should be rejected and repudiated. However, before examining the biblical evidence for these doctrines, it may prove useful to consider the influence they have had on Christian history. If Calvinism is biblical, then we should expect to discover that the church has flourished whenever the doctrines of grace have been taught and practiced. By contrast, we should expect to discover that wherever and whenever these doctrines have come under assault, the church has suffered spiritual, moral, and social decline.

Church history is never that simple, of course. There are many threads in the fabric of time, and it is often difficult to determine the pattern of divine providence. God tends to do more than one thing at a time, which makes it hard to decide what lessons are to be learned from any particular moment in history. Nevertheless, the history of the church is instructive, even edifying, and one way to test the mettle of a theology is to examine the record of its practical effect.

When we apply this method to the doctrines of grace, we find ample evidence to support the claim that Calvinism can have a salutary influence on the life of the church. In this chapter we consider four noteworthy examples from history—thriving Christian communities shaped by a commitment to the sovereignty of God's grace. We will also see what happens when Reformed theology is set aside: the pathway from Calvinism to Arminianism often leads to liberalism. Our purpose in tracing this history is to demonstrate not only the usefulness of the doctrines of grace but also the high cost of abandoning them.

CALVIN'S GENEVA: A GODLY COMMONWEALTH

The place to begin is Geneva, which prior to the Reformation was infamous for its immorality. Among the wealthy city's common vices were drunkenness, disorderly conduct, gambling, prostitution, and adultery. On occasion, Genevans had been known to run naked through the streets singing vulgar and even blasphemous songs. Unfair business practices, such as usury, were common. The city was also troubled by dissension in the form of what one observer described as "ungodly and dangerous factions."

It was hoped that all of the violence and debauchery would cease in the 1530s, when Geneva's governing body voted to make a permanent break with Roman Catholicism and to align the city-state with the churches of the Protestant Reformation. What needed reforming was not simply the city's worship and theology but its entire moral atmosphere. To that end, the Council of Two Hundred passed civic ordinances designed to promote the Protestant religion and restrain public indecency. However, they quickly discovered how difficult it is to legislate morality. In the absence of strong enforcement, the laws themselves made little difference, and Geneva's moral decadence generally went unchecked.

To their credit, the Council recognized that moral transformation would not occur without biblical proclamation, and they decided to hire a better minister. In August of 1536, a brilliant young scholar named John Calvin passed through Geneva on his way to Strasbourg.

He was collared by William Farel, a Reformer in his own right, who recognized that Calvin had both the pastoral gifts and the personal resolve to further the Reformation in Geneva. Calvin got off to a slow start, however, finding on his arrival that the city was in even greater chaos and disorder than he expected. Moreover, his preaching proved to be unpopular, especially when he insisted that in order to exercise its own God-given authority, the church needed to be free of secular control. Within two years Calvin was relieved of his pastoral duties and banished to Strasbourg. Yet the citizens of Geneva found that they could ill afford to do without him, and in 1541 they clamored for his restoration.

Understandably, Calvin was reluctant to resume pastoral ministry in a place where he had experienced both ridicule and rejection, yet he sensed that God was calling him back to Geneva. This time he insisted that the church be governed by a proper constitution, accepted on oath by the citizens. The *Ecclesiastical Ordinances,* as they were called, granted the city's pastors and elders full authority to regulate the worship and discipline of the Genevan church. Armed with this new authority, Calvin resumed his rigorous schedule of preaching and teaching. In addition to preaching twice on Sunday, he preached on average several mornings a week and also gave biblical and theological lectures to students preparing for pastoral ministry.

What Calvin preached, of course, was the Bible—verse by verse, chapter by chapter, and book by book. As he followed this method of consecutive Bible exposition, he eventually produced commentaries on nearly the entire Bible. His doctrinal framework was the theology of the Reformation, as summarized in his famous *Institutes of the Christian Religion.* To put this another way, Calvin was a Calvinist. He taught each of the doctrines later defended at the Synod of Dort, from the totality of depravity to the certainty of persevering grace. Absolute predestination—the doctrine that "God, by his eternal and unchanging will, determined once and for all those whom he would one day admit to salvation"—held an especially important place in Calvin's theology.[1] Some scholars question whether he believed in definite atonement, a doctrine that was not fully clarified until the seventeenth century, when it came under Arminian attack. However, there is no doubt that Calvin believed that Christ's death on the Cross actually achieved what it was designed to accomplish: the redemption of the elect. Nor is there any doubt that he maintained the efficacy of God's grace in the effectual calling of God's Spirit. At every point in his theology, Calvin insisted that salvation is a gift of divine grace rather than an achievement of human effort. The whole aim of his theology, especially his soteriology, was to glorify God for his sovereign grace. His own dependence on God's sovereignty is perhaps best expressed in his famous prayer: "When I remember that I am not my own, I offer up my heart, presented as a sacrifice to the Lord."

Calvin and his Calvinism came to exercise a profound influence on the city of Geneva. This influence did not come through coercion, as is sometimes thought, but primarily through persuasion. Oxford historian and theologian Alister McGrath writes:

> Calvin was no Genevan dictator, ruling the population with a rod of iron. He was not even a citizen of Geneva throughout his time there, and was thus denied access to political authority. His status was simply that of a pastor who was in no position to dictate to the magisterial authorities who administered the city. Indeed, those authorities retained to the end the right to dismiss Calvin, even if they chose not to exercise that right. As a member of the Consistory, he was certainly able to make representations to the magistracy on behalf of the ministers—representations which were frequently ignored, however. . . . Calvin's influence over Geneva rested ultimately not in his formal legal standing (which was insignificant) but in his considerable personal authority as a preacher and pastor.[2]

Daily exposure to Calvin's sound exposition of the Bible transformed the mind and heart of Geneva. The citizens embraced their election as the people of God and their calling to build a holy city. Their motto became *post tenebras lux*—"after darkness, light." As they learned to worship the God of grace, especially through the singing of psalms, Geneva became a happier city. It also became a more wholesome city. In an effort to eliminate drunkenness and adultery, the taverns were closed and the public bathhouse was divided so that men and women could bathe separately. Geneva became a cleaner and safer city. Examples of this include Calvin's own design for a civic sewer system and his insistence that parents protect their children by installing railings around their balconies.

As Calvin's reputation grew, Geneva became a refuge for Protestants fleeing religious persecution elsewhere in Europe. In order to care for these refugees, Calvin established a fund for Christian hospitality. He also organized a diaconate to care for the needs of the poor, who were given opportunities to perform useful labor in the manufacture of clothing. Geneva also became a smarter city, as Calvin established a school—the famous Geneva Academy—to serve as a center for academic excellence. This was in keeping with his goal of universal Christian education (including a school for girls). The Academy helped Geneva become a center for missions: many of the pastors trained there were sent to evangelize France by planting new churches.

In addition to undertaking all of these social measures, Calvin set up a system for the spiritual care of church members. The pastors and elders who formed the Consistory met weekly to resolve disputes and to discipline parishioners who were caught in sin. Depending on the situation, these meetings could serve as a form of conflict-resolution or family counseling. When formal discipline was required, its goal was to encourage genuine repentance. In time, the effect of the Consistory's disciplinary work was a drastic reduction in public immorality.

As a result of these reforms, Geneva became a city for God's glory. One historian summarizes the extent to which Calvin realized his goal of a godly commonwealth:

> Cleanliness was practically unknown in towns of his generation and epidemics were common and numerous. He moved the Council to make permanent regulations for establishing sanitary conditions and supervision of markets. Beggars were prohibited from the streets, but a hospital and poorhouse were provided and well conducted. Calvin labored zealously for the education of all classes and established the famous

Academy, whose influence reached all parts of Europe and even to the British Isles. He urged the council to introduce the cloth and silk industry and thus laid the foundation for the temporal wealth of Geneva. This industry . . . proved especially successful in Geneva because Calvin, through the gospel, created within the individual the love of work, honesty, thrift and cooperation. He taught that capital was not an evil thing, but the blessed result of honest labor and that it could be used for the welfare of mankind.[3]

Calvin's Geneva was a remarkable example of spiritual, moral, and social transformation. It is little wonder that the Scottish Reformer John Knox described the city as "the most perfect school of Christ that there was in earth since the days of the apostles."[4] To another visitor Geneva seemed like "the wonderful miracle of the whole world." This urban transformation was not accomplished by the doctrines of grace alone, of course, but by the plain teaching of Scripture, as understood from the perspective of the Calvinist system of doctrine with its undying passion to see God glorified in all of life.

THE PURITANS: TO GLORIFY AND ENJOY GOD

If ever a group of Christians sought to glorify God in everything they did, it was the Puritans. Although the term "Puritan" has often been used as an insult, the Puritans themselves were simply Christians who wanted to honor God in their worship and doctrine. Richard Baxter, himself a leading Puritan pastor, defined them as "religious persons that used to talk of God, and heaven, and Scripture, and holiness."[5] Their worldview is perhaps best encapsulated in the first answer in the Westminster Shorter Catechism: "Man's chief end is to glorify God, and to enjoy him forever."

The Puritans learned this God-centered lifestyle from John Calvin, for among the many foreigners who crowded into Geneva during Calvin's tenure were Protestant refugees from England. These men and women had been forced to flee the bloody reign of Mary Tudor. In the providence of God, their exile afforded them the opportunity to live in the holy commonwealth of Geneva, where they attended the

English-speaking church pastored by John Knox. There the exiles developed a profound appreciation for Reformed worship, and by the time Elizabeth ascended the throne, they had become part of the burgeoning movement of international Calvinism. They returned to their homeland with the zealous intent of completing the Reformation in England by teaching "the true knowledge of God's Word which we have learned in this our banishment." Various forms of Puritanism flourished in England (and America) for the next one hundred years, culminating in the 1640s with their rise to parliamentary power and Oliver Cromwell's victory over Charles I in the English Civil War.

With few exceptions, the Puritans were committed Calvinists. The mature statement of their theological convictions is contained in the Confession of Faith and Catechisms of the Westminster Assembly (1643–1648). Written several decades after the Synod of Dort, these documents include a clear exposition of the doctrines of grace. At the heart of all Puritan theology was a concern for the glory of God's sovereignty: "God the great Creator of all things doth uphold, direct, dispose, and govern all creatures, actions, and things, from the greatest even to the least, by His most wise and holy providence, according to His infallible foreknowledge and the free and immutable counsel of His own will, to the praise of the glory of His wisdom, power, justice, goodness, and mercy" (Westminster Confession of Faith, Chap. 5, Sec. 1). Included in the "all things" that God disposes to his glory are all things pertaining to the salvation of sinners—everything from election to redemption.

Where the Puritans excelled was at bringing this high view of God down to the level of ordinary life. One Puritan woman—the wife of a soldier in Cromwell's army—defined Christianity as "that universal habit of grace which is wrought in a soul by the regenerating Spirit of God, whereby the whole creature is designed up into the Divine will and love, and all its actions designed to the obedience and glory of its Maker."[6] By defining the Christian faith in this way, she was making a connection between the doctrines of grace and daily experience. God's sovereignty in salvation entails his sovereignty over everything else. Thus Puritanism was a theological interpretation of religious,

social, economic, and political life, the conscious application of
Calvinism to the total structure of human existence.

For the Puritans, Christianity began at home, where God's grace
served to "spiritualize every action," so that even the simplest activities of domestic life, such as "a man's loving his wife or child," became
"gracious acts."[7] In the words of Benjamin Wadsworth, "Every
Christian should do all he can to promote the glory of God, and the
welfare of those about him; and the well ordering of matters in particular families tends to promote these things."[8]

Marriage was a gift from God that established two Christians as
partners in grace. One of its purposes was edification; husbands and
wives were to encourage each other in spiritual things. At the same
time, the Puritans viewed marriage as a romance. This was virtually
an innovation, for the Renaissance ideal was courtly love, in which
romance transgressed the boundaries of marital fidelity. But the
Puritans combined love and matrimony to promote the biblical ideal
of romantic marriage—a passionate partnership in which even the
sexual act of love (or "due benevolence," as they called it) was a means
of glorifying God in the body. To summarize, the Puritans viewed marriage as a "high, holy and blessed order of life, ordained not of man,
but of God, . . . wherein one man and one woman are coupled and knit
together in one flesh and body in the fear and love of God, by the free,
loving, hearty, and good consent of them both, to the intent that they
two may dwell together as one flesh and body, of one will and mind,
in all honesty, virtue and godliness, and spend their lives in equal par-
taking of all such things as God shall send them with thanksgiving."[9]

Another purpose of marriage was procreation. Like marriage
itself, children were a gift from God. The Puritans believed that they
were called to train their children in the love, knowledge, and service
of God. Since this ultimately included their taking a place in public
society, the Puritans placed a high value on Christian education.
According to the poet John Milton, writing in his treatise *Of Education*,
a complete education is one that "fits a man to perform justly, skill-
fully, and magnanimously, all the offices, both private and public, of
peace and war." In other words, it equips a Christian to be a good husband, father, churchman, workman, and citizen. The education

required to achieve this lofty goal was not vocational but liberal (that is, universal); and in addition to theology, the Puritans advocated thorough training in mathematics, astronomy, physics, botany, chemistry, philosophy, poetry, history, and medicine. In keeping with this comprehensive curriculum, when Thomas Shepard sent his son off to college, he urged him to remember "that not only heavenly and spiritual and supernatural knowledge descends from God, but also all natural and human learning and abilities."[10]

The Puritans were leaders in childhood education, and the number of grammar schools in England doubled during the brief period of their governance. But their concern for education also extended to the highest levels of learning. The leading Puritans were educated at Oxford and Cambridge. When some of them later founded Harvard College, its charter eloquently expressed their commitment to Christ-centered education: "Let every student be plainly instructed and earnestly pressed to consider well the main end of his life and studies is to know God and Jesus Christ which is eternal life, and therefore to lay Christ in the bottom, as the only foundation of all sound knowledge and learning."[11] Love of learning was always tempered by the need for grace.

The Puritans were hard workers, largely due to their Calvinist conviction that Jesus Christ is sovereign over all. The Roman Catholic Church had drawn an absolute distinction between the sacred and the secular: whatever religious leaders did was sacred; everything else was secular. Although this distinction was rejected by Calvin (and before him, by Luther), its overthrow was completed by the Puritans, who made secular work part of a person's sacred calling. Every job, no matter how mundane, was intrinsically important because it afforded the opportunity to glorify God and to love one's neighbor. Cotton Mather wrote, "Every Christian ordinarily should have a calling. That is to say, there should be some special business . . . wherein a Christian should for the most part spend the most of his time; and this, that so he may glorify God."[12] This faith in God's sovereign blessing on human labor produced the vaunted Puritan work ethic, which in turn made many Puritans prosperous. Since they believed that God was also sovereign over their wealth, they sought to exercise good stewardship, and in particular to use their money to care for the poor. The Puritans were well known for their charity. One study of English philanthropy from the Middle Ages through the Reformation shows that it was the Puritans who made the most generous contributions to public charity.[13] This was because they were convinced that wealth was a social good rather than a private possession, and therefore that its purpose was not personal pleasure but general welfare.

This concern for the poor is one indication that the Puritans were interested in much more than personal piety. Puritanism was a social vision. In the words of one historian, the "summons to a reformation was a call to action, first to transform the individual into an instrument fit to serve the divine will, and then to employ that instrument to transform all of society."[14] Many Puritans pursued this vision by entering public life. They were scholars, scientists, and politicians. C. S. Lewis went so far as to define them as "young, fierce, progressive intellectuals, very fashionable and up-to-date."[15] Some taught at leading universities, especially in the disciplines of systematic theology and biblical interpretation. Others were members of Parliament. There were many Puritan-trained men among the first members of the Royal Society, then the most prestigious scientific organization in the world. In each of these areas—theology, politics, and science—the Puritans sought to acknowledge God's sovereignty by bringing all of life and thought under the authority of his Word.

The Puritan mind was a God-centered mind, and the result was a God-glorifying life. In the words of John Cotton, "Not only my spiritual life, but even my civil life in this world, all the life I live, is by the faith of the Son of God: he exempts no life from the agency of his faith."[16]

THE GREAT AWAKENING: EVANGELISM BY GRACE

Eventually the Puritan vision was transplanted to American soil, where it helped to shape the moral landscape of a rising nation. Many of the first colonists were Puritans who believed that God had chosen and called them to establish "a city on a hill," a holy community dedicated to the glory of God. Even if they were not wholly successful in fulfilling that calling, their faith in God's sovereignty and their high sense of moral purpose helped to define what it means to be an American.

Among the heirs of Puritanism was Jonathan Edwards, a man universally regarded as having one of the greatest intellects in American history. Edwards was a latter-day Puritan, and therefore a Calvinist. Already during his days as a graduate student at Yale, he took his stand against faculty members who committed "the Great Apostasy" of converting to Arminianism. Upon his graduation, Edwards began to preach the doctrines of grace, as typified in the sermon "God Glorified in Man's Dependence." He not only preached these doctrines but also defended them. Edwards placed a strong emphasis on total depravity, and later wrote a treatise entitled *The Great Christian Doctrine of Original Sin Defended* (1758). In particular, Edwards insisted that choice followed character. He argued that because the will always chooses what the mind thinks best, and because the unregenerate mind never thinks that God's way *is* best, a sinner will never act in a way that pleases God until God first transforms the sinner's inward nature. This is an argument to which we shall return in chapter 3.

Common to all of Edwards's theology and piety was a passion for God's glory. As a young man he reveled in what he called "sweet contemplations of my great and glorious God" and claimed, "Absolute sovereignty is what I love to ascribe to God." In a work entitled *The End for Which God Created the World* (1765), Edwards carefully and logically defended the position that God's ultimate purpose is to glorify himself in all his works. Edwards applied this great truth to his own ministry as a pastor, theologian, scholar, and missionary by making it his passion to proclaim God's glory.

The name of Jonathan Edwards is most closely associated with the Great Awakening, the loosely connected series of evangelical revivals that swept through the American colonies in the 1730s and '40s, with effects that lingered until perhaps 1770. At the time there seemed to have been a general decline in religion and morals, and contemporary observers claimed that although the church still retained the form of godliness, it had lost much of its power. Biblical Christians were distressed by the prevalence of such sins as gambling, adultery, alcoholism, and infanticide. Edwards himself complained that "there is very little appearance of zeal for the mysterious and spiritual doctrines of Christianity; and they never were so ridiculed, and had in contempt, as they are in the present age."[17]

It was during this time that the church Edwards served in Northampton, Massachusetts, experienced revival. As Edwards recounted in *A Faithful Narrative of the Surprising Work of God* (1737), in the weeks and months leading up to this spiritual awakening he had been preaching on the doctrines of grace, and in particular on reprobation and justification by faith alone. Seemingly without warning, churchgoers began to have an almost palpable sense of God's presence and to come under deep conviction of personal sin. Hundreds were converted, including members of the surrounding community. A few years later Edwards's preaching met with a similar response in Enfield, Connecticut, where he preached his famous sermon, "Sinners in the Hands of an Angry God." Members of the congregation came under profound conviction of their depravity and cried out for mercy, saying "What shall I do to be saved?"

The awakenings in Northampton and Enfield were not isolated occurrences. Revival swept through the Connecticut Valley. Soon other ministers began to meet with a similar response in the other colonies. Particularly noteworthy was the dramatic and persuasive preaching of George Whitefield, who in the autumn of 1740 traveled more than 800 miles to visit more than 100 churches. Whitefield preached to large crowds, often out-of-doors, and his celebrated tour was a landmark event in the history of American Christianity. There were others as well, such as William and Gilbert Tennent in Pennsylvania and New Jersey, and Virginia's Samuel Davies, who wrote:

> About sixteen years ago, in the northern colonies, when all religious concern was much out of fashion, and the generality lay in a dead sleep in sin, having at best but the form of godliness, but nothing of the power . . . suddenly a deep, general concern about eternal things spread through the country; sinners started out of their slumbers, broke off from their vices, began to cry out, What shall we do to be saved? and made it the great business of their life to prepare for the world to come.

Then the gospel seemed almighty, and carried all before it. It pierced the very hearts of men with an irresistible power.[18]

Something similar was happening in England, Scotland, and Wales, where the preaching of sovereign grace was favored with many extraordinary demonstrations of the Spirit's power.

The Great Awakening was a decisive experience in the history of American evangelicalism. In the near term it produced more than 300 new churches and some 50,000 or more converts. In many local communities the effect was dramatic. In a letter he wrote to the Rev. Thomas Prince of Boston in 1743, Edwards described the enduring impact of the awakening in Northampton:

> Ever since the great work of God that was wrought here about nine years ago, there has been a great abiding alteration in this town in many respects. There has been vastly more religion kept up in the town, among all sorts of persons, in religious exercises and in common conversation than used to be before. There has been a very great alteration among the youth of the town with respect to reveling, frolicking, profane and unclean conversation, and lewd songs. Instances of fornication have been very rare. . . . There has also been an evident alteration with respect to a charitable spirit to the poor. . . . The minds of the people in general appeared more engaged in religion, showing a greater forwardness to make religion the subject of their conversation, and to meet frequently together for religious purposes, and to embrace all opportunities to hear the Word preached.[19]

The Great Awakening sowed the seeds of the modern missionary movement. Edwards encouraged "concerts of prayer" for the unconverted. He also promoted the missionary work of his friend David Brainerd, who labored among the Native Americans of the Northeast before his tragic death at age 29. Edwards himself became a missionary upon his dismissal from Northampton, moving to Stockbridge, Massachusetts, to evangelize a tribe of Mahican Indians.

In assessing the impact of the Great Awakening, social historian Richard Hofstadter has identified it as nothing less than a Second

Reformation.[20] Although its main result was to bring spiritual renewal to the church, this inevitably had an influence on the wider culture. The Great Awakening led to the founding of several prominent New England colleges, the now venerable institutions of the Ivy League. It has also been linked in various ways to the American Revolution; at the very least it was a creative force in colonial development.

It should be emphasized that nearly all the leaders of the Great Awakening were Calvinists, the noteworthy exception being John Wesley. This is not to suggest that Calvinism somehow produced the Great Awakening. Like all true revivals, the movement was in large measure a genuine work of God's Holy Spirit, who always does as he pleases, sometimes in spite of human effort. The leaders of the revival themselves believed that spiritual awakening was, as Edwards put it, "the great work of God."

What the Great Awakening does show is that the doctrines of grace help to promote the gospel of grace. When it is remembered what these gracious doctrines teach, it is not surprising that God used them to revive his church, for they are the doctrines that most clearly demonstrate his glory in the salvation of sinners. The Great Awakening was characterized by deep conviction of sin. But what better means of encouraging repentance than the doctrine of radical depravity, when combined with the doctrine of freely justifying grace? Further, those renewed by revival had a fresh awareness of God's majesty, which is precisely the kind of awe that the decrees of election and reprobation are intended to produce. Then new converts praised God for his amazing grace—the grace that irresistibly, efficaciously brought them to Christ, and without which they never would have been saved. In short, it was the preaching of sovereign grace that helped people to understand and embrace the gospel. The Great Awakening thus shows that Calvinism is not opposed to evangelicalism, but actually enables it to flourish.

KUYPER'S HOLLAND: CALVINISM AS A WORLDVIEW

A final example shows that the doctrines of grace are able to meet the challenges of the modern world. This example comes from the

Netherlands, where Abraham Kuyper presented Calvinism as a public theology to rival secular culture.

Kuyper was a remarkable man, one of the greatest that Holland has ever produced. During his lifetime he founded two newspapers, a university, a political party, and a Protestant denomination. He was a man with unusually wide and varied talent. Kuyper was a journalist, serving for many decades as the editor of two influential Dutch newspapers: *De Heraut,* a religious weekly; and *De Standaard,* a national daily. Both publications were written from the standpoint of Reformed theology. In addition to a weekly Bible meditation, he wrote articles and editorials on religion, education, and public life. It was through these columns—nearly 20,000 in all—that Kuyper taught Christians how to respond to national issues, and thus came to have a profound influence on Dutch culture and politics. In time he became a politician in his own right. In 1874 he was elected to Parliament, where he served as a representative of the party he helped to found. The Anti-Revolutionary Party, as it was called, was a distinctively Christian political organization that sought to apply Calvinism to public life. Its purpose was to promote—not simply by confession but also by legislation and administration—the absolute sovereignty of God. In 1900 the Anti-Revolutionary Party (as part of a broader coalition with the Catholic party) gained a parliamentary majority, and as party leader, Kuyper served for five years as Holland's Prime Minister.

Kuyper was also a churchman. His public life began with a decade in the pastorate, including prominent pulpit ministries in Utrecht and Amsterdam. Over the years he produced several theological works, including an encyclopedia on *Principles of Sacred Theology* and a three-volume work on the doctrine of common grace (*De Gemeene Gratie*). Kuyper was the leading figure in the *Doleantie,* or Dutch Disruption (1886), in which some 100,000 Calvinists left the State Church to establish a purer form of Calvinism. Eventually Kuyper's followers joined with other Calvinist denominations to form the Reformed Churches in the Netherlands, or *Gereformeerde Kerken in Nederland.* The Disruption was brought about in the first place by the National Synod's decision no longer to require ordination candidates to subscribe to the historic confessions of Dutch Calvinism. The explicit intention of the Reformed Churches was to maintain these confessions—especially *The Canons of the Synod of Dort*—as the basis for reforming their faith and practice.

The new denomination needed new schools, so Kuyper became an educator. He had long been an advocate of Christian schools, believing that it was impossible for any academic institution to be morally neutral. He contended that even the public schools, with their commitment to secularism and opposition to Calvinism, had embraced a religious point of view. What the country needed was "the School with the Bible," and eventually Kuyper persuaded the Dutch Parliament that Christian schools should be state-funded, without state interference. He went on to found a major university, the Free University of Amsterdam (1880). In order to be liberated from the unwholesome influence of liberalism, the Free University accepted the Bible as its basis for every area of human thought. In the words of its original statutes, the faculties of arts, science, law, medicine, and theology were to rest "wholly and exclusively on the foundation of the Reformed principles."

In all of these activities, Kuyper was motivated by a love for both God and country. He wrote:

> One desire has been the ruling passion of my life. One high motive has acted like a spur upon my mind and soul, and sooner than that I should escape from the sacred necessity that is laid upon me, let the breath of life fail me. It is this: that, in spite of all worldly opposition, God's holy ordinances shall be established again in the throne, in the school, and in the state for the good of the people; to carve, as it were, into the conscience of the nation the ordinances of the Lord, to which Bible and creation bear witness; until the nation pays homage again to God.[21]

This vision for national Reformation came from Kuyper's commitment to Calvinism.[22] Although he was raised in the home of an evangelical pastor, he had abandoned his childhood faith when he went off to study at the University of Leiden. The theological community there was dominated by modernism, a worldview that denied the supernatural aspects of Christianity, including the virgin birth and the bodily resurrection of Christ. When Kuyper subsequently entered the pastorate, the liberal theology he had embraced at the university brought him into sharp conflict with his parishioners, who were vibrant Calvinists. One young woman, a miller's daughter named Pietje Baltus, was so dismayed by his sermons that she refused to attend church, or even to greet him in public. When Kuyper went to visit her, Pietje explained that she believed in "full sovereign grace," which did not leave any room at all for human merit in salvation. She also encouraged the new minister to read Calvin's *Institutes*. It was through the counsel and example of such parishioners that Kuyper was led to commit himself to the doctrines of grace, and to begin preaching sermons with titles like "The Comfort of Eternal Election." As he later wrote, "Their unwavering persistence has been the blessing of my heart. . . . They brought me in their simple language to that absolute form in which alone my soul can find rest: in the adoration and exaltation of a God who worketh all things, both to do and to will, according to his good pleasure."[23]

Not only did he embrace the doctrines of grace, but more than that, Kuyper understood that a radically God-centered theology provides the only solid basis for Christian life and work. It is by trusting in sovereign grace that the heart finds "its high and holy calling to consecrate every department of life and every energy at its disposal to the glory of God." Kuyper wrote:

> The starting-point of every motive in religion is God and not Man. Man is the instrument and means, God alone is here the goal, the point of departure and the point of arrival, the fountain, from which the waters flow, and at the same time, the ocean into which they finally return. . . . to covet no other existence than for the sake of God, to long for nothing but for the will of God, and to be wholly absorbed in the glory of the name of the Lord, such is the pith and kernel of all true religion.[24]

This passion for God's glory prompted Kuyper to apply Calvinism to all of life. His theology of culture came to clearest expression in his famous lectures on Calvinism, given at Princeton

Seminary in 1898. We shall return to the subject of these lectures in chapter 9. For now it is sufficient to say that Kuyper presented Calvinism as a total world-and-life view. His belief in divine election led him to draw a sharp distinction, or antithesis, between regenerate and unregenerate thought. Human beings face the choice either to submit to the will of God or to pursue their own will, and this choice has implications for everything else we think and do. Modernism was characterized by an anthropocentric perspective, in which man became his own authority and point of reference. By contrast, a theocentric perspective offers a proper understanding of God, and therefore of the world that he has made for his glory. This viewpoint is superior, Kuyper argued, because the Christian, "at every point of his horizon, views God as God, by honouring him in all things as the almighty Creator who has made all things for his own sake, who, as God, is not bound by anything but himself and determines for every creature both its being and the law thereof, now and for evermore. Not only *Deo Gloria*, but *Soli Deo Gloria.*"[25]

The Christian view of the world includes an awareness of the pervasiveness of sin, which corrupts every human endeavor. At the same time, Kuyper's belief in divine sovereignty persuaded him that God has a purpose and a plan for the secular world as well as the sacred community. God allows the goodness of creation to shine even in places where the lordship of Jesus Christ is not yet acknowledged. This goodness is the product of his common grace, by which he maintains human existence, relaxes his curse against sin, arrests the process of decay, and thus allows human culture to develop. As culture develops, Jesus begins to exercise his supreme lordship over all the spheres of human activity. To quote Kuyper's most famous statement: "In the total expanse of the human life there is not a single square inch of which Christ, who alone is sovereign, does not declare, 'That is mine'."[26]

FROM CALVINISM TO LIBERALISM

The purpose of introducing these examples is not to glamorize the history of Calvinism. Human depravity is a doctrine that Calvinists not only believe but also practice! It was in Calvin's Geneva that Michael

Servetus was burned at the stake for heresy; Puritans executed Ch
I and conducted the witch trials at Salem; Edwards was a slave-own
and some Afrikaners used Kuyper's doctrine of sphere sovereignty
(explained in chapter 9) to justify the oppressive system of apartheid.
These tragedies were not the inevitable outcome of Calvinism, for they
were at odds with its very principles. Nevertheless, they warn us not
to idealize the past. One of the dominant lessons of church history is
that Christians (including Calvinists) never live up to God's ideals,
which is why we are in such desperate need of his saving grace.

Still, the doctrines of grace have made a valuable contribution to
church and culture. Each of our four examples illustrates a slightly different aspect of this contribution. The Reformation in Geneva shows
what Calvinism means for urban renewal. The Puritans worked out
the implications of sovereign grace for the family, and thus for the
nation. As the Puritan Richard Greenham claimed, "if men were careful to reform themselves first, and then their own families, they should
see God's manifold blessings in our land and upon church and commonwealth. For of particular persons come families; of families,
towns; of towns, provinces; of provinces, whole realms."[27] The Great
Awakening demonstrates the power of gracious doctrine in the
church, especially for evangelism and spiritual renewal. Finally, the
example of Abraham Kuyper shows how Calvinism can engage the
modern world, down to the last square inch.

Nor are these the only examples of what the doctrines of grace
have done in history. One thinks of Augustine's vision of the City of
God, built by sovereign grace in opposition to the City of Man. Or of
the Scotsman Thomas Chalmers, who organized an extensive network
of pastoral care and Christian education for poor people in Glasgow.
Then there is the modern missionary movement, which largely arose
out of a Calvinist concern to take the gospel of grace to the ends of
the earth.[28] Or to take a more recent example, consider the salutary
influence of Francis Schaeffer on twentieth-century apologetics.
Christianity has flourished wherever the doctrines of grace have been
clearly understood and rigorously applied.

But what happens when these doctrines disappear? The present
book grew out of a concern for the recovery of Reformed theology in

ee why this is so important, consider what hap-
ecomes deformed. The decline of Calvinism
cent of Arminianism. This is virtually a logical
sists that salvation is by grace alone (*sola gra-*
that can replace salvation by grace alone is salvation by divine grace plus human effort—a move Arminian theology
tends to encourage. Arminianism initially appears in the form of
Pietism, with a warm personal devotion to Jesus Christ. However,
unless Pietism matures in the direction of Calvinism, so that there is
a balance between heart and mind, it eventually gives way to liberalism and ultimately atheism. (We are not speaking here of individual
Christians, primarily, but of long-term trends in the Christian community). This is an oversimplification, and a careful historian would
want to qualify it by pointing out the variety of social, religious, and
cultural factors that contribute to doctrinal declension. Nevertheless,
the basic pattern of theological compromise can be documented in
church history. When divine sovereignty is pushed aside to make
room for human ability, a theological dislocation occurs that inevitably
leads to the abandonment of orthodoxy.

This downward spiral can be traced using each of the examples
mentioned above. First, consider the Calvinism that was prevalent in
Geneva and elsewhere during the Protestant Reformation. It was this
theology that the Arminians opposed, first in Holland and subsequently in the rest of Europe. For a time, Arminianism maintained
something of its spiritual vitality, chiefly in the form of eighteenth-century Pietism. However, by the nineteenth century many Protestant
churches in Europe were in the clutches of liberalism, which began
with an assault on the divine authority of Scripture and proceeded to
evacuate the central dogmas of the Christian faith. By the twentieth
century most Europeans had abandoned Christianity altogether.

Or consider the history of Puritanism in America, especially after
Jonathan Edwards. The men who immediately succeeded Edwards—
men such as Joseph Bellamy, Samuel Hopkins, and Jonathan Edwards,
Jr.—all moved in the direction of Arminianism. The key issue for these
theologians was the freedom of the will; they wanted to preserve a
place for human agency in the process of salvation. Thus their New

England Theology, as it was called, denied the doctrine of total inability and generally downplayed the doctrine of original sin, as well as insisted on a universal atonement. By 1800 Calvinism was in decline. At Yale a more radical form of the New England Theology appeared, known as the New Haven Theology. Men such as Nathaniel Emmons argued that responsibility implies ability, and that if God calls sinners to repent, they must therefore have the power to activate their own regeneration. They must also have what N. W. Taylor called "power to the contrary," or the ability to resist divine grace. One by one, the doctrines of grace were falling. This dilution of Puritan thought prepared the way for liberalism, which triumphed in the nineteenth century and has dominated New England and its institutions ever since.

Although the move from Calvinism to Arminianism began in the seminary classroom, it came to have a profound influence on American culture through the events of the Second Great Awakening. The revivals of the first Great Awakening were supernatural events, wrought by the power of God's Spirit. The same could be said of the new wave of revivals that began in the 1790s and continued well into the nineteenth century. Like its predecessor, the Second Great Awakening began and flourished in Calvinist churches, where it was believed that because revival is a work of God alone, it is "peculiarly illustrative of the glorious doctrines of grace."[29]

However, since it was only natural to want the awakening to continue, some Christian leaders—especially Methodists—sought to devise methods for promoting revival. Their concern for personal salvation was commendable. However, rather than relying on God to bless the ordinary means of grace (prayer, the ministry of the Word, and the sacraments), they adopted the "New Measures" associated with the invitation system: the protracted camp meeting, the "anxious bench," the altar call. These pragmatic techniques were susceptible to manipulation, especially where it was considered important to count the number of converts. Preachers stressed the necessity of "coming forward to receive Christ," with the unintended consequence of confusing a human decision (to come forward) with a divine transformation (spiritual conversion). In short, there was a shift from revival to revivalism.[30]

This transition was rooted in an Arminian theology of conversion, which maintained that sinners were neutral—free to choose their own spiritual destiny. Whereas the Puritans had insisted that depravity prevented anyone from choosing for Christ apart from the prior work of the Holy Spirit, the new revivalists called on people to exercise their own ability to receive the gospel. Gardiner Spring described this as the difference between a revival that is "*got up* by man's device" and one that is "*brought down* by the Spirit of God."[31] The difference can be illustrated by comparing Jonathan Edwards, who described revival as "a very extraordinary dispensation of Providence,"[32] with Charles Finney, who insisted that a revival is not supernatural but the natural "result of the right use of the constituted means." Like most revivalists, Finney explicitly rejected the doctrines of grace. Early in his ministry he left the Presbyterian church and repudiated Calvin's views "on the subject of atonement, regeneration, faith, repentance, the slavery of the will, or any of the kindred doctrines."[33] The view he eventually adopted was not merely Arminian but actually Pelagian. Finney believed that sinners could initiate their own conversion: "Instead of telling sinners to use the means of grace and pray for a new heart, we called on them to make themselves a new heart and a new spirit and pressed the duty of instant surrender to God."[34]

And what of Kuyper's Holland? Although the details are different, the same pattern emerged as Calvinism accommodated itself to liberalism. Here the leading figure is G. C. Berkouwer, who was once a leading Reformed theologian but whose theology traced a liberal trajectory through the twentieth century. Berkouwer's earliest work included a vigorous defense of the Five Points of Calvinism, but by the 1950s he was becoming increasingly doubtful about election and reprobation, and had begun to defend neo-orthodox theology. Berkouwer's compromise was a personal change that mirrored wider trends in the Dutch Church. The Free University became less and less committed to distinctively Christian ideas, and by 1971 it had abandoned its confessional commitment to Calvinism. Today the Reformed Church in the Netherlands is an embattled minority, holding on to its last few seats in the Dutch Parliament as it fights against the rising tide of atheism, with its moral decadence and disdain for human life.

THE PRESENT EVANGELICAL CRISIS

Like any survey, our brief history of Calvinism and its detractors has been necessarily selective. Nevertheless, it serves to illustrate the dangers of rejecting sovereign grace. When Calvinism turns toward Arminianism, the lines of thought run in the direction of liberalism and ultimately atheism. And if this pattern holds true, then it may reveal what to expect in the coming evangelical crisis.

American evangelicalism has never been exclusively Calvinistic, but it has long benefited from the salutary influence of Reformed theology. This influence, which has its roots in Puritanism and the Great Awakening, was perpetuated in the nineteenth century by Princeton Theological Seminary and its stalwart theologians—Archibald Alexander, Charles Hodge, and B. B. Warfield. Princeton's Old School Calvinism was prominent in the Fundamentalist/Modernist debates of the early twentieth century, during which orthodox Christians recommitted themselves to fundamental doctrines such as the virgin birth, divine miracles, substitutionary atonement, bodily resurrection, and the second coming of Jesus Christ. One of the leading orthodox theologians was J. Gresham Machen, who especially in his *Christianity and Liberalism* (1923) showed the difference between a merely human religion (modernism) and a religion of divine sovereignty and grace (Calvinism).

Fundamentalism was a diverse movement, and many of its adherents showed little interest in substantive theology. In time, some Christians began to distinguish themselves from the legalism and anti-intellectualism that characterized much of fundamentalism, and began to call themselves "evangelicals." Here, too, Calvinism has had an influence, especially through the systematic writings of Carl F. H. Henry, J. I. Packer, and others. Yet Arminianism has been in the ascendancy, and as the intellectual influence of Calvinism has been eclipsed, even Calvinists who are sympathetic to evangelicalism increasingly find themselves distanced from the movement as a whole. This trend can be illustrated from the history of Fuller Theological Seminary in California. As historian George Marsden has shown, Fuller regarded itself as being founded largely on Calvinist principles, yet openness to other perspectives gradually led the institution away from Reformed orthodoxy, especially in its doctrine of Scripture.[35] Many other evangelical seminaries, colleges, associations, magazines, and publishing houses followed a similar path during the second half of the twentieth century.

With Arminianism has come Pietism, a fervent devotion to Christ that is nonetheless more interested in personal experience than in biblical doctrine. The current evangelical preference for experience over doctrine can be demonstrated by perusing the shelves of the average Christian bookstore. The problem with this preference, of course, is that even the warmest spirituality cannot be sustained without a solid basis in theology. In the absence of a coherent doctrinal framework, today's Pietists become tomorrow's liberals.

It is not surprising, then, that the winds of profound doctrinal change are already sweeping through the evangelical church. Evangelical theologians are pushing the boundaries (erasing them, in some cases), and the strain is being felt at many Christian institutions. There is a trend toward what some leaders within the movement call "post-conservative" evangelicalism, a theology that transcends the categories of the historic confessions. Evangelical theology is being reoriented in order to introduce postmodern perspectives to Christian thought.

The rise of this new evangelicalism increasingly brings central doctrines of the Christian faith under attack. One area of concern is the doctrine of Scripture. In the 1970s and '80s, the "Battle for the Bible" was won on behalf of biblical inerrancy, or so it seemed. By the end of the century, however, it was apparent that even if the battle had been won, the war could still be lost. Although most evangelicals continue to say that they believe in biblical inerrancy, this belief is often notional rather than foundational, for the Bible itself has an ever lessening influence on the evangelical mind. Many Christian students arrive at college with an appalling ignorance of biblical truth. But this is not surprising, given the dearth of sound biblical exposition or theological instruction coming from most American pulpits. At the academic level, although many evangelicals continue to claim that they are inerrantists, their methods and assumptions are often indistinguishable from those employed by liberal scholars. The difficulty, of course, is that biblical inerrancy is indispensable to theological orthodoxy.

Another alarming development is the trend toward religious relativism, even among Christians who claim to be evangelicals. Religious relativism is the view that all religions (Buddhism, Hinduism, Islam, etc.) are equal. No religion can claim to be superior to any other because in its own way, each is a valid perspective on ultimate truth. This is the age of tolerance, in which the only absolute is that there are no absolutes. In the church this sometimes takes the form of denying that Jesus Christ is the only way to God. According to a study conducted by James Davison Hunter of the University of Virginia, a majority of students at Christian colleges and seminaries doubt whether personal faith in Christ is really necessary for salvation.[36] Theologians such as Clark Pinnock have argued that, in fact, it is *not* necessary. Jesus is revealed through other religions, which offer true but partial salvation. Nor is it necessary to have explicit faith in Christ; anyone who truly loves God is an implicit Christian. Pinnock thus rejects the exclusivity of Christ (although he still believes in what he terms "the finality of Christ").[37]

Then there is the new perspective on Paul, as developed by E. P. Sanders, N. T. Wright, and others. This is an attempt to reinterpret New Testament theology by reassessing the apostle Paul's relationship to first-century Judaism, as well as his doctrine of justification. According to the new perspective, Paul was not (as the Reformers taught) trying to combat the works-righteousness of the Jews, because first-century Judaism was already a religion of grace. Nor did he consider "the righteousness of God" (Rom. 1:17, RSV) to be a gift that God grants to sinners; although righteousness is an attribute of God, it cannot be credited to anyone else. The effect of this change in perspective is to cast doubt on the Reformation doctrine of justification, which properly insists that the righteousness of God is imputed to the sinner who receives Christ by faith alone. According to the new perspective, the Reformation was wrong about Paul, wrong about Judaism, wrong about Roman Catholicism, wrong about justification, and therefore wrong about the gospel![38] The new perspective also tends to dismiss the judicial aspect of the atonement. Some scholars are frankly repelled by the idea of substitution—Christ offering his body and blood as payment for sin. They would prefer to view the crucifixion as a demonstration of love rather than as the satisfaction of a debt. This is part of an overall aversion to understanding salvation in legal categories, with a general preference for relational categories instead. But of course Scripture teaches both. The atonement accomplishes both redemption and reconciliation, and to do away with the former is to remove the legitimacy of the latter.

Another threat to the biblical doctrine of justification comes from the evangelical eagerness to compromise with Catholicism—a threat exposed by the 1994 signing of *Evangelicals and Catholics Together* (*ECT*). This theological statement was intended to provide a basis for Evangelical-Catholic cooperation on social and political issues. To that end, the drafters labored to find doctrinal constructions that were mutually agreeable. The difficulty, of course, was the doctrine of justification. For Roman Catholics, justification is a subjective process that is begun by faith but completed by works. For evangelicals—or for Calvinists, at any rate—justification is an objective declaration that the believer is righteous through faith in Christ alone, apart from works. It would be nice to think that this difference is merely a misunderstanding; but it is, in fact, a principled and irreconcilable disagreement on a matter of vital importance. At issue are the meaning of the gospel and the method of salvation. Here Catholic dogma and evangelical theology are mutually exclusive, and thus the compromise *ECT* reaches on the doctrine of justification (sinners are justified "because of Christ") really amounts to an equivocation.[39] But this is not a cause as much as it is a symptom of a general disregard for doctrine. Perhaps it is not surprising that for an evangelical church that is increasingly non-confessional (i.e., no longer committed to the historic creeds and confessions of the Christian faith), it is becoming difficult to tell the difference between Protestantism and Catholicism.

Another threat to evangelical orthodoxy comes from theologians who advocate "the openness of God." According to this view, also known as "open theism," God neither knows nor determines the future, but he is open to its possibilities. The future is partly foreknown and partly unknown, partly settled and partly unsettled. Although God has knowledge of the future, this knowledge is not exhaustive. Open theism is an open attack on the Reformed understanding of the sovereignty of God. One of its purposes is to increase the role of human agency in achieving one's personal destiny. As Greg Boyd writes in *God of the Possible*, "I have discovered a new appreciation and excitement regarding my own responsibility in bringing about the future. . . . The bottom line is that *life is all about possibilities*. . . . [T]he picture of God as the 'God of the possible' creates a people who do not wait for an eternally settled future to happen. Through God's grace and power, they help *create* the future."[40] However exciting this prospect may seem to some, it comes at the expense of divine sovereignty.[41]

This is not the place to fully refute post-conservative theology, although it should be noted that each of these trends introduces serious doctrinal error, and in some cases heresy. Our purpose here is simply to observe that they are exactly the kinds of doctrines that hold sway when Calvinism is set aside. That is to say, they minimize divine sovereignty by maximizing human agency. Start with the doctrine of Scripture. To believe that the Bible contains errors is to treat it as a human book about God rather than as God's Word to humanity. Or consider the implications of religious pluralism: if sinners can find their way to Christ, even without ever hearing the gospel, then they must be something less than totally depraved. The same is true of any attempt to discredit the biblical doctrine of justification. Justification by faith alone preserves the sovereignty of grace because it welcomes righteousness as a divine gift. The alternative is to regard salvation as in some sense a personal achievement. Finally, open theism restricts the scope of God's plan in order to expand the horizons of human potential.

Since it is doubtful whether evangelicalism has the doctrinal stability or moral courage to resist these departures from orthodoxy, it seems almost certain that its theology will become increasingly postconservative. Sooner or later, evangelical churches will end up in the position that liberal churches now occupy: declining in membership and influence, while at the same time becoming ever more worldly in their agenda and methods. It will probably be sooner. Evangelicalism lacks theological precision and biblical discernment, so the transition from crisis to collapse may be even more sudden. All of this is only a hypothesis, of course, which future events will serve either to confirm or deny. Yet it is a hypothesis with some historical justification. The pathway from Calvinism to liberalism—and even atheism—is well worn, and it usually passes through Arminianism.

All of which leads us to wonder, whatever happened to the doctrines of grace? This book began with the claim that "Evangelicalism stands or falls with Calvinism." While the evangelical church has not yet fallen, many agree that it has begun to totter, and if church history is any indication, it may never regain its balance. While there are many reasons for this, our central argument is that evangelicalism cannot survive without Calvinism because the gospel of grace requires the doctrines of grace.

Is there any hope of recovery? Perhaps not. Still, there may be some hope for Christians who commit themselves to establishing theologically rigorous, biblically literate, culturally engaged, and evangelistically active churches. For this hope to be realized, however, evangelical churches must recognize that maintaining spiritual vitality requires Christians to worship the God of grace, believe the gospel of grace, and confess the doctrines of grace. It is to a biblical exposition and theological defense of these doctrines that we now turn.

Part Two

THE FIVE
POINTS

THREE

Radical Depravity

I once was rebellious, corrupted by sin,
Pursuing the Devil's dark path,
Oblivious, dead to the state I was in,
An object of God's dreadful wrath.

The tremendous optimism that characterized the period immediately prior to World War I, reflected in the writings of H. G. Wells and many others, and that originated in the Age of Enlightenment when Rousseau wrote imaginatively about the noble savages of North America living without the encumbrance of civilization, has disappeared almost entirely. Man is no longer seen as perfectible. Despair has overtaken the humanist idealism of those days, and sin has come to be recognized as a depressing fact of life."[1]

That analysis of the current cultural mood by Canadian writer Arthur Custance may not be universally valid, since not everyone is willing to call sin, sin. Karl Menninger of the Menninger Clinic of Topeka, Kansas, asked the famous question: "Whatever became of sin?" even as he called for its rediscovery as a necessary category for understanding human beings.[2] Menninger himself is an example of the new, increasingly realistic outlook, and Custance's analysis is close enough to what many intelligent spokespersons are saying to be taken seriously. Certainly, in our day humanity no longer seems perfectible, despair has replaced the idealism of the last two hundred years, and sin is no longer reckoned a totally meaningless category for understanding human existence. This new despairing mood is part of what is sometimes called postmodernism.

Yet the point of this chapter is not merely that men and women sin. That truth is established every moment of every day by what we do and by what we see others do. It is documented in our newspapers and magazines, on television and in our own hearts. Nor is the point of this chapter merely that because we sin we are sinners. That is as obvious as saying that the man who murders is a murderer or that the person who steals is a thief. The point of this chapter is more significant than that. Here we are dealing with the nature and extent of sin, and the point is that we are all radically sinful, so much so that we cannot take even the smallest of steps toward God unless he first intervenes.

This is the Bible's teaching. As early as Genesis 6 we are told that "The LORD saw how great man's wickedness on the earth had become, and that every inclination of the thoughts of his heart was only evil all the time" (Gen. 6:5). A person whose heart can only incline toward evil certainly does not and cannot seek God. Jeremiah wrote,

> The heart is deceitful above all things
>   and beyond cure.
> Who can understand it? (Jer. 17:9).

Jesus said, "No one can come to me unless the Father who sent me draws him" (John 6:44). Paul, quoting from two of the best known psalms (Ps. 14:1-3; 53:1-3), declared:

> There is no one righteous, not even one;
>   there is no one who understands,
>   no one who seeks God.
> All have turned away,
>   they have together become worthless;
> there is no one who does good,
>   not even one (Rom. 3:10-12).

This teaching is the first of the famous "Five Points of Calvinism," commonly called "total depravity." But that wording of the point, like the wording of most of the others, is a bit misleading. To most persons "total" means "utterly," and utter depravity would mean that people are as bad as they can possibly be. That is not true, of course. Given the finite circumstances of our lives, civil laws, and various social and religious restraints, each of us could undoubtedly be much worse than we are. What total depravity is meant to convey is the idea that sin has affected the whole person down to the very core or root of his or her being. That is why many writers prefer the words "radical depravity" or "radical corruption" instead.

Loraine Boettner, whose book on *The Reformed Doctrine of Predestination* has probably helped as many people to understand the Calvinistic system as any other modern work, wrote:

> This doctrine of Total Inability, which declares that men are dead in sin, does not mean that all men are equally bad, nor that any man is as bad as he could be, nor that anyone is entirely destitute of virtue, nor that human nature is evil in itself, nor that man's spirit is inactive, and much less does it mean that the body is dead. What it does mean is that since the fall man rests under the curse of sin, that he is actuated by wrong principles, and that he is wholly unable to love God or to do anything meriting salvation.[3]

THE FALL OF THE RACE IN ADAM

The Bible's teaching about sin begins with the story of the fall of humanity recorded in Genesis 3, a story that highlights several steps in the first temptation: 1) doubting the benevolence of God, 2) doubting the Word of God, and 3) aspiring to be as God. But that is not our primary concern here. Our concern here is with the *result* of the Fall, its consequence not only for our first parents but also for the race. And what is significant about the Genesis account in this regard is that the consequence of Adam and Eve's sin is described as death—not mere imperfection or a weakening of one's innate capacity to do good, but death: God said, "You are free to eat from any tree in the garden; but you must not eat from the tree of the knowledge of good and evil, for when you eat of it you will surely die" (Gen. 2:16-17).

Most Bible readers recognize that God's warning was not merely about physical death (though it was that) but included spiritual death as well since Adam and Eve showed their newly won depravity by attempting to hide from God when he came to them in the garden, and by blaming each other and the devil for their sin when God confronted them about it. Genesis is pointing to Adam and Eve's moribund condition before God after having fallen. It is a way of saying that Adam and Eve were as unable to love and rightly respond to God as a corpse is unable to respond to attempts at resuscitation.

This is a point the world does not even begin to grasp, even though many may think of sin as a not entirely useless concept for understanding human beings. For that matter, it is something that even many Christians do not grasp. Sinners? Yes, we admit that much because the Bible calls us sinners, but we would like to think that we are able to help ourselves, at least if we are aided by God. However, that is not the Bible's view of sin. According to the Bible, to be a sinner is not merely to be morally imperfect or to be unable to achieve one's full potential without God. It is rather a description of human beings in an utterly ruined state, a state from which we are unable to deliver ourselves and in which we might all have been left to perish, and justly so.

If sin is only an imperfection, a marring of something once perfect and able to become so again, then it is not really right to call it sin, or even to look down on it as something less desirable than the next inevitable stage of evolution. This line of thinking eliminates the possibility of any meaningful talk about virtue. Nobody can be said to be better or worse than someone else. No action can ever be viewed as inherently wrong. Yet if sin is only an imperfection to be eliminated over time as a result of the inevitable upward movement of the race, why has so much evil been around for so long? If sin is merely imperfection, why hasn't the imperfection been eliminated long before this? Looking at the historical record honestly, is it even possible to say that there has been such a thing as progress? Are we really morally better than our predecessors? Are we more virtuous than the Greeks? Are we more noble even than the barbarians? It is hard to say so.

This fact alone suggests that sin is a much greater problem than the secularist allows, and it pushes us to seek a better understanding of the Bible's teaching about it.

PAUL'S TEACHING IN EPHESIANS 2

One place to look for a better understanding of the nature and effect of sin is Ephesians 2:1-3, a passage in which Paul describes the condition of an individual before he or she became a Christian. He says four things about it:

1. *The sinner is "dead in . . . transgressions and sins."* That is precisely what we found in Genesis, of course, and the Genesis account of the Fall is certainly one important source of Paul's teaching. Dead in transgressions! Dead in sins! This leads to the observation that in the entire history of the human race there have been only three basic views of human nature apart from God's grace, namely: 1) that man is well, 2) that man is sick, and 3) that man is dead.

The first view is the view of all *optimists*. Optimists may vary as to how healthy they believe human beings are. Some would argue that people are very, very well. Others would admit that they are not as morally healthy as one day they may be. But all would say that the world is getting better and better, and the reason is that there is nothing basically wrong with humanity. This view—as suggested at the beginning of this chapter—is being abandoned, at least by thinking people.

The second view is that man is sick, even mortally sick. This is the view of *realists*. They observe rightly that if people are as healthy as the optimists say, then surely war, disease, starvation, poverty, and other problems we face should have been fixed by now. Since such problems have not been fixed, realists conclude that something is basically wrong with human nature. Still, they contend, the situation is not hopeless—bad, or even desperate, but not hopeless. People are still around, after all. We have not yet blown ourselves off the surface of the planet. No need to call the mortician yet!

The third view, which Paul articulates in classic language in this passage, is that man is neither well nor sick. He is dead, at least so far as his relationship to God is concerned. Abraham Kuyper observed that, prior to regeneration, a sinner "has all the passive properties belonging to a corpse. . . . [Therefore] every effort to claim for the sinner the minutest co-operation in this first grace destroys the gospel, severs the artery of the Christian confession and is anti-scriptural in the highest degree."[4] Like a spiritual corpse, he is unable to make a single move toward God, think a right thought about God, or even respond to God—unless God first brings this spiritually dead corpse to life. And this is exactly what Paul says God does.

2. *The sinner actively practices evil.* There is something even worse about humanity, according to the biblical view. Ephesians 2:1 teaches that human beings are spiritually dead. But this is a strange kind of death since, although the sinner is dead, he is nevertheless up and about, actively practicing sin. Paul says that we "followed the ways of this world and of the ruler of the kingdom of the air, . . . gratifying the cravings of our sinful nature and following its desires and thoughts" (v. 2). To put it differently, though the sinner is indeed dead to God, he nevertheless is very much alive to wickedness.

John Gerstner, who was a professor at Pittsburgh Theological Seminary, compared Paul's description of our sinful state to what horror stories call a zombie. A zombie is a person who has died but who is still up on his feet walking around. It is a gruesome concept, which is why it appears in horror stories. But it gets worse. This upright, walking human corpse is putrefying. It is rotting away, which is probably the most disgusting thing most people can imagine. But this is a fair description of what Paul is saying about human nature in its lost condition. Apart from Jesus Christ, these sinning human corpses are "the living dead."

3. *The sinner is enslaved.* Another way to speak of our sinful state is to say that men and women are enslaved to sin, so that they cannot escape from it. Peter wrote, "a man is a slave to whatever has mastered him" (2 Pet. 2:19). What has mastered us? There is a tradition in the church that identifies the Christian's three great enemies as "the world, the flesh and the devil"; with that in mind, what Paul seems to be say-

ing in Ephesians 2, though he does not use the word *slave,* is that in
our natural state we are in bondage to each one of these three.

We are enslaved to the world because we follow "the ways of this
world" (v. 2). We think as the world thinks, without regard for our
relationship to God or our final destiny; and because we think as the
world thinks, we also act as the world acts. We are enslaved to the flesh
because our natural desire is to "[gratify] . . . the cravings of our sinful nature and [follow] its desires and thoughts" (v. 3). We want what
we want, regardless of God's law or the effect that what we want to do
has on other people. Jesus said, "Everyone who sins is a slave to sin"
(John 8:34). We are enslaved to the devil because, just as we follow
the ways of this world, so also we follow "the ruler of the kingdom of
the air, the spirit who is now at work in those who are disobedient"
(Eph. 2:2). We are Satan's playthings, and never so much as when we
are unaware of his presence. Paul wrote to Timothy that sinners are
taken "captive" by Satan "to do his will" (2 Tim. 2:26).

4. *The sinner is by nature an object of God's wrath.* The worst thing
about our sinful condition apart from God's grace in Jesus Christ is
that we are objects of God's wrath. Most people can hardly take this
seriously. They do not take wrath seriously because they do not take
sin seriously. But if sin is as bad as the Bible declares it to be, nothing
is more reasonable than that the wrath of a holy God should rise
against it. The Old Testament uses more than twenty words to express
the idea of God's wrath, and more than six hundred important passages deal with it. There are other equally important passages in the
New Testament. The Bible says, "'It is mine to avenge; I will repay,' and
again, 'The Lord will judge his people.' It is a dreadful thing to fall into
the hands of the living God" (Heb. 10:30-31).

Paul's Teaching in Romans 3

A third key passage for understanding what the Bible has to say about
sin is Romans 3:9-20, in which the apostle Paul summarizes the condition of every human being apart from the grace of God in Jesus
Christ. According to Paul, Jews are no better off than Gentiles, and

Gentiles are no better than Jews. Instead, all are alike under sin, and all are thus subject to the wrath and final judgment of Almighty God:

There is no one righteous, not even one;
  there is no one who understands,
  no one who seeks God (Rom. 3:10-11).

This is a serious, indeed a devastating picture of the race, because it portrays human beings as unable to do even a single thing either to please, understand, or seek after God. Sin corrupts the heart, the mind, and the will:

1. *The moral nature: None are righteous.* In the first part of his summary of the hopeless condition of humanity, Paul speaks of our moral nature and concludes that we are unrighteous. This does not mean merely that we are a bit less righteous than we need to be to please God and somehow get to heaven. When Paul says that there are none righteous he means that, from God's point of view, sinners have no righteousness at all. The words "from God's point of view" are not meant to suggest that any view other than God's is ever ultimately valid, but merely to make clear that it is from this viewpoint that we need to assess the situation. If we assess the human condition from our perspective, we will always conclude that at least some people are good—simply because they are better than what we think we have observed in others.

Our problem at this point is that we think of the good we can do—our righteousness—as the same thing as God's righteousness, when actually it is quite different. We assume that by accumulating human goodness we can please God. Taken this way, human righteousness is like Monopoly money. It is useful in the game we call life; however, it is not the currency of God's kingdom. God requires divine righteousness, just as in America one needs United States dollars to pay bills. We find Paul making this distinction a bit further along in Romans, writing of Israel's failure to find God: "Since they did not know the righteousness that comes from God and sought to establish their own, they did not submit to God's righteousness" (Rom. 10:3). That is, Israel wanted God to accept its own currency rather than the currency that Christ alone could provide them. This is not simply Israel's problem, but the failure of our entire race. As Paul goes on to say, "All have turned away, they have together become worthless; there is no one who does good, not even one" (Rom. 3:12).

2. The sinful mind: None understands. The second pronouncement Paul makes about human beings in their sin is that no one understands spiritual things. Again, we need to think of this as a lack of spiritual perception and not merely a lack of human knowledge. If we think on the human level, comparing the understanding of one person with that of another, we will observe that some people seem to understand a great deal about God. They probably do, but only from a human point of view. What we need to see is that in spiritual matters, no one either truly understands or seeks God.

The best commentary on the phrase "no one who understands" is the first two chapters of 1 Corinthians. The Corinthians were mostly Greeks and therefore highly prized the wisdom of the philosophers, as virtually all Greeks did. But Paul writes that when he was with them he did not attempt to impress them with such wisdom; rather, he determined to know nothing among them "except Jesus Christ and him crucified" (1 Cor. 2:2). He explains his decision in two ways. First, human wisdom has shown itself bankrupt so far as coming to know God is concerned. Paul says:

> The message of the cross is foolishness to those who are perishing, but to us who are being saved it is the power of God. For it is written:
>
> > "I will destroy the wisdom of the wise;
> > the intelligence of the intelligent I will frustrate."
>
> Where is the wise man? Where is the scholar? Where is the philosopher of this age? Has not God made foolish the wisdom of the world? For since in the wisdom of God the world through its wisdom did not know him, God was pleased through the foolishness of what was preached to save those who believe (1 Cor. 1:18-21).

In making this indictment, Paul was only echoing what the Greeks had concluded themselves. The best of the philosophers knew that they had been unable to discover God by philosophy.

The second way Paul explains his decision to know nothing among the Greeks but Christ crucified is the statement that spiritual things can be known only by God's Spirit. He writes that "the man without the Spirit does not accept the things that come from the Spirit of God, for they are foolishness to him, and he cannot understand them, because they are spiritually discerned" (1 Cor. 2:14).

This does not mean that a person cannot have a rational understanding of Christianity or of what the Bible teaches apart from the illumination of his or her mind by the Spirit. In one sense, a scholar can understand and even teach theology as well as any other branch of human knowledge. An unbelieving philosopher can lecture accurately on the Christian idea of God. An unbelieving historian can analyze the causes of the Reformation and describe the meaning of justification by faith. At universities such as Oxford and Harvard, non-Christian professors present the doctrines of Christianity so brilliantly that even Christians marvel at their lectures. But such professors do not believe what they are teaching. If they are asked their personal opinion of what they present, they say that it is all nonsense. It is in this sense that they, not being "spiritual," are unable to understand Christianity.

3. *The captive will: None seeks God.* Here again we must not think in merely human terms. If we do, we will conclude, contrary to Paul's teaching, that "seeking after God" is an accurate description of human history. Human beings are religious. There are very few genuine atheists. Even primitive tribes have well-developed religious concepts. However, as anthropologist Robert Brow argues in *Religion: Origins and Ideas,* the study of primitive peoples suggests not that the human race has moved from primitive conceptions of God to higher conceptions of him—thus seeking after "God" constantly, but rather that the human race consistently has been running away from ideas of a high and holy God. Brow argues that primitive peoples generally have a truer picture of God than we do, though they do not worship him.

They believe in a great and true God who stands behind their pantheon of animistic deities or lesser gods, but they do not worship this God because they do not fear him as much as they do the immediate and hostile powers.[5]

In any case, what people actually do with their "religion" today is use it to avoid any real contact with God. They may say that they have been seeking him in the Baptist church, the Presbyterian Church, the Episcopal church, the Methodist church, or any other church. But what they are actually doing is running away from God. They make the round of the churches, and at the end of the line, they look around to see if anyone is watching and then jump back in at the beginning. They are not seeking God. They are running away from God. They are using religion to disguise their true intentions.

According to Romans 3, no one unaided by God 1) has any righteousness by which to lay a claim upon God, 2) has any true understanding of God, or 3) seeks God. But what we do not have, and cannot and have not done, God has done for those who are being saved. First, God sought us. We ran from him, but as the "Hound of Heaven" God pursued us relentlessly. If God had not pursued us, we would have been lost. Second, God gave us understanding. He did it by making us alive in Jesus Christ by the power of the Holy Spirit, as a result of which our eyes were opened to see things spiritually. This does not mean that we understand things perfectly, but what we do understand about God we now truly do understand—in the sense that we believe it and respond accordingly. Third, God has given us a righteousness that we did not have and could never have had on our own—his very own righteousness, which is the righteousness of Jesus Christ, the ground of our salvation.

THE BONDAGE OF THE WILL

If we are as desperately lost in sin as the Bible says we are, then no one can come to God, choose God, or even believe on Jesus Christ and be saved—unless God first makes that person alive in Christ and draws him. But this is what troubles many. It does not seem consistent with what they know of their ability to choose what they want to choose and reject what they want to reject. What is more, it seems inconsistent with the many free offers of the gospel found throughout Scripture. The Bible says we are "dead in . . . transgressions and sins" (Eph. 2:1), that no one can come to me "unless the Father . . . draws him" (John 6:44), but the Bible also gives numerous invitations for sinners to repent of their sins and come to Christ. What about invitations like:

> Come, all you who are thirsty,
>   come to the waters;
> and you who have no money,
>   come, buy and eat! (Isa. 55:1)?

Or Jesus' words: "Come to me, all you who are weary and burdened, and I will give you rest" (Matt. 11:28). One of the last verses in the Bible says, "Whoever wishes, let him take the free gift of the water of life" (Rev. 22:17). Don't these verses imply that every person has a will that is able to choose Christ when the gospel is presented? And if they do, how can it be said, even on the basis of Romans 3:11, that "no one seeks . . . God"?

We might suspect that a question as important as this must have been discussed often in church history, and this is indeed the case. In fact, the best way of approaching the subject is through the debates that took place between the theological giants of past days.

1. *Augustine and Pelagius.* The first important debate on this issue was between the British monk Pelagius and the great Saint Augustine of Hippo, toward the end of the fourth and the beginning of the fifth century. Pelagius argued for the existence of free will. He did not want to deny the universality of sin, at least at the beginning. He knew that "all have sinned and fall short of the glory of God" (Rom. 3:23). In this he wanted to remain orthodox. But Pelagius could not see how we can be responsible for something if we do not have free will in that matter. If there is an obligation to do something, he argued, there must be an ability to do it. Pelagius said that the will, rather than being bound by sin, is actually neutral—so that at any moment or in any given situation it is free to choose either good or evil.

This position worked itself out in several ways. For one thing, it led to a view of sin as only those deliberate and unrelated acts in which the will actually chooses to do evil. Thus any necessary connection between sins, or any hereditary principle of sin within the race, going back to Adam, was forgotten. Pelagius argued further that:

1. The sin of Adam affected no one but himself;
2. Those born since Adam have been born into the same condition Adam was in before his fall, that is, into a position of neutrality so far as sin is concerned; and
3. Today human beings are able to live free from sin, if they want to.

This is probably the root view of most people today, including many Christians. But it is faulty because it limits the nature and scope of sin and because it leads to a denial of the necessity of God's unmerited grace in salvation. Moreover, even when the gospel is preached to a fallen sinner (according to this view), what ultimately determines whether he or she will be saved is not the supernatural working of God through the Holy Spirit but rather the person's will, which either receives or rejects the Savior. This gives human beings glory that ought to go to God.

In his early life Augustine had thought along the same lines. But as he studied the Bible, he came to see that Pelagianism does not do justice either to the biblical doctrine of sin or to the grace of God in salvation. Augustine saw that the Bible always speaks of sin as more than mere isolated and individual acts. It speaks of an inherited depravity as a result of which it simply is not possible for the individual to stop sinning. Augustine had a phrase for this fundamental human inability: *non posse non peccare*, which means "not able not to sin." Unaided by God, a person simply is unable to stop sinning and choose God. Augustine said that man, having used his free will badly in the Fall, lost both himself and his will. The will is free of righteousness, but enslaved to sin. It is free to turn away from God, but not to come toward him.[6]

As far as grace is concerned, Augustine saw that apart from grace no one can be saved. Moreover, it is a matter of grace from beginning to end, not just prevenient or partial grace to which the sinner adds his or her efforts. Otherwise, salvation would not be entirely of God, God's honor would be diminished, and human beings would be able to boast in heaven. Any view that leads to such consequences must be wrong, for God has declared: "It is by grace you have been saved, through faith—and this not from yourselves, it is the gift of God—not by works, so that no one can boast" (Eph. 2:8-9). Eventually Augustine won the day and the church condemned Pelagius at the Synod of Carthage in A.D. 418. But the church gradually drifted back toward Pelagianism in the Middle Ages.

2. *Luther and Erasmus*. At the time of the Reformation the battle erupted again, first between Martin Luther and the Dutch humanist Erasmus of Rotterdam, and then later between the followers of Jacob Arminius and the followers of John Calvin.

The more interesting debate was between Luther and Erasmus. Erasmus had been sympathetic to the Reformation in its early stages, because, like most perceptive people of the time, he saw that the church badly needed to be reformed. But Erasmus did not have Luther's spiritual undergirdings, and at last he was prevailed upon to challenge the Reformer. Erasmus chose to write upon the freedom of the will. He said that the will must be free—for reasons similar to those given by Pelagius. Still, the subject did not mean a great deal to Erasmus, and he counseled moderation, no doubt hoping that Luther would do likewise.

It was no small matter to Luther, however, and he did not approach the subject with detachment. Instead, he approached the matter zealously, viewing it as an issue upon which the very truth of God depended. In one place, in the midst of demolishing the Dutch humanist's views, Luther wrote: "I give you hearty praise and commendation on this further account—that you alone, in contrast with all others, have attacked the real thing, that is, the essential issue."[7]

In this work, *The Bondage of the Will*, which he considered his greatest theological writing, Luther did not deny the psychological fact that men and women do make choices. This is so obvious that no one can deny it. What Luther insisted, however, was that in the specific area of an individual's choice of God or failure to choose God, the will is impotent. In this area Luther was as determined to deny the will's freedom as Erasmus was determined to affirm it. We are wholly given over to sin, said Luther:

> [A] man without the Spirit of God does not do evil against his will, under pressure, as though he were taken by the scruff of the neck and dragged into it, like a thief . . . being dragged off against his will to punishment; but he does it spontaneously and voluntarily. And this willingness of volition is something which he cannot in his own strength eliminate, restrain or alter. He goes on willing and desiring to do evil; and if external pressure forces him to act otherwise, nevertheless his will within remains averse to so doing and chafes under such constraint and opposition.[8]

Therefore, our only proper role is humbly to acknowledge our sin, confess our blindness, and admit that we can no more choose God by our enslaved wills than we can please him by our sullied moral acts. All we can do is call upon God for mercy, knowing that as we seek to do so, we cannot even call for mercy unless God is first active to convict us of sin and lead us to embrace the Lord Jesus Christ for salvation.

3. *Edwards's "Freedom of the Will."* It is sometimes suggested that although we have free will in many areas, we do not have free will in all areas. That is, we can choose what we want in some things—little things like what we will select from a menu, what color tie we will put on, what job we will take—but we do not have free will in the important areas. A person with an intelligence quotient of 120 cannot make it 140 by the exercise of free will. Someone who is not an Olympic class athlete does not have the free will to run a mile in four minutes or the 100-yard dash in nine seconds. In exactly the same way, none of us by the mere exercise of our will can choose God.

This explanation is attractive. However, Jonathan Edwards's treatise on "The Freedom of the Will" persuades us to take a different approach, not on the basic issue or in our conclusions, but in the way the will is defined.

It can hardly escape anyone who looks at this treatise that on the surface Edwards seems to be saying the opposite of what Augustine and Luther said. Augustine said that the will is not free. Luther titled his study *The Bondage of the Will* in opposition to Erasmus's *Freedom of the Will*. But Edward's treatise is called "A Careful and Strict Inquiry into the Prevailing Notions of the Freedom of the Will."[9] Of course, the title does not specifically state that Edwards is asserting the will's "freedom" (though he actually does so in the treatise), only that he is going to investigate the prevailing notions about the will's freedom. But it is not by chance that Edwards uses words entirely opposite from Luther's. In the end, Edwards comes out on the same side as Luther and all the great biblical theologians before him. But along the way he makes a unique contribution to the subject for which the idea of the "freedom" of the will is appropriate.

First, Edwards *defined the will.* It is strange that no one had done this previously. Everyone had operated on the assumption that we all know what the will is. We call the will that thing in us that makes choices. Edwards saw that this was not accurate and instead defined the will as "that by which *the mind* chooses anything." That may not seem to be much of a difference, but it is a major one. It means, according to Edwards, that what we choose is not determined by the will itself (as if it were an entity to itself) but by the mind. We choose what we think is the most desirable course of action.

Second, Edwards spoke of *motives.* Why is it that the mind chooses one thing rather than another? Edwards asked. He answered that the mind chooses what it does because of motives. The mind is not neutral. It thinks some things are better than other things, and because it thinks some things are better than other things it chooses what it judges to be best. If a person thought one course of action was better than another, and yet chose the undesirable alternative, the person would be acting irrationally or, to use other language, he would be insane. Does this mean that the will is bound, then? Quite the contrary. It means that the will is free. It is always free. It is free to choose (and always will choose) what the mind thinks best.

But what does the mind think best? Here we get to the heart of the problem as it involves seeking or choosing God. When confronted with God, the mind of a sinner never thinks that God's way is good. The will is free to choose God. Nothing is stopping it. But the mind does not regard submission to and service of God as desirable. Rather, it turns from God, even when the gospel is presented most winsomely. It turns away because it does not want God to be sovereign over it. It does not consider the righteousness of God to be the way to personal fulfillment or happiness. It does not want its sinfulness exposed. The mind is wrong in its judgments, of course. The way it chooses is actually the way of alienation and misery, the end of which is death. But human beings think that sin is best. Therefore, unless God changes the way we think—which he does by the miracle of the new birth—our minds always tell us to turn from God. And we do turn from him. Loraine Boettner says, "As the bird with a broken wing is 'free' to fly but not able, so the natural man is free to come to God but not able. How can he repent of his sin when he loves it? How can he come to God when he hates him?"[10]

Third, Edwards distinguished between *moral and natural inability*. Because man's inability is moral and not natural, according to Edwards, the individual is responsible for the choices he or she makes. Here is a simple illustration: in the natural world there are animals that eat nothing but meat. They are called carnivores, from *caro, carnis,* which means "meat." There are other animals that eat nothing but grass or plants. They are called herbivores, from *herba,* which means vegetation. Imagine taking a lion, who is a carnivore, and placing a bundle of hay or a trough of oats before him. He will not eat the hay or oats. Why not? It is not because he is physically or naturally unable to eat them. Physically, he could munch on the oats and swallow them. But he does not and will not, because it is not in his nature to eat this kind of food. Moreover, if we were to ask why he will not eat the herbivore's meal, and if the lion could answer, he would say, "I can't eat this food, because I hate it. I will only eat meat."

Now think of the verse that says, "Taste and see that the LORD is good" (Ps. 34:8), or of Jesus' saying, "I am the living bread that came down from heaven. If anyone eats of this bread, he will live forever"

(John 6:51). Why won't a sinful person "taste and see that the Lord is good" or feed upon Jesus as "the living bread"? To use the lion's words, it is because he "hates" such food. The sinner will not come to Christ because he does not want to. Deep in his heart he hates Christ and what he stands for. It is not because he cannot come naturally or physically.

Someone who is opposed to this teaching might say, "But surely the Bible says that anyone who will come to Christ may come to him. Didn't Jesus invite us to come? Didn't he say, 'Whoever comes to me I will never drive away' (John 6:37)?" The answer is, "Yes, that is exactly what Jesus said, but it is beside the point." Certainly, anyone who wants to come to Christ may come to him. That is why Jonathan Edwards insisted that the will is not bound. However, this liberty is what makes our refusal to seek God so unreasonable and increases our guilt. Who is it who wills to come? The answer is, No one, except those in whom the Holy Spirit has already performed the entirely irresistible work of the new birth, so that, as a result of this miracle, the spiritually blind eyes of the natural man are opened to see God's truth, and the depraved mind of the sinner, which in itself has no spiritual understanding, is renewed to embrace the Lord Jesus Christ as Savior.

OLD AND PRACTICAL DOCTRINE

This is not new teaching, of course, although it may seem new to many who hear it for the first time in our superficial age. It is merely the purest and most basic form of the Christian doctrine of humanity embraced by most Protestants and even (privately) by some Catholics. Perhaps some examples from church history will help:

The Belgic Confession (1561) has this statement: "We believe that through the disobedience of Adam original sin is extended to all mankind; which is a corruption of the whole nature and a hereditary disease, wherewith even infants in their mother's womb are infected, and which in man produces all sorts of sin, being in him as a root thereof, and therefore is so vile and abominable in the sight of God that it is sufficient to condemn all mankind" (Art. XV: "Original Sin").

The Thirty-Nine Articles of the Church of England (1562) say: "The condition of man after the fall of Adam is such, that he cannot

turn and prepare himself by his own natural strength and good works
to faith, and calling upon God; wherefore we have no power to do
good works, pleasant and acceptable to God, without the grace of God
by Christ preventing us [that is, being present beforehand to motivate
us], that we may have a good will, and working with us when we have
that will" (Art. 10).

The Westminster Larger Catechism (1647) states, "The sinfulness
of that state whereinto man fell, consisteth in the guilt of Adam's first
sin, the want of that righteousness wherein he was created, and the
corruption of his nature, whereby he is utterly indisposed, disabled,
and made opposite to all that is spiritually good, and wholly inclined
to all evil, and that continually" (A. 25).

The Westminster Confession of Faith (1647) says, "Man, by his
fall into a state of sin, hath wholly lost all ability of will to any spiritual good accompanying salvation; so as, a natural man, being altogether averse from that good, and dead in sin, is not able, by his
own strength, to convert himself, or to prepare himself thereunto"
(Chap. 9, Sec. 3).

The Baptist Confession (1689) says, "Our first parents, by this sin,
fell from their original righteousness and communion with God, and
we in them, whereby death came upon all: all becoming dead in sin,
and wholly defiled in all the faculties and parts of soul and body"
(Chap. 2: "Of the Fall of Man, of Sin, and of Punishment Thereof").

There may be people who are willing to admit that the inability
of the will to choose God or believe in Christ is the prevailing doctrine
of the church, and perhaps even the true teaching of the Bible, but who
are still not certain of the value of this doctrine and may even consider
it harmful. "If we teach that men and women cannot choose God,
don't we destroy the main impetus to evangelism and undercut the
missionary enterprise?" they ask. "Isn't it better just to keep quiet
about it?" It should be a sufficient answer to say that the very person
who gave us the Great Commission said, "No one can come to me
unless the Father who sent me draws him" (John 6:44).

But another way to answer is to say that, contrary to being a hindrance, this doctrine is actually the greatest possible motivation for
evangelism. If it is true that sinners, left to themselves, never naturally

seek out God, then how are they ever going to find God unless people like ourselves, sent by God, carry the gospel to them? It is by the preaching of the gospel that God calls people to faith, and the one who obeys God by taking the gospel to the lost can know that God will work through this means.

"But surely we must not tell the sinner that he cannot respond unless God first does a work of regeneration in him!" someone argues. "That will make him complacent, or even despairing." On the contrary, that is exactly what the sinner needs to know. For it is only in such understanding that sinful human beings learn how desperate their situation is, and thus how absolutely essential God's grace is. If we are hanging on to some confidence in our own spiritual ability, no matter how small, we will never seriously worry about our condition. There will be no sense of urgency. Life is long. There will be time to believe later on. We can always bring ourselves to believe when we want to—perhaps on our deathbed, after we have done what we wish with our lives. Or so we think. At least we can take a chance on it. But if we are truly dead in sin, as the Bible says we are, and if that involves our will as well as all other aspects of our psychological and spiritual make-up, then we will find ourselves in near despair. We will see our state as hopeless apart from the supernatural and totally unmerited workings of the grace of God.

And that is what God wants! He will not have us boasting of even the smallest human contribution to salvation. It is only as we renounce all such vain possibilities that he will show us the way of salvation through Christ and lead us to him.

Perhaps one final illustration will serve to confirm this point. During the 1840s, when revival was sweeping through Savannah, a young man came to the Rev. Benjamin Morgan Palmer to complain about his Calvinism. "You preachers are the most contradictory men in the world," he said. "Why, you said in your sermon that sinners were perfectly helpless in themselves—utterly unable to repent or believe—and then turned round and said they would all be damned if they did not."

Palmer sensed that his visitor was wrestling with the great issues of life and death. To make sure that the man really dealt with the gospel, he gave him an indifferent response: "Well, my dear sir, there is no use in our quarreling . . . ; either you can or you cannot. If you can [repent and believe], all I have to say is that I hope you will just go and do it." Palmer describes what happened next:

> As I did not raise my eyes from my writing . . . I had no means of marking the effect of these words, until, after a moment's silence, with a choking utterance, the reply came back: "I have been trying my best for three whole days and cannot." "Ah," [I] responded, raising [my] eyes and putting down [my] pen, "that puts a different face upon it; we will go . . . and tell the difficulty straight to God."
>
> We knelt down and I prayed as though this was the first time in human history that this trouble had ever arisen; that here was a soul in the most desperate extremity, which must believe or perish, and hopelessly unable of itself, to do it; that, consequently it was just the case for divine interposition. . . . Upon rising I offered not one single word of comfort or advice. . . . So I left my friend in his powerlessness in the hands of God, as the only helper. In a short time he came through the struggle, rejoicing in the hope of eternal life.[11]

Far from keeping us away from Christ, the true knowledge of radical depravity actually helps us abandon ourselves to his grace.

FOUR

⁘

Unconditional Election

Foreknown before the world began,
According to his gracious plan,
God destined I must be
Conformed to Jesus Christ, the man,
Who lived and loved as no man can:
A glorious decree.

Election is probably not the doctrine with which a person normally would begin a biblical theology. It has been pointed out that even John Calvin, who is famous for this doctrine, does not deal with it until near the end of the third volume of his four-part systematic theology. Calvin began as a biblical theologian, teaching what God has done for us in Jesus Christ. Only after that did he look back to explore the matter in its fullest perspective, showing, on the one hand, that salvation begins in eternity past in God's determination to save a people for himself and, on the other hand, that it continues into the eternal future by God's final perseverance with his saints.

Nevertheless, election is an important measuring rod for someone's theology, since an acceptance or rejection of this doctrine reveals at once whether a person is biblically correct on such other doctrines as the nature and extent of sin, the bondage of the will, the full grace of God in salvation, and even the presentation of the gospel.

After discussing the doctrine of man's radical depravity, Loraine Boettner noted the connection between depravity and election, writing,

It follows . . . from what has been said that salvation is absolutely and solely of grace—that God is free, in consistency
with the infinite perfections of his nature, to save none, few,
many, or all, according to the sovereign good pleasure of his
will. It also follows that salvation is not based on any mer-
its in the creature, and that it depends on God, and not on
men, who are, and who are not, to be made partakers of
eternal life. God acts as a sovereign in saving some and passing by others who are left to the just recompense of their
sins.[1]

It is this doctrinal "measuring rod" that we need to discuss in this
chapter.

THE MOST IMPORTANT PASSAGE

Throughout the Bible there are countless passages that deal with election, some of which will be noted in the course of this discussion. But
the most extensive biblical treatment of the subject is the apostle Paul's
exposition in Romans 9. Here are the most important verses:

It is not as though God's word had failed. For not all who are
descended from Israel are Israel. Nor because they are his
descendants are they all Abraham's children. On the contrary,
"It is through Isaac that your offspring will be reckoned." In
other words, it is not the natural children who are God's children, but it is the children of the promise who are regarded as
Abraham's offspring. For this was how the promise was
stated: "At the appointed time I will return, and Sarah will
have a son."
  Not only that, but Rebekah's children had one and the
same father, our father Isaac. Yet, before the twins were
born or had done anything good or bad—in order that
God's purpose in election might stand: not by works but by
him who calls—she was told, "The older will serve the
younger." Just as it is written: "Jacob I loved, but Esau I
hated."
  What then shall we say? Is God unjust? Not at all! For he
says to Moses,

> "I will have mercy on whom I have mercy,
>   and I will have compassion on whom I have
>   compassion."

It does not, therefore, depend on man's desire or effort, but on God's mercy. For the Scripture says to Pharaoh: "I raised you up for this very purpose, that I might display my power in you and that my name might be proclaimed in all the earth." Therefore God has mercy on whom he wants to have mercy, and he hardens whom he wants to harden (Rom. 9:6-18).

This is one of the most difficult sections of the entire Bible, more difficult even than those very confusing sections of Daniel and Revelation that deal with prophecy and the end times. But it is not only its treatment of election that makes this chapter difficult. What is especially hard is that it also deals with two related matters: first, the negative counterpart to election, which is the doctrine of reprobation (reprobation refers to God's passing over of those who are not elected to salvation); and second, that God is right in electing some and passing over others.

The proper name for this second matter is *theodicy*. "Theodicy" is composed of two Greek words: *theos,* which is the word for "God," and *dikei,* meaning what is "just" or "right." Thus a theodicy is an attempt to vindicate the justice of God in his actions. The question is, Is it right and just for God to choose some but not others?

A BASIS IN FACT

The best place to begin any discussion of election is precisely where Paul begins in Romans 9, namely, with the fact of election itself. The reasons are obvious. First, there is no sense arguing over the justice of God in electing some to salvation and passing over others if we are not convinced first of all that he does just that. If we do not believe this, we will not waste our time puzzling over it. Second, if we are convinced that God does elect some to salvation, as Paul is going to insist he does, then we will approach even the theodicy question differently. We will approach it in order to find understanding, rather than arrogantly trying to prove that God cannot do what the Bible clearly teaches he does. To seek understanding is one thing. God urges us to seek it. But to demand that God conform to our limited insights into what is just or right is another matter entirely.

As long as we believe that God exercises *any* control over history or the lives of his people, then we must come to terms with the doctrine of election in one way or another. It is simply inescapable. Why? For this reason. When Jesus called his first disciples, he called twelve and not more. Others might very well have profited by spending three years in close association with Jesus, but Jesus chose only twelve for this privilege. Moreover, when Jesus sent his disciples into the world to tell others about him, by necessity these early preachers went in one direction rather than another. Philip went to Samaria. Barnabas went to Antioch. Then Paul and Barnabas went north to Asia Minor. Still later, Paul and other missionary companions went to Greece, then Italy, and eventually farther west. In each case a choice was involved: north rather than south; west rather than east. If God was directing his servants at all, as virtually every Christian believes that he was, then he was choosing that some should hear the gospel rather than others, which is a form of election—even apart from the matter of a determination to call some to active faith by means of an internal, Spirit-empowered call.

The same is true in our experience. If you believe that God is leading you to speak to someone about the gospel, it is a fact that you are speaking to that person rather than to another. And even if a Christian friend should join you and speak to that other person, there are still millions who inevitably are passed by. Election is an inescapable fact of finite human life and history.

Loraine Boettner distinguishes between four biblical types of election: 1) the election of some individuals to salvation, 2) the election of some nations to special spiritual privileges, 3) the election of some individuals to the external means of grace apart from regeneration, and 4) the election of individuals to receive different kinds of gifts. But he says rightly that these four types of election are alike in principle, namely, that what God withholds from one he graciously bestows on another: "Why precisely this or that one is placed in circumstances which lead to saving faith, while others are not so placed, is indeed, a mystery. We cannot explain the workings of Providence; but we know that the Judge of all the earth shall do right, and that when we attain to perfect knowledge we shall see that He has sufficient reasons for all His acts."[2]

THREE GENERATIONS OF ELECTION

This is not the way Paul presents the doctrine, of course, though it is close enough to get us thinking along the right lines. At this point in the letter Paul is explaining why not all Jews are saved, and why the fact that they are not all saved does not mean that God's purposes for Israel have failed. The reason is that God does not choose everybody . . . and never has. He does not even choose all Jews, which is the meaning of Paul's opening statement: "It is not as though God's word had failed. For not all who are descended from Israel are Israel. Nor because they are his descendants are they all Abraham's children" (Rom. 9:6-7). He means that not everyone who has descended physically from Israel (the patriarch who was the grandson of Abraham, who was the father of the heads of the twelve Jewish tribes, and whose other name was Jacob) is a member of the true, elected, spiritual Israel of God. In the verses that follow he demonstrates that the three fathers of the nation—Abraham, Isaac, and Jacob—became what they were by election, and that others were not given this privilege.

1. *Abraham.* Election is obvious in the case of Abraham, which is one reason why Paul does not discuss his case in detail, though he does mention him. Abraham had a pagan ancestry, having been born in the ancient city of Ur in Mesopotamia. He had no knowledge of the true God, because no one in Ur had knowledge of the true God. In fact, Abraham's family worshiped idols. Joshua said this explicitly in the sermon recorded in the twenty-fourth chapter of the book that bears his name: "This is what the LORD, the God of Israel, says: 'Long ago your forefathers, including Terah the father of Abraham and Nahor, lived beyond the River and worshiped other gods'" (Josh. 24:2). Years later, even after God had called Abraham out of this pagan

environment and had instructed his son and grandson about himself as the true God, idols were still possessed and cherished in this family, for Rachel, the wife of Jacob, hid them from her father (see Genesis 31). Since God's call of Abraham is recorded clearly in Genesis 12, every knowledgeable Jew would have to confess that Jewish history began with that election.

2. Isaac. "But that is beside the point," some might have answered. "God had to start somewhere." They would have argued that the important matter is not whether God had elected the nation of Israel to some specific destiny apart from other nations. That was conceded. Paul had already written of "the adoption as sons, . . . the divine glory, the covenants, the receiving of the law" and other privileges that were granted only to Israel (Rom. 9:4-5). No one disputed the election of the nation. The real issue was whether all the descendants of Abraham (that is, all Jews) were saved by reason of their having come from him, or whether the principle of choice and rejection also applies after the initial choice of Abraham. In other words, does God continue to choose some but not all for salvation, both Jews and Gentiles, but not all from either category?

Since this is the issue, Paul begins his actual argument in verse 7 with the case of Abraham's son Isaac. The point is that Abraham had another son, Ishmael, begotten of Hagar thirteen years before Isaac was born. Ishmael was Abraham's son, but Ishmael was not chosen. Ishmael was Abraham's physical descendant, but he was not a child of promise as Isaac was.

There is something else in this example: the contrast between *natural* in the phrase "natural children" and *promise* in the phrase "children of the promise" (v. 8). The contrast shows that the difference between Isaac and Ishmael was not merely that God elected Isaac and passed over Ishmael, though that was an obvious truth, but also that God's choice of Isaac involved a supernatural intervention in the case of his conception. Ishmael was born of Abraham's *natural* sexual powers. But Isaac was conceived when Abraham was past the normal age for engendering children and when Sarah was past the age of conceiving and giving birth.

It is the same with our spiritual conception and new birth. Our spiritual conception, which is the outworking of God's electing choice, is likewise supernatural. We cannot engender spiritual life in ourselves, since according to Ephesians 2:1 we are spiritually dead in sins. We studied that in the last chapter. A dead person cannot do anything. In order for us to become spiritually alive God must do a miracle, which is exactly what he does. It is called the new birth, or regeneration.

3. *Jacob.* Yet there is still another objection. Paul's opponents could have argued that Ishmael was not a pure-blooded Jew. "It is true," they might have said, "that Ishmael was the son of Abraham. Yet he was not the son of Sarah. He was the son of Hagar, and Hagar was only an Egyptian and Sarah's servant. That is why Ishmael was not chosen."

In order to answer this point, Paul proceeds to the third generation of election, to the case of Rebekah's twin children, the sons Jacob and Esau. The words "not only that" show that he is continuing the argument: "Not only that, but Rebekah's children had one and the same father, our father Isaac. Yet, before the twins were born or had done anything good or bad—in order that God's purpose in election might stand: not by works but by him who calls—she was told, 'The older will serve the younger'" (vv. 10-12).

This is a remarkably effective example, since it proves everything that Paul needed to make his point.

First, Jacob and Esau were born of the same Jewish parents. That is, each was "a Hebrew of Hebrews," the phrase Paul used to describe his own pure-blooded Jewish ancestry in Philippians 3:5. So this was not a case of one having been chosen on the basis of a better ancestry and the other having been rejected because of a lesser one. The possible explanation of Paul's opponents for the choice of Isaac over Ishmael was invalidated by this case.

Second, the choice of Jacob rather than Esau went against the normal standards of primogeniture, according to which the elder should have received the greater blessing. True, the boys were twins, but Esau actually emerged from Rebekah's womb first. In spite of that, however, Jacob was chosen. There is nothing to explain this except God's right to dispose of the destinies of human beings as he pleases.

Third, the choice of Jacob was made before either child had opportunity to do either good or evil. The choice was made while the children were still in the womb. This means—we cannot miss it—that election cannot be on the basis of anything done by us. Moreover, Paul argues, the choice of Jacob rather than Esau was made specifically to teach election. This is what verses 11 and 12 say: "Yet, before the twins were born or had done anything good or bad—*in order that God's purpose in election might stand . . .*" (emphasis added). This means that God made his choice before the birth of Rebekah's sons to show that his election is apart from anything a human being might or might not do. It is a proof of what Paul says later, namely: "God has mercy on whom he wants to have mercy" (v. 18).

A BASIS IN SCRIPTURE

There are countless Bible texts that teach the doctrine of election, though Romans 9 is the most extensive treatment of the subject. There are probably several hundred of these texts—more than we can discuss or even list—but it might be valuable to mention some of the most explicit ones:

> *Deuteronomy 7:7-8.* "The LORD did not set his affection on you and choose you because you were more numerous than other peoples, for you were the fewest of all peoples. But it was because the LORD loved you and kept the oath he swore to your forefathers that he brought you out with a mighty hand and redeemed you from the land of slavery, from the power of Pharaoh king of Egypt."

> *John 15:16.* "You did not choose me, but I chose you and appointed you to go and bear fruit—fruit that will last."

> *Acts 13:48.* "When the Gentiles heard this, they were glad and honored the word of the Lord; and all who were appointed for eternal life believed."

Romans 11:5-6. "So too, at the present time there is a remnant chosen by grace. And if by grace, then it is no longer by works; if it were, grace would no longer be grace."

Romans 11:7. "What then? What Israel sought so earnestly it did not obtain, but the elect did."

Ephesians 1:4-5. "For he chose us in him before the creation of the world to be holy and blameless in his sight. In love he predestined us to be adopted as his sons through Jesus Christ, in accordance with his pleasure and will—to the praise of his glorious grace, which he has freely given us in the One he loves."

1 Thessalonians 5:9. "For God did not appoint us to suffer wrath but to receive salvation through our Lord Jesus Christ."

2 Thessalonians 2:13. "We ought always to thank God for you, brothers loved by the Lord, because from the beginning God chose you to be saved through the sanctifying work of the Spirit and through belief in the truth."

MIGHT ELECTION BE "CONDITIONAL"?

The existence of numerous texts like these means that every Christian has to believe in some kind of election. The concept appears too frequently to deny it. However, some who have trouble with the doctrine accept the word but try to reduce its force by arguing for what they call "conditional election." This means that God bases his election of an individual on foresight, foreseeing whether or not a particular individual will have faith. This destroys the very meaning of the word, of course, for such election is really not election at all. It actually means that men and women elect themselves, and God is reduced to a bystander who responds to their free choice. Logically and causally, even if not chronologically, God's choice follows man's choice.

Here is an even more potent objection to "conditional election": if election is based on what God foresees an individual might do, what could he possibly foresee in a spiritually dead sinner other than rejection of the gospel? To suppose that God could see something that is impossible apart from his determining will is irrational. On the other hand, to suppose that faith actually could be there denies the doctrine of man's radical depravity. We are beginning to see that the doctrines of grace are all interrelated. In Calvin's sermons on Genesis 25–27, which focus on election and reprobation, the Geneva Reformer wrote, "What could he [God] foresee, but this corrupted mass of Adam, that brings forth no other fruit but malediction. . . . Take away election, and what shall remain? As we have declared, we remain altogether lost and accursed."[3]

There is a philosophical objection, too. Election cannot rest on foreknowledge of what might happen, because in the sovereignty of God, the only things that can be foreknown are those that are predetermined, and this means that election must be prior to faith. Boettner sees this clearly:

> The Almighty and all-sovereign Ruler of the universe does not govern himself on the basis of a foreknowledge of things which might haply come to pass. Through the Scriptures the divine foreknowledge is ever thought of as dependent on the divine purpose, and God foreknows only because he has predetermined. His foreknowledge is but a transcript of his will as to what shall come to pass in the future, and the course which the world takes under his providential control is but the execution of his all-embracing plan. His foreknowledge of what is yet to be, whether it be in regard to the world as a whole or in regard to the detailed life of every individual, rests upon his pre-arranged plan.[4]

The verse that is most often used in support of conditional election is Romans 8:29, which says, "For those God foreknew he also predestined to be conformed to the likeness of his Son." However, that verse is not about God's foresight, if by foresight we mean simply God's ability to predict the future. The word "know" (in "foreknew") actually indicates God's choice, just as in Amos 3:2 ("You only have I known of all the families of the earth," KJV), which the New International Version rightly renders: "You only have I chosen. . . ."

Besides, the text does not say that God foreknew what certain individuals might do, only that he foreknew them as individuals to whom he would extend the grace of salvation.

Arthur Custance gives twelve renderings of Romans 8:29 by a variety of scholars, not many of whom are Calvinistic. Yet they all understand "foreknow" to refer to election and not to God's foreseeing faith. Here are some examples: "For those whom he had marked out from the first he predestinated" (*An American Translation*, Smith and Goodspeed); "For those whom God had already chosen he had also set apart to become like his Son" (*Good News for Modern Man*); "They are the ones he chose specially long ago and intended to become images of his Son" (*The Jerusalem Bible*); "For long ago, before they ever came into being, God both knew them and marked them out to become like the pattern of his Son" (*The New Testament: A New Translation*, Barclay); "For he decreed of old that those whom he predestined should share the likeness of his Son" (*The New Testament: A New Translation*, Moffatt); "For those whom God chose from the first he also did predestinate to be conformed to the image of his Son" (*The Twentieth Century New Testament*).[5] To summarize, when the Bible speaks of divine foreknowledge, it has in view the gracious doctrine of unconditional election.

REPROBATION: THE DIFFICULT DOCTRINE

Here we have to think about the difficult doctrine of reprobation, the teaching that God rejects or repudiates some persons to eternal condemnation in a way that is parallel but opposite to his ordaining others to salvation. We have to think about it here because it is brought into Romans 9 by two Old Testament quotations: Malachi 1:2-3 ("Jacob I loved, but Esau I hated," as cited in v. 13); and Exodus 9:16 ("I raised you [Pharaoh] up for this very purpose, that I might display my power in you and that my name might be proclaimed in all the earth," as cited in v. 17). Paul summarizes the teaching in those texts by concluding, "Therefore God has mercy on whom he wants to have mercy, and he hardens whom he wants to harden" (v. 18).

The place to begin is with the fact of reprobation, regardless of any questions we may have. In other words, we must follow the same procedure with reprobation as we followed with election. Many texts teach reprobation:

> Proverbs 16:4. "The LORD works out everything for his own ends—even the wicked for a day of disaster."

> John 12:39-40. "They could not believe, because, as Isaiah says elsewhere: 'He has blinded their eyes and deadened their hearts, so they can neither see with their eyes, nor understand with their hearts, nor turn—and I would heal them.'"

> John 13:18. "I know those I have chosen. But this is to fulfill the scripture: 'He who shares my bread has lifted up his heel against me.'"

> John 17:12. "While I was with them [the disciples], I protected them and kept them safe by that name you gave me. None has been lost except the one doomed to destruction so that Scripture would be fulfilled."

> 1 Peter 2:7-8. "Now to you who believe, this stone [Jesus Christ] is precious. But to those who do not believe, 'The stone the builders rejected has become the capstone,' and, 'A stone that causes men to stumble and a rock that makes them fall.' They stumble because they disobey the message—which is also what they were destined for."

> Jude 4. "Certain men whose condemnation was written about long ago have secretly slipped in among you."

Each of these verses (and others) teaches that God passes by some persons, destining them to destruction rather than to salvation. Clear enough. But here we need to make several important distinctions between election on the one hand and reprobation on the other.

First, we need to ask: Does God determine the destinies of individuals in exactly the same way, so that without any consideration of what they do (or might do), he assigns one to heaven and the other to hell? We know he does that in the case of those who are being saved, because we have been told that election has no basis in any good seen or foreseen in those who are elected. Paul's chief point in Romans 9 is that salvation is due entirely to God's mercy and not to any good that might be imagined to reside in us. The question is whether this can be said of the reprobate, too. Has God consigned them to hell apart from anything they have done, that is, apart from their deserving it?

Here there is an important distinction to be made, as I said. It is one, in fact, that has been made by the majority of Reformed thinkers and that has been embodied in many of the church's creeds. Take the Westminster Confession of Faith as a primary example. Here are the two paragraphs concerning election and reprobation:

> Those of mankind that are predestinated unto life, God, before the foundation of the world was laid, according to his eternal and immutable purpose, and the secret counsel and good pleasure of his will, hath chosen in Christ, unto everlasting glory, out of his mere free grace and love, without any foresight of faith or good works, or perseverance in either of them (Chap. 3, Sec. 5).

> The rest of mankind God was pleased, according to the unsearchable counsel of his own will, whereby he extendeth or withholdeth mercy as he pleaseth, for the glory of his sovereign power over his creatures, to pass by, and to ordain them to dishonor and wrath for their sin, to the praise of his glorious justice (Chap. 3, Sec. 7).

Those statements teach that in some ways election and reprobation are the same: both flow from the eternal counsel or will of God rather than the will of man, and both have as their ultimate purpose the revelation of God's glory. But there are two important points of difference.

First, the Confession speaks of the reprobate being "passed by." Some will argue that in its ultimate effect there is no difference between being passed by and being actively ordained to condemnation. But while that is true of the ultimate effect, there is nevertheless a major difference in the cause. The reason why some believe the gospel and are saved by it is that God intervenes in their lives to bring them to faith. He does it by the new birth or regeneration. But those who are lost—and this is the crucial point—are not caused by God to disbelieve. They do that all by themselves. To ordain their end, God needs only to withhold the special grace of regeneration.

Second, the Confession speaks of God ordaining the lost "to dishonor and wrath *for their sin.*" That makes reprobation the opposite of an arbitrary action. The lost are not sent to hell because God consigns them to it arbitrarily, but as a judgment for their sins. "We dare not forget," wrote Abraham Kuyper, "that while God, according to the secret of his counsel, elects those who are to be saved . . . this same omnipotent God has made us morally responsible, so that we are lost, not because we could not be saved, but because we would not."[6] Kuyper's theology was based on *The Canons of the Synod of Dort,* which state: "Not all, but some only, are elected, while others are *passed by* in the eternal decrees" and these are punished *"not only on account of their unbelief, but also for all their other sins"* (Chap. 1, Art. 15). Election is active; reprobation is passive. In election God actively intervenes to rescue those who deserve destruction, whereas in reprobation God passively allows some to receive the just punishment they deserve for their sins.

A USEFUL DOCTRINE

If the doctrine of reprobation is as difficult as it seems, then why should we speak about it at all? One reason, as we have seen, is that the Bible itself speaks of it. This is also the primary answer to a person who says, "I could never love a God like that." Fair enough, we may say; nevertheless, that is the God with whom you have to deal. However, this is not a completely satisfying answer, and there are other meaningful things to say about reprobation:

1. *Reprobation assures us that God's purpose has not failed.* The first benefit of this doctrine is the very thing Paul is concerned about in Romans 9, namely, assuring his readers that God's word has not failed (v. 6). God has determined all things from before the beginning of creation, and his word does not fail in regard to either the elect or the

reprobate. This means that if you have heard God's promises and believed his word, you can be sure that he will be faithful to you. If others are lost, it is because God has determined that they should be. Their loss does not mean that you will follow them. Nor does it mean that God has somehow failed in his plans for the evangelization of the world.

"Am I one of the elect?" you might ask. The answer to that question is easy: believe on the Lord Jesus Christ. If you do that, you are among the elect. That is the only way anyone can ever discover who God's elect are. It you need further assurance of your election, examine the fruit of the Holy Spirit in your Christian experience. However, the only infallible proof of election is found in Christ himself, and in his saving work.

2. Reprobation helps us deal with apostasy. We all know people who seemed to believe at one time but who have subsequently fallen away from the church. It is a disturbing occurrence. Does it mean that God has failed them? No. It only means that if they continue in their unbelieving state, they are not among God's elect people.

3. Reprobation reminds us that salvation is entirely of divine grace and that no human works contribute to it. If none were lost, then we would assume that God somehow owed us salvation. We would think that he saved us either because of who we are or because of who he is; either way, he has to do it. But this is not the situation. All are not saved. Therefore, the salvation of the elect is due to divine mercy only. This is the chief teaching of these important texts in Romans.

4. Reprobation glorifies God. As soon as we begin to think that God owes us something or that God *must* do something, we limit him and diminish his glory. Election and reprobation surround and protect God's glory, for they remind us that God is absolutely free and sovereign. God does whatever he wants with his universe. He is glorified in the damnation of the reprobate as well as in the salvation of the elect; his justice and his mercy are both glorious because they both demonstrate his divine sovereignty.

When we understand these things, we also understand that reprobation is a gospel doctrine. Why? Because reprobation highlights
mercy and reduces those who hear and accept the doctrine to a position of utter suppliance. It forces us to cry, "Jesus, Son of David, have
mercy on me" (Mark 10:47). As long as we believe that we are in control of our own destinies, we will never assume this posture. But when
we understand that we are in the hands of a just and holy God, and
that we are without any hope of salvation apart from his free and
utterly sovereign intervention, then we will call for mercy, which is the
only right response.

"I will have mercy on whom I will have mercy," says the Almighty.
If we believe that sentence, our cry will be that of the tax collector:
"God, have mercy on me, a sinner" (Luke 18:13). Who can fault a doc-
trine that does that?

BUT IS GOD JUST?

Still, there are people who fault God on the matter of election itself.
Even if we are convinced that God does operate in this way (which
many are not convinced of, but which we must be if we study the Bible
honestly), we nevertheless cry out fiercely that it is not right for God
to be selective. "Is God unjust?" That is the way Paul puts the question in Romans 9:14. But he answers by an emphatic denial: "Not at
all!" The King James Bible has "God forbid!" which is the strongest
denial Paul could muster.

That answer is not calculated to satisfy most people today, of
course, and there is more to say. Paul says more in the very next verses.
But this is the proper starting place. Why? Because it puts us in our
proper place as fallen human beings, which is the only position from
which we can begin to learn about spiritual things. The very nature of
sin is wanting to be in God's place. But as long as we try to be in God's
place, we will never be able to hear what God is saying to us. We will
argue with him instead. In order to learn, we must begin by confessing that God is God and that he is therefore right and just in his
actions, even though we may not understand what he is doing.

But how are we to understand God's justice? We can start with the fact that God is just, as well as with the fact that he elects some persons to salvation and passes by others. But how are we to think about his justice in doing so? This is the theodicy question mentioned earlier. Here are the essential elements of the answer:

1. *All human beings deserve hell, not heaven.* The important word here is "deserve." We are not talking about whether people actually end up in hell, or whether only some end up in hell and some in heaven. We are talking about what all deserve, and what all deserve is condemnation. That is justice. The justice of God, if it were to operate apart from any other factor, could do nothing other than to send every human being to hell. In fact, apart from the electing grace of God and the gracious death of Christ, this is exactly what would happen.

2. *If any individual is to be saved, it must be by mercy only, and mercy falls in an entirely different category from justice.* "Deserving" has to do with what people have done. "Mercy" has nothing to do with what people have done but is something that finds its source exclusively in the will of God. Romans 9:15 quotes Exodus 33:19, where God says, "I will have mercy on whom I have mercy, and I will have compassion on whom I have compassion." Notice that God says nothing about his justice, but speaks only of his mercy. The two attributes belong to two different categories, and election is a matter of mercy rather than justice.

3. *Even if God should save people on the basis of something in them—faith, good works, or something else—this actually would be an injustice, since individuals and their backgrounds are unequal.* Think it through. If God saved some people and not others on the basis of good works, which is what many people expect God to do, there would never be justice, because some people have inherited kinder, gentler temperaments than others, and because environmental factors always play a part. It is easier for a person who has been raised by two loving, moral parents to follow in their way, to make wise choices, and to do good as the world thinks of good. Not all do, of course, but that is irrelevant. The point is only that it is easier for such persons to do good than

it is for others who have been neglected by their parents or have been raised in a vicious, immoral environment. Or consider faith. Isn't it true that some persons are born more trusting than others, and others are instinctively more skeptical? Some people have a hard time believing anything. They have a hard time believing people, and it follows that they will have an even harder time believing God.

So election is not only just. It *is* just, and God is right in choosing some and passing by others. But—and here is the important thing—election is the *only* thing that is just. Election alone starts with all people at the same point and on the same level, all of them deserving hell. Then it saves some and passes by others, entirely apart from anything in the elect or reprobate persons themselves.

Two Irrepressible Objections

The answer to the theodicy question lies in the points just made, but objections still crowd our minds. Two objections are particularly common:

1. *Shouldn't God show mercy to everyone?* Anyone who asks that question still has not grasped the situation. The operative word in the question is "should," which means "ought" or "must," if justice is to be done. But as soon as we use that word we are back in the category of justice and are no longer dealing with mercy. If there is any "should" in the matter, the issue is no longer mercy. We are talking about justice, and as we have seen, justice can do nothing but send every human being to hell. It is not justice that we need from God; it is grace.

2. *Why doesn't God show mercy to everyone?* This question sounds like the first one, but it is really quite different. It is the question raised by a person who understands the difference between justice and mercy but still wonders why God is selective. After all, God could show mercy to everyone, couldn't he? He doesn't have to, but he could. And if he doesn't, why not? "Forget the word 'should,'" this person argues. "My question is simply: Why doesn't God save everyone?"

This is a proper question to ask because it is seeking understanding rather than demanding that God submit to human standards of right and wrong. But it is also more difficult than the questions posed so far since it asks about God's reasons for doing something, and there is no way we can know those reasons unless God reveals them to us. Does he? Romans 9:15 seems to say that God does not. We are only told that this is the way God operates: "I will have mercy on whom I have mercy, and I will have compassion on whom I have compassion." In other words, a perfectly legitimate answer to our question is that the "why" is none of our business! God does not owe us an answer.

There is one revealed answer, though not everyone will like it. In verse 17 Paul quotes Exodus 9:16: "For the Scripture says to Pharaoh: 'I raised you up for this very purpose, that I might display my power in you and that my name might be proclaimed in all the earth.'" This verse deals with reprobation, and it explains that at least one purpose of God's passing over some persons is to display his "power," so that his sovereign name might be proclaimed throughout the earth. In other words, God considers it important that we should know that he is all-powerful, especially in overcoming and judging those who stand against him, as Pharaoh did at the time of the Exodus.

A few verses later Paul enlarges on this idea, showing that God's "wrath," "power," "patience," "glory," and "mercy" are displayed in election, on the one hand, and in reprobation, on the other: "What if God, choosing to show his wrath and make his power known, bore with great patience the objects of his wrath—prepared for destruction? What if he did this to make the riches of his glory known to the objects of his mercy, whom he prepared in advance for glory—even us, whom he also called, not only from the Jews but also from the Gentiles?" (vv. 22-24). This means that God considers the display of his attributes to be worth the whole drama of human history—to be worth creation, the Fall, election, reprobation, and everything else. From God's point of view, the revelation of his glory—meaning the revelation of all his glorious attributes—is the grand priority.

Not everyone will be satisfied by this. It may not satisfy you. But if you do not find it satisfying, if you still ask, "But why should it be necessary for God's name to be glorified?" here is the answer: It is necessary because it is right for God to be glorified. God *is* glorious. He should be recognized as such. And because this is a universe run by God, not by us, what is right will be done in the end. God will be honored, and all will bow before him.

Do you see where this is moving? We began with the theodicy question: Is God right to act as he does? We asked that question because it did not seem right for God to select some for salvation and to pass by and judge others for their sin. But when we examine the question, as we have, we find that the matter is exactly the opposite of what we imagined it to be. We have found that God acts as he does precisely *because* he is just. He glorifies his name in displaying wrath toward sinners and the riches of his glory toward those who are being saved because this is the only right thing for God to do. It is his very justice, not his injustice, that causes him to operate in this fashion.

If we object to this, then our objection only shows that we are operating by a different and therefore by a sinful standard. Hence Paul's confrontational question: "Who are you, O man, to talk back to God?" (Rom. 9:20a).

THE BENEFITS OF THIS DOCTRINE

That would be a good place to stop, ending with the glory and justice of God. But we should also mention some benefits of this doctrine. This is because so many people think that election is useless and perhaps even pernicious. It is nothing of the sort. It is part of the Bible's inspired teaching and is therefore "useful," as Paul insisted all Scripture is (2 Tim. 3:16-17).

1. *Election is humbling.* Those who do not understand election often suppose the opposite, and it is true that those who believe in election sometimes appear prideful or smug. But this is an aberration. God tells us that he has chosen some by grace entirely apart from merit or even an ability to receive grace, precisely so that pride will be eliminated: "For it is by grace you have been saved, through faith—and this not from yourselves, it is the gift of God—not by works, so that no one can boast" (Eph. 2:8-9).

2. *Election encourages our love for God.* If we have a part in salvation, however small, then our love for God is diminished by just that amount. If it is all of God, then our love for him must be boundless. Sadly, today's church frequently takes the love of God for granted. "Of course, God loves me," we say. "I love myself; why shouldn't God love me too?" Consider the little girl who loved the Barney theme song from television ("I love you, you love me; we're a happy family"). But she sang it this way: "I love me, you love me; we're a happy family." That is how we tend to think of God's love. We think we deserve it. Understanding that we are elected by grace alone undermines our self-centered, self-satisfied way of thinking.

3. *Election will enrich our worship.* Who can admire a God who is frustrated by the rebellious will of human beings? Martin Luther wrote, "It is not irreligious, idle, or superfluous, but in the highest degree wholesome and necessary, for a Christian to know whether or not his will has anything to do in matters pertaining to salvation. . . . For if I am ignorant of the nature, extent and limits of what I can and must do with reference to God, I shall be equally ignorant and uncertain of the nature, extent and limits of what God can and will do in me—though God, in fact, works all in all. Now, if I am ignorant of God's works and power, I am ignorant of God himself; and if I do not know God, I cannot worship, praise, give thanks, or serve Him, for I do not know how much I should attribute to myself and how much to Him. We need, therefore, to have in mind a clear-cut distinction between God's power and ours, and God's work and ours, if we would live a godly life."[7]

4. *Election encourages us in our evangelism.* People suppose that if God is going to save certain individuals, then he will save them, and there is no point in our having anything to do with it. But it does not work that way. Election does not exclude the use of the means by which God works, and the proclamation of the gospel is one of those means (1 Cor. 1:21).

Moreover, it is only the truth of election that gives us any hope of success as we proclaim the gospel to unsaved men and women. If the heart of a sinner is as opposed to God as the Bible declares it to be, and if God does not elect people to salvation, then what hope of success could we possibly have in witnessing? If God does not call sinners to Christ effectively, it is certain that we cannot do so either. Even more, if the effective agent in salvation is not God's choice and call—if the choice is up to the individual or to us, because of our powers to persuade others to accept Christ—how could we even dare to witness? For what if we make a mistake? What if we give a wrong answer? What if we are insensitive to the person's real questions? In that case, people will fail to believe. They may eventually go to hell, and their eternal destiny will be partly our fault, and how could any thinking, feeling Christian live with that?

But on the other hand, if God has elected some to salvation and if he is calling those elected individuals to Christ, then we can go forth boldly, knowing that our witness does not have to be perfect, that God uses even weak and stuttering testimonies to his grace and, best of all, that all whom God has chosen for salvation will be saved. We can be fearless, knowing that all who are called by God will come to him.

FIVE

Particular Redemption

He bore my sin on Calvary's tree
And righteousness bestowed on me
That I might see his face.
God justified me, set me free,
And glorified I soon will be:
How marvelous this grace.

For whom did Christ die? That is a question the vast majority of today's Christians would answer easily, without any special need for reflection: "Why, for the whole world, of course. The death of Christ is of infinite value. Anyone who believes on the Lord Jesus Christ can be saved." Yes, but things are not that simple. Calvinists believe that Jesus died for the elect alone and that this has important implications for how we are to understand the nature, character, and effect of Christ's death, as well as for how we understand its extent. Yet the idea of a "limited atonement" is so foreign to most of today's Christians, and is so misunderstood even by those who have heard of it, that it needs to be carefully explained.

Admittedly, these misunderstandings are due in some measure to the way Calvinists have often expressed the doctrine. Following the TULIP acronym, they have called the third of the five points "limited atonement," which is an unfortunate way of speaking. Limited atonement suggests that the death of Christ was of limited value, and this is not what any true Calvinist wants to say. We believe, as do most Christians, that the death of Christ is of infinite value. It was sufficient to save not only our world but an infinite number of sinful worlds besides, if they should exist. But that is not what lies behind this question. The question we are raising is this: What did Jesus accomplish by his death? What did his death do? Did Jesus' death merely make salvation possible for everyone, because he died for all, without actually saving anyone? Or did his death actually accomplish the salvation of those for whom he died? The Bible seems to teach the latter. But if it does, then those who will be in heaven are those for whom Christ died and those alone. He did not accomplish salvation for those who will not be in heaven, or they would be there.

When Calvinists speak of a "limited atonement," those holding to the contrary view express their view as an "unlimited atonement," which sounds much better. That probably explains why even some professed Calvinists pull back at this point, calling themselves "four-point" rather than "five-point" Calvinists. But what happens when we express our understanding of Christ's death by the words in the title for this chapter? What if we call our doctrine "definite atonement" or "particular redemption"? Will our opponents respond, "But I believe in an 'indefinite atonement'"? In this contrast, "definite atonement" or "particular redemption" sounds much better.

But the controversy is not really about words. It is about how the gospel doctrines hold together. If God planned from eternity to save one portion of the human race and not another, which is what election affirms, then it is a contradiction to say that he sent his Son to die for those he had previously determined not to save *in the same way* that he sent his Son to die for those he had determined actually to save. This does not mean that the death of Christ has no benefit for the whole of mankind, short of salvation. It does have benefit. It has brought an ethic into the flow of human history from which even non-Christians benefit. But it does mean that, so far as the work of salvation itself is concerned, Jesus came into the world specifically to save those individuals whom the Father had given him, and not others.

A MINORITY POSITION

When we speak of particular redemption we have to acknowledge that Reformed thinkers occupy a minority position within Christendom today, though that was not always true in church history. We believe that the doctrine is biblical, but we recognize that large segments of today's church see things differently.

The opposite view to particular redemption is universal redemption, and if one asks informed Roman Catholics, knowledgeable members of the Greek Orthodox or Russian Orthodox communions, or even orthodox Lutherans or Arminians, they will say that this is what they believe. In fact, even many Presbyterian and Reformed people will say this, though they are not supported at this point by their confessional standards. These people all believe that Jesus died for all men and women and that the only thing that keeps them from the benefits of his death (if, indeed, there are some who do fail to benefit from it) is their unbelief or lack of faith. Those who hold to the Reformed position affirm that Jesus died for a select number of people, those whom the Father specifically had given him, that his atonement accomplished their salvation, and therefore that all of these are certain to be saved.

A good place to begin is by emphasizing certain points of agreement, since there are important matters that are not at all in dispute:

1. *There is agreement about the value of Jesus' atonement.* When Calvinists speak of "limited atonement," as they sometimes unwisely do, they seem to suggest that somehow the death of Jesus was inadequate to save all men and women. But this is not what Reformed people believe. All of us stand together in affirming that the value of Jesus' death was so great—in fact, infinite—that it is more than sufficient to atone for all the sins of all the people in all ages of this world. The value of the death of Jesus Christ is not limited in any way. His atonement is of infinite value.

2. *We agree that there are benefits of the death of Jesus Christ for all people, benefits short of salvation.* Some of those benefits are of a

temporal nature. Before the coming of Christ there was an outpour-
ing of what theologians call common grace. God was patient with sin
and delayed his judgment of it. Paul referred to this in his sermon
on Mars Hill when he said that "in the past God overlooked such
ignorance, but now he commands all people everywhere to repent"
(Acts 17:30). That is true in the present as well. That is, while the
gospel of grace is preached throughout the world, judgment is
delayed. This is what Peter referred to when he observed that God
"is patient with you, not wanting anyone to perish, but everyone to
come to repentance" (2 Pet. 3:9).

There are also common benefits of the life and death of Christ for
human society. Who can doubt that the demonstration of God's love,
mercy, and compassion at Calvary—particularly as this has worked
itself out in the transformed values of Christian people, blessing their
homes and giving them a new concern for others in all other areas of
life—has blessed people wherever the gospel of grace has penetrated?
The world would be a far less gentle place were it not for Christianity.
Calvinists, as well as other Christians, confess that freely.

3. We are not in disagreement as to whether or not all people will be
saved. There are some universalists, of course. In fact, an increasingly
small minority within the evangelical church affirms universalism. But
for the most part, nearly all evangelicals are united in the confession,
based on Scripture, that not all people will be saved, that hell is a real
place, and that there are and will be people in it. We would be glad to
teach that all will be saved, if we thought that this is what the
Scriptures teach. If we should get to heaven one day and discover that
God had saved every person who has ever walked upon the face of the
earth, we would be as delighted as anyone. But that is not what
Scripture teaches. Therefore, like the apostles, we attempt to warn all
men and women to turn from the wrath to come.

In each of the areas mentioned, Reformed people as well as
those of other evangelical theological persuasions are in substantial
agreement. Furthermore, we all agree that the atonement must be
limited in one way or another. Unless a person is a genuine uni-

versalist, and believes that every individual eventuall he or she inevitably circumscribes the atonement. E ited in its *effects* (Christ died for all, but not all get saved), or it is limited in its *scope* (Christ did not die for all, but all for whom he died will be saved). Loraine Boettner, who has written so many helpful books explaining Reformed theology, has compared the situation to two bridges. One is a very broad bridge, but it only goes halfway across the chasm. The other is a narrow bridge, but it spans the divide.[1] When things are put this way, anyone can see that it is far better to have a narrow bridge that actually does the job. This is the Reformed position: that the narrow way of the Cross reaches all the way to salvation.

Charles Spurgeon took this argument one step further, arguing that those who deny particular redemption are the ones who actually limit the atonement. Spurgeon said:

> We are often told that we limit the atonement of Christ, because we say that Christ has not made a satisfaction for all men, or all men would be saved. Now, our reply to this is, that, on the other hand, our opponents limit it: we do not. The Arminians say, Christ died for all men. Ask them what they mean by it. Did Christ die so as to secure the salvation of all men? They say, "No, certainly not." We ask them the next question—Did Christ die so as to secure the salvation of any man in particular? They answer "No." They are obliged to admit this, if they are consistent. They say "No. Christ has died that any man may be saved if"—and then follow certain conditions of salvation. Now, who is it that limits the death of Christ? Why, you. You say that Christ did not die so as infallibly to secure the salvation of anybody. We beg your pardon, when you say we limit Christ's death; we say, "No, my dear sir, it is you that do it." We say Christ so died that he infallibly secured the salvation of a multitude that no man can number, who through Christ's death not only may be saved, but are saved, must be saved and cannot by any possibility run the hazard of being anything but saved. You are welcome to your atonement; you may keep it. We will never renounce ours for the sake of it.[2]

THE DESIGN OF THE ATONEMENT

The real question is not whether the death of Jesus Christ has sufficient value to atone for the sins of the entire world, or whether his
death benefits all people in some limited sense, or whether everyone
will be saved. The real question concerns the *design* of the atonement;
that is, what did God the Father actually intend to do in sending his
Son to die for us? And did Jesus do it? We can express the matter with
such questions as these: Did Jesus' death actually redeem anyone? Did
his sacrifice of himself make a true propitiation for our sins? Did Jesus'
death reconcile any specific individual to God? Was Jesus' death an
actual atonement? If the answer to these questions is "Yes," then for
whom did he do these things? As we phrased things before, did Jesus'
death actually save anyone, or did it only make the gift of salvation
possible? When the question is asked in this way, we can see that there
are only three possible answers:

- Jesus' death was not an actual atonement, but only something that makes atonement possible. The atonement
  becomes actual when the sinner repents of his or her sin
  and believes on Jesus.[3]

- Jesus' death was an actual atonement for the sins of God's
  elect people with the result that these, and only these, are
  delivered from sin's penalty.

- Jesus' death was an actual atonement for the sin of all people with the result that all people are saved.

We can dismiss the third possibility immediately, for all orthodox
Christians agree that not all persons will be saved. On the contrary, the
Bible teaches clearly that some will not be saved; in some cases, specific individuals are lost. Pharaoh is one example. Paul described him
as someone whom God had raised up for the very purpose of displaying his power, judgment, and wrath (Rom. 9:17-22). Judas is
another. Jesus said that "it would be better for him if he had not been

born" (Matt. 26:24). The rich man in Christ's parable of the rich man and Lazarus is yet another.

If we eliminate the third possibility mentioned above, which is universalism, we are left with options one and two:

• Jesus' death was not an actual atonement but only made atonement possible,

or

• Jesus' death was an actual atonement for the sins of those elect persons whom the Father previously had determined to give to him.

This is a very manageable alternative, for it requires us only to study the terms the Bible actually uses to talk about Christ's death on the Cross. What words does the Bible use to speak of his sacrifice?

1. *Redemption.* Redemption is a commercial term, meaning "to buy back." Except for bankers who speak of redeeming bonds, ordinarily we use this word only in reference to pawnshops. If you are temporarily short of money but have something of value that can be pawned, you can take it to a pawnbroker and he will give you a fraction of its value in cash for the object. Later, if you come into sufficient money and want your possession back, you can go back to the pawnbroker and redeem your possession by paying the amount you borrowed plus interest. In the ancient world redemption frequently pertained to slavery. By paying the redemption price a benevolent person might set a favored slave free.

The terminology of redemption is used many times of Jesus' death for us. For example, Peter wrote, "You know that it was not with perishable things such as silver and gold that you were redeemed from the empty way of life handed down to you from your forefathers, but with the precious blood of Christ, a lamb without blemish or defect" (1 Pet. 1:18-19). Paul said, "Christ redeemed us from the curse of the law by becoming a curse for us" (Gal. 3:13). And John wrote, "with your blood you purchased men for God from every tribe and language and people and nation" (Rev. 5:9b).

Now let's ask the question: What kind of a redemption would it be in which the death of Jesus only makes redemption possible and in which, as a result, some of those for whom he died are still in bondage? Imagine that a friend of yours is in trouble with the law and has been taken to jail. He is arraigned before a judge, and bail is set. He has no money, but you hear of his plight and immediately take money down to the courthouse to bail him out. You appear before the judge, pay the bail price, and go home. Your wife asks, "Where is your friend?"

"He's in prison."

"In prison?" she asks. "But didn't you take the bail money down there?"

"Yes," you say. "I paid the money to redeem him, but he's still in prison. I didn't actually bring him out." What kind of redemption would that be? If there is a real redemption, then the person who has been redeemed must be set free. When the Bible says that Jesus redeemed us by his death on the Cross, that redemption must be an effective redemption, and those who have been redeemed must be actual beneficiaries of it.

2. *Propitiation.* Propitiation is a religious term meaning "to turn aside wrath," specifically the wrath of God. Propitiation presupposes God's wrath against sin but shows how another person can die to bear that wrath in the guilty one's place. Paul uses this word in Romans 3 when he says, "God presented him [Jesus] as a sacrifice of atonement, through faith in his blood" (v. 25). The phrase "sacrifice of atonement" translates the word *hilasterion,* which means "propitiation."

Someone who denies that Christ's death was an actual atonement must also deny that it was an actual propitiation. But what kind of propitiation would it be in which Jesus turns the wrath of God aside by his death, but in which God nevertheless pours it out on the sinner? Even in human law there is a generally recognized principle that a crime cannot be punished twice. Legal statutes pertaining to "double jeopardy" prohibit what lawyers call "multiple penalty." If a person is sentenced to ten years in prison for a crime and then serves his time, he is entitled to go out as a free man. No one can send him back to prison and make him pay for his crime again. Or to take another example, if someone pays the fine for another person's parking violation, the traffic court cannot require the offender to pay the fine, too. It is the same with God. God does not punish a sin twice. Therefore, if sin was actually punished in the person of Christ by his dying for it, God cannot also punish the sinner for the same crime.

If Jesus made propitiation for sin by his death, that propitiation must either be for all the sins of all the people of the world, as a result of which all people are or will be saved (the view of universalists), or else it must be a propitiation for the sins of his elect people, who alone are saved.

3. *Reconciliation.* Reconcile means "to make one" or "to establish peace" between warring parties. Paul refers to this in writing to the Corinthians, saying, "God . . . reconciled us to himself through Christ and gave us the message of reconciliation: that God was reconciling the world to himself in Christ, not counting men's sins against them" (2 Cor. 5:18-19). What kind of reconciliation would it be in which the parties who have been reconciled are still fighting? It would not be true reconciliation at all.

Yet reconciliation is what the Bible says Jesus accomplished by his death on Calvary. Apart from Christ everyone is at war with God, regardless of what some may believe or say. We are God's enemies. We resist him in every way we possibly can; we would kill him if we could. And that is what we did, when God became man in the person of Christ! Jesus' death has brought God and those whom God has given him together. Paul told the Romans that while "we were God's enemies, we were reconciled to him through the death of his Son" (Rom. 5:10). What kind of a reconciliation would it be if the parties involved should go on fighting?

4. *Atonement.* Atonement means just what it sounds like: "to make at one" those who formerly were at odds. Atonement has much the same meaning as reconciliation. But the unique flavor of atonement

is its overtone of sacrifice, for it is said over and over again in the Bible, beginning with the sacrificial religion of Israel, that sacrifices make atonement for sin. The author of Hebrews wrote of Jesus that "he had to be made like his brothers in every way, in order that he might become a merciful and faithful high priest in service to God, and that he might make atonement for the sins of the people" (Heb. 2:17). This verse is particularly telling, for the chief point of Hebrews is that Jesus really accomplished by his death what the Old Testament sacrifices merely prefigured. They pointed forward to Christ's work. But when Jesus died, atonement actually was made, with the result that it never needs to be repeated.

When we put these terms together, looking at their precise meanings, we see that Jesus did not come merely to make salvation possible, but actually to save his people. He did not come to make redemption possible; he died to redeem his people. He did come to make propitiation possible; he turned aside God's wrath for each of his elect people forever. He did not come to make reconciliation between God and man possible; he actually reconciled to God those whom the Father had given him. He did not come merely to make atonement for sins possible, but actually to atone for sinners.

In his small theological classic *Redemption Accomplished and Applied,* John Murray summarized the matter like this:

> The very nature of Christ's mission and accomplishment is involved in this question. Did Christ come to make the salvation of all men possible, to remove obstacles that stood in the way of salvation, and merely to make provision for salvation? Or did he come to save his people? Did he come to put all men in a salvable state? Or did he come to secure the salvation of all those who are ordained to eternal life? Did he come to make men redeemable? Or did he come effectually and infallibly to redeem? The doctrine of the atonement must be radically revised if, as atonement, it applies to those who finally perish as well as to those who are the heirs of eternal life. In that event we should have to dilute the grand categories in terms of which the Scripture defines the atonement and deprive them

of their most precious import and glory. This we cannot do. The saving efficacy of expiation, propitiation, reconciliation, and redemption is too deeply embedded in these concepts, and we dare not eliminate this efficacy. We do well to ponder the words of our Lord himself: "I have come down from heaven, not to do my own will but the will of him who sent me. And this is the will of him who sent me, that of everything which he hath given to me I should lose nothing, but should raise it up in the last day" (John 6:38-39). Security inheres in Christ's redemptive accomplishment. And this means that, in respect of the persons contemplated, design and accomplishment and final realization have all the same extent.[4]

Christ's work on the Cross was not a hypothetical salvation for hypothetical believers, but a real and definite salvation for God's own chosen people. A redemption that does not redeem, a propitiation that does not propitiate, a reconciliation that does not reconcile, and an atonement that does not atone cannot help anybody. But a redemption that redeems, a propitiation that propitiates, a reconciliation that reconciles, and an atonement that atones reveal a most amazing grace on God's part and draw us to rest in him and in his completed work, rather than our own.

BELIEF AND UNBELIEF

There is only one possible way to avoid the view that the Bible teaches definite or particular redemption, and even this turns out not to be a true possibility, once it is examined carefully. Some argue that the atonement is an actual atonement for all the sins of all the world but that all persons are not saved, not because their sins are not atoned for but because they do not believe in Jesus and therefore will not accept the gospel. "It's like a gift," a person might say. "The gift has been selected and paid for, but no one can be forced to take a gift. In the same way, the world has been saved, but many will not be saved because they will not believe on Jesus."

Does that sound reasonable?

It does until we explore the nature of unbelief. Is unbelief a morally neutral choice, merely deciding to accept or not to accept sal-

vation? Or is it a sin? It is a sin, of course. In fact, it is the most damning of all sins, for it is the equivalent of trampling the very blood of
the Son of God underfoot. But this means—if Jesus died for all the sins
of all men, including this sin of unbelief—that all are saved, and we
are back once again to universalism.

No one has put this better or more plainly than John Owen, the
great Puritan preacher and theologian. Owen's classic treatise *The
Death of Death in the Death of Christ* (1647) is an attempt to show
that the doctrine of universal atonement is unbiblical and therefore
antithetical to the gospel. Early in the treatise Owen puts the options
like this:

> God imposed his wrath due unto, and Christ underwent the
> pains of hell for,
>
>> either all the sins of all men,
>> or all the sins of some men,
>> or some sins of all men.
>
> If the last, some sins of all men, then have all men some sins
> to answer for, and so shall no man be saved.

That is clearly false. Some will be saved. So option number three is
eliminated. The second option, according to Owen, is the one "we
affirm, that Christ in their stead and room suffered for all the sins of
all the elect in the world."

But what about the first? This is the point to which we have come
in our study. It is what the universalists say: Christ died for all the sins
of all men. But, wrote Owen,

> Why are not all free from the punishment of all their sins? You
> will say, "Because of their unbelief; they will not believe." But
> this unbelief, is it a sin, or not? If not, why should they be
> punished for it? If it be, then Christ underwent the punish-
> ment due to it, or not. If so, then why must that hinder them
> more than their other sins for which he died from partaking
> of the fruit of his death? If he did not, then did he not die for
> all their sins? Let them choose which part they will.[5]

If Jesus died for all the sins of all men, unbelief included, then all are saved, which the Bible denies. If he died for all the sins of all men, unbelief excluded, then he did not die for all the sins of anybody and all must be condemned. There is no other position, save that he died for the sin of his elect people only.

Of course, this is what the Bible teaches. Here are some representative texts (emphases added):

Isaiah 53:8. "For the transgression of *my people* he was stricken."

Matthew 1:21. "You are to give him the name Jesus, because he will save *his people* from their sins."

Matthew 20:28. "The Son of Man did not come to be served, but to serve, and to give his life as a ransom *for many.*"

Luke 1:68. "Praise be to the Lord, the God of Israel, because he has come and has redeemed *his people.*"

John 10:11. "I am the good shepherd. The good shepherd lays down his life for *the sheep.*"

John 13:1. "It was just before the Passover Feast. Jesus knew that the time had come for him to leave this world and go to the Father. Having loved *his own* who were in the world, he now showed *them* the full extent of his love."

John 17:1-2, 9. "Glorify your Son, that your Son may glorify you. For you granted him authority over all people that he might give eternal life to *all those you have given him.* . . . I pray for *them.* I am not praying for the world."

Galatians 3:13. "Christ redeemed *us* from the curse of the law by becoming a curse *for us.*"

Ephesians 5:25. "Husbands, love your wives, just as Christ loved *the church* and gave himself up *for her.*"

Romans 8:28-32. "We know that in all things God works for the good of those who love him, *who have been called according to his purpose.* For those God foreknew he also predestined to be conformed to the likeness of his Son, that he might be the firstborn among many brothers. And those he predestined, he also called; those he called, he also justified; those he justified, he also glorified.

"What, then, shall we say in response to this? If God is *for us,* who can be against *us?* He who did not spare his own Son, but gave him up *for us* all—how will he not also, along with him, graciously *give us* all things?"

In this last passage, those who have been foreknown, predestined, called, justified, and glorified are also those for whom Christ died. They are those who have been chosen by God to belong to Jesus Christ before the foundation of the world.

THE PROBLEM TEXTS

Even as we refer to these verses, some will think of other verses that they believe teach that Jesus died for everyone. What about those texts? This is a serious matter, for if there are texts that do teach that Jesus died for everyone, then we are going to have to revise our theology or at least reconcile the two sets of passages. For it must be the Scriptures and not mere logic on our part that determines our convictions in theological matters.

There are three types of problem passages:

1. *Passages that seem to teach that God has a will to save everyone.* Here are some examples: "I take no pleasure in the death of anyone, declares the Sovereign LORD. Repent and live!" (Ezek. 18:32); "This is good, and pleases God our Savior, who wants all men to be saved and to come to a knowledge of the truth" (1 Tim. 2:3-4); or, perhaps the most often cited of these passages—"The Lord is not slow in keeping his promise, as some understand slowness. He is patient with you, not wanting anyone to perish, but everyone to come to repentance" (2 Pet. 3:9).

However, none of these verses is really to the point. The most frequently cited verse, 2 Peter 3:9, is not talking about the salvation of all men and women, but only of the elect. The issue is the delay of Christ's return, and Peter is explaining that God has delayed it, not out of indifference to us and what we may be suffering, but because he wants to bring to repentance all whom he has determined in advance will be gathered in. If Christ should come now, there would be generations of yet unborn people, containing generations of Christians yet to come, who would not be in heaven. Therefore, "The Lord is not slow in keeping his promise, as some understand slowness. He is patient with you, not wanting [any of his elect ones] to perish, but everyone to come to repentance."

This is how John Owen understood the text. He wrote:

Who are these of whom the apostle speaks, to whom he writes? Such as had received "great and precious promises," chap. 1:4, whom he calls "beloved" (chap. 3:1); whom he opposeth to the "scoffers" of the "last days," verse 3; to whom the Lord hath respect in the disposal of these days; who are said to be "elect" (Matt. 24:22). Now, truly, to argue that because God would have none of those to perish, but all of them to come to repentance, therefore he hath the same will and mind towards all and everyone in the world (even those to whom he never makes known his will, nor ever calls to repentance, if they never once hear of his way of salvation), comes not much short of extreme madness and folly.[6]

In 1 Timothy 2 Paul is urging that prayers be made for everyone—not just the poor and oppressed but also "for kings and all those in authority" (v. 2). In this context, verse 4 is best understood as Augustine and Calvin understood it, namely, that God is saving people from all categories of humanity. He is willing even to save kings, as unlikely as that may seem. So pray for them, says Paul, even though they may be the very ones who are persecuting you at this time.

As far as the passage in Ezekiel goes, the verses say only that God does not find joy in taking vengeance. On the contrary, he finds joy in the salvation of his people, much as we are told that the angels rejoice in heaven over even one sinner who repents. Besides, in that chapter, where Ezekiel is explicitly citing the requirements of the law of Moses, it may well be that it is physical and not spiritual rewards and punishments that are in view; that is, physical death which is the punishment for some of these transgressions. Since this was written during the time of the Babylonian exile, it may even be the contrast between the death of the people *versus* their survival as a nation that the prophet has in mind.

   2. *Passages in which it is suggested that some people for whom Jesus Christ died will perish.* In this category are such passages as these: "Do not by your eating destroy your brother for whom Christ died" (Rom. 14:15); "So this weak brother, for whom Christ died, is destroyed by your knowledge" (1 Cor. 8:11); "If we deliberately keep on sinning after we have received the knowledge of the truth, no sacrifice for sins is left, but only a fearful expectation of judgment and of raging fire that will consume the enemies of God" (Heb. 10:26-27); "There were also false prophets among the people, just as there will be false teachers among you. They will secretly introduce destructive heresies, even denying the sovereign Lord who bought them" (2 Pet. 2:1).
   The first two of these passages are entirely off the mark, for in them Paul is not speaking of a believer being lost. He denies elsewhere that this is even possible. He is speaking only to Christians who by their irresponsible behavior show disregard for the welfare of their fellow believers. They do not care if they hurt them in regard to their spiritual walk.
   Hebrews 10:26-27 is closer, but again it is not quite on target. These verses should be seen in the context of the entire book of Hebrews, which was written to Jews who had received knowledge of Christ and Christianity, but who were not yet at the point of abandoning their Judaism, with its ritual feasts and sacrifices for sin, in order to accept the perfect sacrifice provided by Jesus through his death on Calvary. People in that position are warned that if, after having been taught the only true way of salvation, they should go back to their empty forms and ceremonies, thereby rejecting Christ, there will remain no other sacrifice for them and they will be lost. They will be

lost because they were not true believers in the first place. Those who claim to benefit from Christ's blood yet remain defiant in their sin deceive themselves into a false assurance.

Second Peter 2:1 is the most powerful of the texts in this category, for it seems to speak of those who have actually been redeemed by Jesus' death and yet perish. But we have to look closely at the nature of those about whom Peter is speaking. They are "false prophets," "false teachers" who teach "destructive heresies." Are they Christians? No. Therefore, they are not saved people who perish, but rather unsaved people.

How is it, then, that Peter can speak of them "denying the Sovereign Lord who bought them"? The best approach is to think of this as describing what these unbelieving teachers claimed rather than what they had actually received from Jesus. But even if this is not the answer, if it is supposed that the people in view actually are Christians, we should recognize that the verse will also present difficulties in regard to the doctrine of perseverance, which most people who deny the doctrine of particular redemption nevertheless want to uphold. It is not merely a problem for five-point Calvinists but also for four-point Calvinists.

3. *Passages in which the work of Jesus seems to be intended for the entire world.* To many this is the most important group of passages. They are numerous (emphases added): "We all, like sheep, have gone astray, each of us has turned to his own way; and the LORD has laid on him the iniquity of *us all*" (Isa. 53:6); "Look, the Lamb of God, who takes away the sin of *the world!*" (John 1:29); "We no longer believe just because of what you said; now we have heard for ourselves, and we know that this man really is the Savior of *the world*" (John 4:42); "Consequently, just as the result of one trespass was condemnation for all men, so also the result of one act of righteousness was justification that brings life for *all men*" (Rom. 5:18); "He who did not spare his own Son, but gave him up for *us all*—how will he not also, along with him, graciously give us all things?" (Rom. 8:32); "Christ . . . died for *all*, and therefore all died. And he died for *all*, that those who live should no longer live for themselves but for him who died for them

and was raised again" (2 Cor. 5:14-15); "For there is one God and one mediator between God and men, the man Christ Jesus, who gave himself as a ransom for *all men*" (1 Tim. 2:5-6); "He is the atoning sacrifice for our sins, and not only for ours but also for the sins of *the whole world*" (1 John 2:2).

What do we do with these passages and others like them?

First, we need to point out that the words assumed to include all people—"all" and "world"—do not necessarily have that scope, either in our own speech or in the Bible. That is to say, they often refer to all of a particular class, but not to all people universally. If someone at a meeting says, "Everyone is now free to go to lunch," "everyone" would obviously refer only to those who were at the meeting and not to everyone in the world.

Many of the Bible passages cited above are like that. Isaiah 53:6 says that God laid on Jesus "the iniquity of us all." But it is clear from the verse immediately before this that the ones for whom Jesus bore iniquity are those who have been brought to a state of "peace" with God, that is, those who have been justified (cf. Rom. 5:1). Again, they are those who have been "healed" (v. 5), not those who continue to be spiritually sick or dead. In the same way, the passages in John's Gospel that speak of Jesus being the Savior of the world mean only that Jesus is the only Savior the world will ever have, not that he will save every individual in it. Many other scattered passages that use the word "all" mean only "all of us."

The most difficult of all the passages mentioned is the one cited last—1 John 2:2, which says that Jesus is "the atoning sacrifice for our sins, and not only for ours but also for the sins of the whole world." It is difficult because, alone of all these passages, it seems to make a distinction between a merely limited atonement and a universal one, affirming the latter.

There are several different ways in which this verse might be understood, however. First, John may be stressing *the universal application of Christ's work*. Since "sacrifice of atonement" is a strongly Jewish term and something associated in Jewish minds with the propitiation made at the temple on the Day of Atonement, John may be saying, "Jesus made propitiation for our sins; but not just the sins of us who are Jews, which we might think since atonement is a Jewish tradition, but for all the peoples of the world. In that sense, he is a universal Savior."

Second, John may be stressing *the exclusiveness of the work of Jesus as the means of salvation*. In this case, his words would mean something like this: "Jesus died for our sins, and not just for the sins of us Christians who have the wrath of God propitiated for us by his death, as if other people might have other means of having their sins propitiated. No, Christ is the propitiation for the sins of all the people of the world who ever will have their sins propitiated. There is no salvation outside of him."

Third, John may be stressing *the timeless character of the atonement*. In this case, he would be saying, "Christ is the propitiation, not only for the sins of those of us who live in this present age, but for all who will ever be born into this world, until Jesus comes again." In any case, if the scope of this verse is not restricted in some way, it teaches universal salvation and not merely universal atonement. But as we have already seen, most evangelicals are not prepared to accept this, because of other clear teaching in the Bible.

"WHOSOEVER WILL MAY COME"

There may still be strong objections to the doctrine of definite atonement or particular redemption in some people's minds. A common objection holds that if God did not intend to save all people indiscriminately, and if Christ did not die in order to take away the sins of all the people in the world, then it is not possible for Christians to offer salvation to all without distinction. In fact, it would not be possible to offer salvation to anybody, since we would have no way of knowing whether or not the person to whom we are speaking is one for whom Jesus actually died.

There are two answers to this. First, we are to offer salvation to everyone because we are told to do it and because we have ample biblical examples to that effect. If God tells us to proclaim the gospel to everyone, we can be sure that this makes sense. But we are to do it even if it does not seem to make sense to us. We must remember

Ezekiel 33:11: "As surely as I live, declares the Sovereign LORD, I take no pleasure in the death of the wicked, but rather that they turn from their ways and live. Turn! Turn from your evil ways! Why will you die?" Or Isaiah 55:1, which makes free offer of the gospel:

> "Come, all you who are thirsty,
>   come to the waters;
> and you who have no money,
>   come buy and eat!
> Come, buy wine and milk
>   without money and without cost."

Or Jesus' words in Matthew 11:28: "Come to me, all you who are weary and burdened, and I will give you rest." We are called to offer Christ, as he offers himself, freely to everyone.

But second, and speaking strictly, the gospel is not so much an offer—that people may politely accept or refuse, according to their own pleasure—as it is a command to turn away from sin and come to Jesus. We have gotten into the habit of treating the gospel as an offer, which in one sense it is. But we have forgotten that, even more than an offer, it is a command to sinners to repent and believe. It is only after people have done this and have turned to Jesus that they can know that they are among those for whom Christ died.

J. I. Packer has pointed out that the statement "Christ died for you," which has become so common in today's evangelism, simply cannot be found in any of the sermons recorded for us in Scripture (see, for example, the sermons in the book of Acts, chapters 2–5, 7, 10, 13, 17, and 22). Packer writes:

> The fact is that the New Testament never calls on any man to repent on the ground that Christ died specifically and particularly for him. The basis on which the New Testament invites sinners to put faith in Christ is simply that they need Him, and that He offers Himself to them, and that those who receive Him are promised all the benefits that His death secured for His people. What is universal and all-inclusive in the New Testament is the invitation to faith, and the promise

of salvation to all who believe. . . . The gospel is not "believe that Christ died for everybody's sins, and therefore for yours," any more than it is, "believe that Christ died only for certain people's sins, and so perhaps not for yours." The gospel is, "believe on the Lord Jesus Christ, who died for sins, and now offers you Himself as your Saviour." This is the message which we are to take to the world. We have no business to ask them to put faith in any view of the extent of the atonement; our job is to point them to the living Christ, and summon them to trust in Him.[7]

A good example of the kind of preaching Packer describes is Charles Spurgeon. Spurgeon was a great Calvinist who believed in a definite atonement. But this did not stop him from becoming one of the most effective evangelists of his age. He did not lie to people. He did not say, "I know you are elect; therefore, Christ died for you." For Spurgeon, it was enough to say, "You are a sinner, and Jesus died for sinners. If you would be saved, you must repent of your sin and believe the gospel."

Does this weaken the gospel message? Far from weakening the message, the doctrine of definite atonement strengthens it and alone makes it a genuine gospel. Suppose we go to the lost with the message that Jesus died for everyone but without the conviction that his death actually accomplished salvation for those who should believe. Suppose, in other words, that we proclaim a redemption that did not redeem, a propitiation that did not propitiate, a reconciliation that did not reconcile, and an atonement that did not atone? That would be a fool's errand. But if we can say, "Christ died for sinners to restore them to God; if you believe on him, you are saved and can know that he has died for you," then we have a message worth proclaiming and our hearers have a gospel worth believing.

God does not honor falsehood or lies. He honors truth. Therefore, is it not more likely that he will honor this kind of honest presentation, though there is precious little of it today? Let's speak the truth, especially since it is such a wonderful truth. For what we proclaim is no mere possibility of salvation, but salvation itself. We preach that Jesus died for his people, actually dying in their place. He redeemed them from the terrible bondage of their sin. He propitiated the wrath of the Father on their behalf. He reconciled them to God. He is a sufficient and entirely suitable Savior. And when he said, "It is finished" (John 19:30), it really was finished! Salvation was accomplished. Therefore, all who will believe on him have been saved by him, and there is nothing more to add.

But here is the other side. If those to whom we speak do not repent of their sin and trust in Christ, they are not potentially saved, as some would have it; they are actually and finally lost. This gracious doctrine thus sets before the unbeliever not only the availability of salvation but also the necessity of trusting in Christ, which no other gospel truly does.

Do not say, "But I do not know if Jesus died for me or not." You cannot know the answer to that in the abstract. The only way you will ever know is if you will come to Jesus. If you do come, then you know that you are one for whom he died. Therefore, come to Jesus! And if you have not done so before, come now!

SIX

Efficacious Grace

But God who is rich in compassion and love,
Not leaving my soul to the grave,
Has given me life; born again from above,
By God's sov'reign grace I've been saved.

Unconditional election is the work of God the Father. Particular redemption is the work of Jesus Christ, the second person of the Trinity. In this chapter we come to the work of the Holy Spirit, the third member of the Trinity, whose efficaciously gracious work it is to apply the benefits of Christ's work to those elect persons whom Jesus has redeemed.

If we are following the TULIP acronym, this is the doctrine called "irresistible grace," which refers to the way God calls us to Jesus Christ. But again the words themselves are somewhat misleading, for they do not mean (as they seem to imply) that God will drag us kicking and screaming into his kingdom. Nor do they mean that grace is never resisted by us. Obviously it is. What they mean is that we do not resist effectively. Or, to put it the other way around, they mean that when God calls us to faith in Jesus Christ he calls effectively, succeeding in his purpose to save us. The grace of God's calling is overwhelmingly efficacious. A good way of expressing this is to say that the Holy Spirit regenerates us, giving us a new nature, as a result of which we naturally do what the new nature does: that is, we believe the gospel, repent of our sin, and trust in Christ unto salvation.

This puts the determining factor in a person's salvation in God's

hands, where it clearly belongs. When the Jewish authorities opposed
Jesus Christ they were allowed to do so to the very last (Acts 7:51). But
although the apostle Paul also resisted, he was allowed to do so only to
a point, after which God brought his resistance to an end (Acts 9:5-6).

The Westminster Confession of Faith expresses the doctrine of
efficacious grace in particularly effective language:

> All those whom God has predestinated unto life, and those only,
> he is pleased, in his appointed and accepted time, effectually to
> call, by his Word and Spirit, out of that state of death, in which
> they are by nature, to grace and salvation by Jesus Christ;
> enlightening their minds spiritually and savingly, to understand
> the things of God; taking away their heart of stone, and giving
> them a heart of flesh; renewing their wills, and by his almighty
> power determining them to that which is good; and effectually
> drawing them to Jesus Christ, yet so as they come most freely,
> being made willing by his grace (Chap. 10, Sec. 1).

Martin Luther was saying the same thing when he wrote, "When
God works in us, the will is changed under the sweet influence of the
Spirit of God. Once more it desires and acts, not of compulsion, but
of its own desire and spontaneous inclination."[1] Or again, consider
this definition from John Murray: "God's call, since it is effectual, carries with it the operative grace whereby the person called is enabled
to answer the call and to embrace Jesus Christ as he is freely offered
in the gospel."[2]

It is this doctrine that we need to examine in this chapter, answer-
ing the question why, if the gospel is freely offered to all men (as it is),
some respond to it and are saved while others reject it and are lost. The
Arminian says that this is because of something in the individual, so
that the individual ultimately is responsible for his own destiny. The
Calvinist says that it is God who makes the difference, and that this is
due entirely to his grace.

TWO KINDS OF CALLS

A husband and his wife are walking down the street. Someone calls so
that they can hear the voice but cannot quite distinguish the words.

The woman assumes that the person is calling her and turns around. Her husband assumes that the person is calling someone else and keeps on going. The man ignores the call; it must be for someone else. His wife thinks someone is trying to get her attention. What this illustrates is the word that we need to look at first. The word is "called," and it occurs in the statement, "those he [that is, God] predestined, he also called . . ." (Rom. 8:30). The point of this word is that—like the woman in the story—those whom God calls effectively not only hear his call but actually respond to it by turning around and by believing on or committing their lives to Christ.

1. A general call. There are two kinds of calls in Scripture. The first is external, general, and universal. It is an invitation to all persons to repent of sin, turn to the Lord Jesus Christ, and be saved. It is the call that Jesus gave when he cried, "Come to me, all you who are weary and burdened, and I will give you rest" (Matt. 11:28). Or again, when he said, "If anyone is thirsty, let him come to me and drink" (John 7:37).

The latter invitation was spoken in Jerusalem on the last day of the Feast of Tabernacles, when people from many lands and nationalities were assembled. There were Jews from every part of Palestine as well as from many regions of the Roman Empire. There were also Gentiles, some who had become Jewish proselytes but also some who, no doubt, were merely interested bystanders. We get a feeling of what this audience must have been like by remembering the composition of the crowd that assembled at Pentecost when Peter preached the first sermon of the Christian era, likewise extending a general call to believe on Jesus. We are told that on that occasion Jerusalem was filled with "Parthians, Medes and Elamites; residents of Mesopotamia, Judea and Cappadocia, Pontus and Asia, Phrygia and Pamphylia, Egypt and the parts of Libya near Cyrene; visitors from Rome (both Jews and converts to Judaism); Cretans and Arabs" (Acts 2:9-11). When Jesus (and later Peter) issued that call, the call was universal. It was for everyone. Anyone who wanted to respond could come to Jesus Christ and be saved. Today that same call flows from every true Christian pulpit and from all who bear witness to Jesus Christ as Lord and Savior in every land.

The difficulty with this external, universal, and (in itself) ineffectual call is that if people are left to themselves, no one ever actually responds to it. People hear the gospel and may even understand it up to a point, but the God who issues the call is undesirable to them, and so they turn away.

Jesus told a story about a man who prepared a great banquet and invited many guests. When the feast was prepared, he sent servants with the invitation, "Come, for everything is now ready." But the guests began to make excuses:

"I have just bought a field, and I must go and see it," said one.

"I have just bought five yoke of oxen, and I'm on my way to try them out," said another.

A third replied, "I just got married, so I can't come" (Luke 14:15-24).

Jesus was not making this story up out of thin air. That was the way the people of his day actually responded to his call. They would not receive the invitation. They rejected it, preferring to go their own way.

The Howard newspaper organization has as its logo a lighthouse beneath which are the words: "Give the people the light, and they will find their way." The idea is that people make foolish mistakes and bad decisions because they do not know the right way. Show it to them and they will follow it. However, that is not the way the Bible describes our condition spiritually. When Jesus was in the world, he was the world's light. The light was shining. But the people of his day did not respond to Jesus by walking in the right path. Instead, they hated the light and tried to put it out. They crucified the lighthouse. John was there. He saw what happened, and he had this damning observation: "This is the verdict: Light has come into the world, but men loved darkness instead of light because their deeds were evil" (John 3:19).

2. The specific call. The second kind of call is internal, specific, and effectual. It not only issues the invitation but also provides the willingness or ability to respond. It is a case of God bringing to spiritual life those who without that call would remain spiritually dead forever.

Probably the greatest illustration of God's grace in calling a dead sinner to life is the raising of Lazarus, recorded in John 11. When Jesus reached Bethany, at the request of the dead man's sisters, he was told that Lazarus had been dead for three days and that he was already putrefying: "But Lord," said Martha, "by this time there is a bad odor, for he has been there four days" (v. 39). What a graphic description of the state of our moral and spiritual decay because of sin! There was no hope that anything could be done for Lazarus in his helpless condition. His case was not serious or grim; it was altogether hopeless. Using this as an illustration, the great eighteenth-century evangelist George Whitefield used to say that the sinner's condition is worse than hopeless. In our decaying spiritual state we stink; we are offensive to God's nostrils. Hopeless? Yes, but only to man, not to God, with whom all things are possible (Matt. 19:26). Having prayed, Jesus called, "Lazarus, come out!" (John 11:43), and the call of God brought the dead man to life.

That is what the Holy Spirit does today. The Holy Spirit operates through the preaching and teaching of the Word to call to faith those whom God previously has elected to salvation and for whom Jesus specifically died. Apart from those three actions—the act of God in electing, the work of Christ in atoning, and the power of the Holy Spirit in calling—there would be no hope for anyone. No one could be saved. But because of those actions—because of God's sovereign grace—even the worst of blaspheming rebels may be turned from his or her folly to the Savior.

Perhaps the best discussion of the effectual call is in John Murray's book *Redemption Accomplished and Applied*. Murray begins by making the distinction just made, showing that there is such a thing as a general or universal call and that there are examples of it in the Bible. But then he points out that "in the New Testament the terms for calling, when used with reference to salvation, are almost uniformly applied, not to the universal call of the gospel, but to the call that ushers men into a state of salvation and is therefore effectual. There is scarcely an instance where the terms are used to designate the indiscriminate overture of grace in the gospel of Jesus Christ."[3]

Here are some examples:

> *Romans* 1:6-7. "You also are among those who are called to belong to Jesus Christ . . . called to be saints."

Romans 11:29. "God's gift and his call are irrevocable."

1 Corinthians 1:9. "God, who has called you into fellowship with his Son Jesus Christ our Lord, is faithful."

Ephesians 4:1. "As a prisoner for the Lord, then, I urge you to live a life worthy of the calling you have received."

2 Timothy 1:8-9. "Do not be ashamed to testify about our Lord, or ashamed of me his prisoner. But join with me in suffering for the gospel, by the power of God, who has saved us and called us to a holy life."

2 Peter 1:10. "Therefore, my brothers, be all the more eager to make your calling and election sure."

In each of these texts (and many others), the call of God effectively saves those to whom it is addressed. Putting the above texts together, it is a call that unites us to Jesus Christ, bringing us into fellowship with him and setting before us a holy life in which we will be sure to walk if we truly have been called. Anticipating subjects to be introduced later in this chapter, effectual calling is the point at which the eternal foreknowledge and predestination of God pass over into time and start the process by which the individual is drawn from sin to faith in Jesus Christ, is justified through that faith, and is then kept in Christ until his or her final glorification.

Why is this internal or specific call so effective? The answer is not difficult. The reason the call is so effective is that it is God's call. It issues from his mouth, and everything that issues from the mouth of God accomplishes that for which it is sent:

> As the rain and the snow
>   come down from heaven,
> and do not return to it
>   without watering the earth
> and making it bud and flourish,
>   so that it yields seed for the sower and bread for the eater,
> so is my word that goes out from my mouth:

It will not return to me empty,
but will accomplish what I desire
and achieve the purpose for which I sent it (Isa. 55:10-11).

THREE IMPORTANT OBSERVATIONS

There are, however, a number of serious misunderstandings of what "calling" means. So let me add here three significant clarifications of what has been said so far about the two calls.

1. *Two responses.* The trouble with the general call is that men and women do not naturally respond to it. But although they do not respond to the general call to salvation, they can respond by such outward actions as coming forward at a religious meeting, making a profession of faith, or even joining a church. Not only can they respond in these ways, but many do. That is why Peter told apparent believers, "make your calling and election sure" (2 Pet. 1:10). He meant that we must be sure that we really have been called by God and are truly born again, and that we have not merely been called by the preacher.

Donald Grey Barnhouse, who served as minister of Tenth Presbyterian Church from 1927 to 1960, wrote:

> If men heed no more than the outward call, they become members of the visible church. If the inward call is heard in our hearts, we become members of the invisible church. The first call unites us merely to a group of professing members; but the inward call unites us to Christ himself, and to all that have been born again. The outward call may bring with it a certain intellectual knowledge of the truth; the inward call brings us the faith of the heart, the hope which anchors us forever to Christ and the love which must ever draw us back to him who first loved us. The one can end in formalism, the other in true life. The outward call may curb the tendencies of the old nature and keep a soul in outward morality; the inward call will cure the plague that is in us and bring us on to triumph in Christ.[4]

2. *The importance of the general call.* Everything said thus far has stressed the necessity of the special or internal call of the individual

to salvation by God. No one naturally responds to God on the basis of the general call alone. Although that is true, nevertheless it is also true that the general call is necessary, since it is through the general or universal call that God calls specifically.

The effectual or specific call comes through the general call. In other words, it is through the preaching of God's Word by evangelists and ministers, and through the telling of the good news of the gospel by Christians everywhere, that God calls sinners. He does not call everyone we call. We sow the seed broadly; some of it falls on stony or shallow soil, just as some of it also falls on good soil. But when the seed falls on the soil God previously has prepared and when God, the giver of life, blesses the work of sowing so that the seed takes root in the good soil and grows, the result is a spiritual harvest. People are saved and enter the golden chain of God's saving acts—including foreknowledge, predestination, calling, justification, and glorification—that is outlined in Romans 8.

To put it still another way, if God calls effectively through the general call, then if some are to be saved, the general call is as necessary as the specific and effectual call. The call we give does not regenerate. God alone is the author of the new birth. All must be born "from above." Nevertheless, the way God does that is through the sowing of the seed of his Word, which is entrusted to us.

Nobody but God could invent this way of saving human beings. If it were left to us, we would say that either: 1) God has to do it; we can do nothing; or 2) we have to do it; God can do nothing. As it is, the work of effectively calling people to Christ is God's work, although he uses human beings to do it.

3. *Am I elect?* Sometimes people get bogged down by the mistaken thought, "If God is going to elect me to salvation, he will just have to do it. There is nothing I can do." Or they get hung up on knowing whether or not they are among the elect. They say, "How can I know I am elect? If I am not, there is no hope for me." This question bothered John Bunyan, the author of *Pilgrim's Progress,* and caused extraordinary anxiety for him. But there is no reason for either such passivity or such despair. How do you know whether or not you are elect? The

answer is, Have you responded to the gospel? Have you answered God's call?

Consider some of the biblical examples. How do we know that Noah was chosen by God for salvation? It is because, when God told him of the destruction that was to come upon the world by the great flood, Noah believed God and built an ark to save his family. The Bible says, "By faith he condemned the world and became heir of the righteousness that comes by faith" (Heb. 11:7).

How do we know that the patriarch Abraham was an elect man? It is because, when God called to him to leave Ur of the Chaldeans and go to a land that he would afterward inherit, Abraham "obeyed and went, even though he did not know where he was going" (Heb. 11:8), and because he persevered in that obedience to the end of his life. "He was looking forward to the city with foundations, whose architect and builder is God" (v. 10).

How do we know that Moses was predestined to be saved? It is because, though raised in the lap of Egyptian luxury, when he had grown up he "refused to be known as the son of Pharaoh's daughter," choosing "to be mistreated along with the people of God rather than to enjoy the pleasures of sin for a short time" (Heb. 11:24-25). He sided with God's people.

How do we know that Paul was elected to salvation? It is because, though breathing hatred against God's people and though trying to kill some of them, when Jesus appeared to him on the road to Damascus, calling, "Saul, Saul, why do you persecute me?" (Acts 9:4) the future apostle to the Gentiles was transformed. He saw his sin for what it was and turned from it. He saw the righteousness of Christ and believed on Jesus. He obeyed and served God from that time on.

How do you know if you are among the elect?

There is only one way to know this, and it is not by trying to peer into the eternal counsels of God, stripping the cover from the book of his divine foreknowledge and predestination. The only way you will ever know if you are among the elect is if you respond to the gospel. The Bible says, "Believe in the Lord Jesus Christ, and you will be saved" (Acts 16:31). When you believe in Christ, you can know that God has set his electing love upon you and that, having loved you, he will continue to love you and keep you to the end. It is in Christ that you have been chosen (Eph. 1:4), and it is to Christ that you must look for the assurance of your salvation.

THE ORDER OF SALVATION (ORDO SALUTIS)

We must not think, however, that the specific or effective call, as decisive as it is, is all that is involved in God's efficacious grace. The effective call is only one point in a long chain of actions (and responses) by which God saves an individual sinner. Some of these actions were mentioned a moment ago. In theology this chain is called the *ordo salutis*, meaning the "order of salvation." It is a long chain beginning with God's eternal purpose to save and ending with the glorification of the justified sinner.

What are the links in this chain? As we saw back in chapter 4, one link is the electing choice of God, which precedes the new birth. Verses like John 1:13 point to this. It says that those who become children of God are "born not of natural descent, nor of human decision or a husband's will, but born of God." This means that God is the cause of our spiritual birth, just as a father is responsible for the conception of a child. Similarly, James 1:18 says that God "chose to give us birth through the word of truth, that we might be a kind of firstfruits of all he created."

Other acts and processes follow the new birth. John 3:3 tells us that "no one can see the kingdom of God unless he is born again"; and John 3:5 adds, "No one can enter the kingdom of God unless he is born of water and the Spirit." In other words, we must be born again before we are able to believe in Christ and be saved.

Another helpful verse is 1 John 3:9: "No one who is born of God will continue to sin, because God's seed remains in him; he cannot go on sinning, because he has been born of God." John is not talking about perfection in this verse, for earlier he has insisted that Christians do sin. If they claim differently, they are either deceived or deceitful—"If we claim to be without sin, we deceive ourselves and the truth is not in us" (1 John 1:8). Rather, he is talking about sanctification, which follows regeneration and is the progressive growth in holiness of one who has become God's child.

Romans 8:28-30 adds justification and glorification: "And we know that in all things God works for the good of those who love him, who have been called according to his purpose. For those God foreknew he also predestined to be conformed to the likeness of his Son, that he might be the firstborn among many brothers. And those he predestined, he also called; those he called, he also justified; those he justified, he also glorified." In these verses foreknowledge and predestination deal with the prior determination of God; calling, justification, and glorification deal with the application of redemption to us. We know from Paul's teaching elsewhere that justification presupposes faith (Rom. 5:1), so we can insert faith before justification, but after regeneration. Adoption must follow justification, because only justified people are admitted to God's spiritual family. Sanctification is the process that follows justification. It also comes before glorification. Therefore, in the final list of these acts or responses we have: foreknowledge, predestination, the effectual call, regeneration, repentance and faith, justification, adoption, sanctification, and glorification.[5]

1. *Foreknowledge.* Of the many terms in this list, foreknowledge is probably the most frequently misunderstood. It has two parts: "fore," which means beforehand, and "knowledge." It has been taken to mean that, since God knows all things, God knows beforehand who will believe on him and who will not, and as a result he has predestined those whom he foresees will believe on him for salvation. What he foreknows or foresees is their faith.

However, the matter is not as simple as that. For one thing, Romans 8:29 does not say that God foreknew what certain of his creatures would do. It is not talking about human actions at all. Rather it is speaking entirely of what God does. Each of the terms in Romans 8:29-30 is like that: *God* foreknew, *God* predestined, *God* called, *God* justified, *God* glorified. Besides, the object of divine foreknowledge is not the actions of certain people but the people themselves. In this sense foreknowledge can only mean that God has fixed a special attention upon certain people or has loved them in a saving way. As we learned back in chapter 4, this is the way the word generally is used in the Old Testament.

And there is this problem, too. If all the word *foreknowledge* means is that God knows beforehand what people will do in response to him or to the preaching of the gospel, and then determines their destiny on that basis, what could God possibly foresee or foreknow except opposition to him? If the hearts of all men and women are as depraved as Paul has been teaching they are, if in fact "There is no one righteous, not even one; there is no one who understands, no one who seeks God" (Rom. 3:10-11), then what could God possibly foresee in any human heart but unbelief?

Murray puts it in a slightly different way:

> Even if it were granted that "foreknew" means the foresight of faith, the biblical doctrine of sovereign election is not thereby eliminated or disproven. For it is certainly true that God foresees faith; he foresees all that comes to pass. The question would then simply be: whence proceeds this faith, which God foresees? And the only biblical answer is that the faith which God foresees is the faith he himself creates (cf. John 3:3-8; 6:44, 45, 65; Eph. 2:8; Phil. 1:29; 2 Pet. 1:2). Hence his eternal foresight of faith is preconditioned by his decree to generate this faith in those whom he foresees as believing.[6]

Foreknowledge means that salvation has its origin in the mind of God, not man. To know, in the biblical sense, is to love; to foreknow is to "forelove." Foreknowledge thus focuses our attention on the everlasting love of God, according to which some persons are graciously chosen to be conformed to the character of Jesus Christ.

2. *Predestination*. A common objection to this understanding of foreknowledge is that, if it is correct, then foreknowledge and predestination (the term that follows) mean exactly the same thing, and therefore that Paul is redundant. But the terms are not synonymous. In reality, predestination carries us an important step further.

Like foreknowledge, predestination is composed of two parts: "pre," meaning "beforehand," and "destiny" or "destination." It means to determine a person's destiny beforehand, and this is the sense in which it differs from foreknowledge. Foreknowledge means to fix one's love upon or to elect, but this "does not inform us of the destination to which those thus chosen are appointed."[7] Predestination supplies this element. It tells us that, having fixed his distinguishing love upon us, God next appointed us "to be conformed to the likeness of his Son, that he might be the firstborn among many brothers" (Rom. 8:29). He does this, as the next terms show, by calling, justifying, and glorifying those whom he has chosen.

3. Effectual calling. The next step in this chain is what was discussed in the first part of this chapter. As we explained there, one kind of calling is external, general, and universal. It is an open invitation to all persons to repent of sin, turn to the Lord Jesus Christ, and be saved. It is what Jesus was speaking of when he said, "Come to me, all you who are weary and burdened, and I will give you rest" (Matt. 11:28). The problem with this type of call is that, left to ourselves, none of us would ever respond positively. We hear the call, but we turn away, preferring our own ways to God. That is why Jesus also said, "No one can come to me unless the Father who sent me draws him" (John 6:44).

The other kind of call is internal, specific, and effectual. That is, it not only issues the invitation but also provides the ability or willingness to respond. It is God drawing to himself or bringing to spiritual life the one who without that call would remain spiritually dead and far from him. This is the way Jesus called Lazarus from the tomb. Lazarus was dead, but the call of God created in the dead man life and the ability to respond. This is also how God calls those whom he has foreknown and predestined to salvation.

4. Regeneration. When we say that God's call brings forth life in the one who is called, what we mean is that the call of God regenerates or brings about the new birth. This is the next critical step. Regeneration is a work of God by which a spiritually dead man or woman is brought to life in Christ (John 5:24), having been given a new nature in which what was once a heart of stone now becomes a heart of flesh (Ezek. 11:19), and the individual is brought out of darkness into God's wonderful light (1 Pet. 2:9). It involves a change of one's character so that he or she becomes "a new creation" in Christ (2 Cor. 5:17).

The Bible speaks of the new birth often. For example:

Deuteronomy 32:18. "You deserted the Rock, who fathered you; you forgot the God who gave you birth."

John 1:13. " . . . children born not of natural descent, nor of human decision or a husband's will, but born of God."

John 3:3. "I tell you the truth, no one can see the kingdom of God unless he is born again."

1 Peter 1:3. "Praise be to the God and Father of our Lord Jesus Christ! In his great mercy he has given us new birth into a living hope through the resurrection of Jesus Christ from the dead."

1 Peter 1:23. "For you have been born again, not of perishable seed, but of imperishable, through the living and enduring word of God."

Those are important verses, and when we put them together we have an analogy of what happens when a person becomes a Christian. No one is responsible for his or her physical birth. It is only as a human egg and sperm join, grow, and finally enter this world that birth occurs. The process is initiated and nurtured by the parents. Likewise spiritual rebirth is initiated and nurtured by our heavenly Father and is not our own doing. John develops the analogy in precisely this way in a verse cited earlier: "Yet to all who received him, to those who believed in his name, he gave the right to become children of God—children born not of natural descent, nor of human decision or a husband's will, but born of God" (John 1:12-13). These verses have three important negatives: not of natural descent, nor of human decision or a husband's will.

The first negative teaches that regeneration is not by physical birth or merit. Some people are very proud of their bloodline, like the Jews of Jesus' day. There were thousands who thought that they were right with God simply because physically they were descended from Abraham (John 8:33). They were like Paul, who boasted that he was "circumcised on the eighth day, of the people of Israel, of the tribe of Benjamin, a Hebrew of Hebrews" (Phil. 3:5). They thought they had it made because they were descended from Abraham physically. Jesus pointed out that God is interested in a spiritual relationship and that their actions indicated that they were actually children of the devil (John 8:44). In the same way, many people today think that they are right with God simply because they have been born of Christian parents or live in a so-called Christian country. But this saves no one.

The second and third negatives deny the role of the human will in salvation by the analogy of a husband's role in the conception of a child, the point being that no one can become a child of God by mere volition. A person can accomplish much by sheer willpower and hard work, pushing himself to get ahead. He can become successful in the world's terms. But no one conceives or gives birth to himself. Nor can any amount of willpower make someone a son or daughter of one set of parents if he or she has been born to another set of parents. Similarly, nothing will make a person a child of God unless God himself engenders spiritual life and brings about a new birth. Becoming a child of God is a matter of God's grace. It is true that we must believe on Jesus Christ to be saved. This is what we will come to next. But we believe only because God has already taken the initiative to plant his divine life within us. People only believe because God has quickened them. If they fail to believe, it is because God has withheld that special, efficacious grace that he was under no obligation to bestow. In other words, new life comes before saving faith; it is never the other way around.

5. *Repentance and faith.* The immediate effect of the divine regeneration of the soul is that the sinner now abhors the sin that he once cherished, and trusts in Christ for his salvation. This involves two actions: 1) turning from sin, which is repentance; and 2) turning to Christ, which is faith. These are both things that we do. That is, God does not repent for us, nor does he believe for us. We must repent. We

must believe. Nevertheless, both repentance and faith occur in us because of God's prior work of regeneration.

Which comes first, repentance or faith? In some systems of theology, faith is placed before repentance on the grounds that it is only when we see Christ in his holiness, and come to desire and trust him, that we perceive sin for what it is and reject it. This was John Calvin's point of view. He said, "Repentance not only immediately follows faith but is produced by it," though he added, "When we speak of faith as the origin of repentance, we dream not of any space of time which it employs in producing it; but we intend to signify that a man cannot truly devote himself to repentance unless he knows himself to be of God."[8] In other systems of theology, repentance is placed first on the grounds that we cannot come to Christ unless we have turned from sin. Robert L. Dabney was adopting this position when he wrote, "The very first acting of faith implies some repentance as the prompter thereof." But, like Calvin, Dabney also insisted that there is "no gap of duration between the birth of the one or the other."[9] Since the proponents of neither view want to preserve a time gap between faith and repentance or repentance and faith, we seem to be dealing with an unnecessary distinction.

Actually, repentance and faith are two parts of the single experience that we call conversion. Conversion means to turn around. Before God's regenerating work in our hearts, we were going in a wrong direction. But when God gave us a new nature to desire him and what he desires for us, we turned a full 180 degrees to go in the opposite direction: 90 degrees is repentance, a turning from sin, and 90 degrees is faith, turning to Christ. There is no salvation without both turnings.

6. *Justification*. The next step in God's chain of saving actions is his gracious justification of the sinner. So here we are back to what God himself does. Justification is his act, not ours. It is the judicial function by which God declares sinful men and women to be in a right standing before him, not on the basis of their own merit—for they have none—but on the basis of what Jesus Christ has done by dying in their place on the Cross. Jesus bore their punishment, taking the

penalty of their sins upon himself. Those sins have been punished, and God now imputes the perfect righteousness of the Lord Jesus Christ to their account.

What needs to be discussed here is the relationship of the effectual call to justification. Or to put it in the form of a question: Why does Paul place calling where he does in Romans 8? Why does calling come *after* foreknowledge and predestination, and *before* justification and glorification?

There are two reasons. First, calling is the point at which the things determined beforehand in the mind and counsel of God pass over into time. We speak of "fore" knowledge and "pre" destination. But these two time references only have meaning for us. Strictly speaking, there is no time in God, for whom the end is as the beginning and the beginning as the end. "Fore" and "pre" are meaningless from his perspective. God simply "knows" and "determines," and that eternally. But what he thus decrees in eternity becomes actual in time, and calling is the point where his eternal foreknowledge and predestination find concrete manifestation. We are creatures in time. So it is by God's specific calling of us to faith in time that we are saved.

Second, justification, which comes after calling in Paul's list of divine actions, is always connected with faith or belief, and it is through God's call of the individual that faith is brought into being. God's call creates or quickens faith. Or, as we could perhaps more accurately say, it is the call of God that brings forth spiritual life, of which faith is the first true evidence or proof. The Bible never says that we are saved *because* of our faith. That would make faith something good in us that we somehow contribute to the process. But the Bible does say that we are saved *by* or *through* faith, meaning that God must create faith in us before we can be justified.

7. *Adoption.* Adoption, like justification, is a judicial act. However, it differs from justification in that justification concerns our standing before the bar of God's justice, while adoption has to do with our being brought into God's spiritual family, with all the blessings that entails. Adoption brings us all the benefits of sonship, including the right to

approach God in prayer. It assures us of God's love and protection. It
contributes to our assurance that we have been saved. Paul refers to
some of these blessings in Galatians 4:6-7, where he writes, "Because
you are sons, God sent the Spirit of his Son into our hearts, the Spirit
who calls out, 'Abba, Father.' So you are no longer a slave, but a son;
and since you are a son, God has made you also an heir."

8. *Sanctification.* Foreknowledge, predestination, calling, regeneration, justification, and adoption are exclusively God's work. But
sanctification is a process in which, having been given a new nature
by God, the redeemed sinner now can and must cooperate. To put
it in other language, justification is monergistic; it is the work of
God. By contrast, sanctification is synergistic; it is a joint work of
both God and man.

Murray argues that no verse shows this more clearly than
Philippians 2:12-13, which says, "continue to work out your salvation with fear and trembling, for it is God who works in you to will
and to act according to his good purpose." He goes on to argue:
"God's working in us is not suspended because we work, nor our
working suspended because God works. Neither is the relation
strictly one of co-operation as if God did his part and we did ours. . . .
The relation is that because God works we work. . . . What the apostle is urging is the necessity of working out our own salvation, and
the encouragement he supplies is the assurance that it is God himself who works in us. The more persistently active we are in working, the more persuaded we may be that all the energizing grace and
power is of God."[10]

9. *Glorification.* Glorification is our ultimate spiritual destiny. It
means to become like Jesus Christ, as fully and as gloriously as possible. When Paul mentions glorification in Romans 8:30 he refers to it
in the past tense ("glorified") rather than in the future ("will glorify")
or even a future passive tense ("will be glorified"), which is what we
might have expected him to do. Why is this? The obvious reason is
that he is thinking of this final step in our salvation as being so certain that it is possible to refer to it as already having happened. And,

of course, he does this deliberately to assure us that this is exactly what *will* happen. He wrote to the Christians at Philippi, "I always pray with joy, . . . being confident of this, that he who began a good work in you will carry it on to completion until the day of Christ Jesus" (Phil. 1:4, 6). That is shorthand for what Paul wrote in Romans 8. God began the process of salvation by foreknowledge, predestination, calling, justification, and adoption. And because God never goes back on anything he has said or ever changes his mind, we can know that he will carry it on until the day when we will be made like Jesus Christ.

ALL THIS IS FROM GOD

The bottom line of this discussion of the *ordo salutis* is that the decisive acts in this sequence are God's, and even the matters for which we are responsible—repentance and faith, sanctification—are possible only because of God's prior working. It is the acts of God that matter. Without them, not one of us would be saved.

Do we have to believe? Of course, we do. But even faith is of God or, as it is better to say, it is the result of his working in us. Ephesians 2:8-9 says, "It is by grace you have been saved, through faith—and this not from yourselves, it is the gift of God—not by works, so that no one can boast." When we are first saved, we think quite naturally that we have had a great deal to do with it, perhaps because of wrong or shallow teaching, but more likely because at that stage of our Christian lives we know more about our own thoughts and feelings than we do about God. However, the longer we are Christians the further we move from any feeling that we are responsible for our salvation or even any part of it, and the closer we come to the conviction that it is all of God.

Harry A. Ironside, a great Bible teacher, told a story about an older Christian who was asked to give his testimony. He told how God had sought him out and found him, how God had loved him, called him, saved him, delivered him, cleansed him, and healed him—a great witness to the grace, power, and glory of God. But after the meeting a rather legalistic Christian took him aside and criticized his testimony, as some Christians like to do. He said, "I appreciated all you said about what God did for you. But you didn't mention anything about your part in it. Salvation is really part us and part God. You should have mentioned something about your part."

"Oh yes," the older Christian said. "I apologize for that. I really should have said something about my part. My part was running away, and his part was running after me until he caught me."[11]

If we understand the truth of that, we understand a great deal about the true gospel. All of us have run away. But God has set his gracious love upon us, predestined us to become like Jesus Christ, called us to faith and repentance, justified us, adopted us as his spiritual sons and daughters, begun a work of sanctification within us that will continue until the day of Jesus Christ, and has even glorified us, so certain of completion is his plan.

SEVEN

Persevering Grace

What can separate my soul
From the God who made me whole,
Wrote my name in heaven's scroll?
Nothing. Hallelujah!
Trouble, hardship, danger, sword
Brought by those who hate my Lord?
Slander here? Or no reward?
Nothing. Hallelujah!

The doctrine we are dealing with in this chapter is perseverance, which is also called eternal security. Or, as some say colloquially, "once saved, always saved." It is the truth that those who have been brought to faith in Jesus Christ—having been foreknown and predestined to faith by God from eternity past, having been called, regenerated, and justified in this life, and having been so set on the road to ultimate glorification that this culminating glorification can even be spoken of in the past tense—that these persons never will and never can be lost. Perseverance is implied in each of the other doctrines we have studied and is a logical consequence of salvation being the work of an eternally loving and utterly immutable God.

SOME COMMON MISUNDERSTANDINGS

Yet we do not want to distort the doctrine of perseverance by over-simplifying it, as some do. We want to understand it as it is taught in

Scripture, and this means that first we need to eliminate some common misunderstandings.

1. *Perseverance does not mean that Christians are exempted from all spiritual danger just because they are Christians.*

On the contrary, the opposite is true. They are in even greater danger, because now that they are Christians, the world and the devil will be doggedly set against them and will try to destroy them—and would destroy them, if that were possible. One of the greatest statements of the believer's eternal security in the entire Bible is Romans 8:35-39. But this section of Scripture is bold in listing the dangers Christians face. Paul writes of trouble, hardship, persecution, famine, nakedness, danger, and sword, concluding, "For your sake we face death all day long; we are considered as sheep to be slaughtered" (v. 36, quoting Ps. 44:22). But in spite of these many hostile forces, the Christian will be kept by God's power and love. It is because we really do face these spiritual dangers that the doctrine of perseverance is so important.

2. *Perseverance does not mean that Christians are always kept from falling into sin, just because they are Christians.*

Sadly, Christians do sin. Noah fell into drunkenness. Abraham lied about his wife Sarah, claiming that she was his sister rather than his wife, thinking to protect his own life. David committed adultery and then arranged for the murder of Uriah, Bathsheba's husband. Peter denied the Lord. These examples lead us to conclude that perseverance does not mean that Christians will not fall, only that they will not fall away. Jesus predicted Peter's denial, but he added, "I have prayed for you, Simon, that your faith may not fail. And when you have turned back, strengthen your brothers" (Luke 22:32).

Loraine Boettner points out that the elect are often like the prodigal son in that they are deluded by the world and led astray by their own corrupt desires. They waste their substance on wrong living. They feed on the world's husks, which do not satisfy. But sooner or later they come to their senses and say, "How many of my father's hired men have food to spare, and here I am starving to death! I will set out and go back to my father and say to him: Father, I have sinned against heaven and against you" (Luke 15:17-18). And when they return they find a loving Father and a joyful reception. Boettner says that "this is a thoroughly Calvinistic parable in that the prodigal was a son, and could not lose that relationship. Those who are not sons never have the desire to arise and go to the Father."[1]

3. Perseverance does not mean that those who merely profess Christ without actually being born again are secure.

We live in a day when many claim to be Christians but are destitute of any true knowledge of the faith and any genuine Christian experience or character. Others know a great deal about religion and may be able to pass even the strictest examination for church membership. But knowledge like this is no guarantee that the individual is actually saved, and membership in a church is no guarantee, either. None who are in any of these categories of religious profession can assume that the doctrine of perseverance applies to them.

This sad truth explains the many warnings that appear in Scripture to the effect that we should give diligent attention to make our "calling and election sure" (2 Pet. 1:10). Jesus' statements are among the most direct. For example, he said, "All men will hate you because of me, but he who stands firm to the end will be saved" (Matt. 10:22). We are able to stand firm only because God perseveres with us. But it is also true that we must stand firm. In fact, the final perseverance of believers is the only ultimate proof that we have been chosen by God and truly have been born again.

The Christian doctrine of perseverance does not lead to a false assurance or presumption, though some who claim to be saved presume on God by their sinful lifestyles and willful disobedience. Perseverance does not make us lazy. As Calvin insisted, "It is not enough that God should choose any people for himself, except the people themselves persevere in the obedience of faith."[2] Nor does perseverance make us proud.

The doctrine of perseverance is precisely what Paul declares it to be in Romans 8, namely, that those whom God has foreknown and predestinated to be conformed to the likeness of his Son will indeed come to that great consummation. They will be harassed and con-

stantly tempted. Frequently, they will fall. Nevertheless, in the end
they will be with Jesus and will be made like him, because this is the
destiny that God in his sovereign and inexplicable love has predetermined for them, and because he accomplishes this end through his
sovereign acts of calling, regenerating, justifying, and glorifying the
believer.

This doctrine has a logical connection to the other Calvinistic dis-
tinctives, of course. Because we are radically depraved and because salvation depends on God's sovereign acts in our salvation, we have a
security that is based on his ability and will rather than our own. If salvation depended in any measure on what we were able to do or contribute to it, we would not be secure at all. But there is a strange
anomaly in contemporary evangelicalism at this point. The great
majority of evangelicals are theologically Arminian. That is, they do not
believe in radical depravity or election. They believe that the deciding
factor in whether a person becomes a Christian and is saved is not
God's regenerating power but the individual's free will, by which he can
choose either to believe or disbelieve. In other words, he is able to put
himself into the kingdom or keep himself out. But in spite of this synergistic (see chapter 1) and ultimately man-determined theology, most
evangelicals nevertheless believe in perseverance, insisting that when
a person is once saved, he is saved forever. It is a correct point, but
Arminian theology provides no basis for it.

The Westminster Confession of Faith rightly and wisely grounds
our security in God's acts when it says of perseverance, "They whom
God hath accepted in his Beloved, effectually called and sanctified by
his Spirit, can neither totally nor finally fall away from the state of
grace; but shall certainly persevere therein to the end, and be eternally
saved" (Chap. 17, Sec. 1).

MANY PERSEVERANCE VERSES

One reason why many contemporary Arminians believe in perseverance in spite of its being inconsistent with their basic theology is that
so many Bible verses teach it, not to mention the fact that it is a com-
forting doctrine to embrace. Here is a selection:

Psalm 34:7. "The angel of the LORD encamps around those who fear him, and he delivers them."

Jeremiah 31:3. "I have loved you with an everlasting love."

Jeremiah 32:40. "I will make an everlasting covenant with them: I will never stop doing good to them, and I will inspire them to fear me, so that they will never turn away from me."

Ezekiel 11:19-20. "I will give them an undivided heart and put a new spirit in them; I will remove from them their heart of stone and give them a heart of flesh."

John 5:24. "I tell you the truth, whoever hears my word and believes him who sent me has eternal life and will not be condemned; he has crossed over from death to life."

John 6:51. "I am the living bread that came down from heaven. If anyone eats of this bread, he will live forever."

Romans 11:29. "God's gifts and his call are irrevocable."

2 Corinthians 4:8-9, 14. "We are hard pressed on every side, but not crushed; perplexed, but not in despair; persecuted, but not abandoned; struck down, but not destroyed. . . . We know that the one who raised the Lord Jesus from the dead will also raise us with Jesus and present us with you in his presence."

Hebrews 10:14. "By one sacrifice he has made perfect forever those who are being made holy."

1 Peter 1:3-5. "In his great mercy he has given us new birth into a living hope through the resurrection of Jesus Christ from the dead, and into an inheritance that can never perish, spoil or fade—kept in heaven for you, who through faith are shielded by God's power until the coming of the salvation that is ready to be revealed in the last time."

1 John 5:11-13. "This is the testimony: God has given us eternal life, and this life is in his Son. He who has the Son has life;

he who does not have the Son of God does not have life. I
write these things to you who believe in the name of the Son
of God so that you may know that you have eternal life."

These verses are taken from many places in the Bible and are all
plain statements that the one who called the believer to faith will also
preserve him in that state to the end. It is a double security. We are told
that, on the one hand, God will never depart from us but will keep,
preserve, and defend us; and that, on the other hand, and because he
acts in this way, we for our part will not depart from him. Left to ourselves we surely would. But Christ has prayed for us, as he did for
Peter, and therefore our faith will not fail. God perseveres with his
saints, and because he does, the saints themselves also persevere.

THREE GREAT PERSEVERANCE VERSES

The previous list of verses that teach perseverance omits three passages that are among the strongest, and thus deserve to be discussed
in a little more detail. The verses are Philippians 1:6; John 10:27-30;
and Romans 8:35-39.

1. *Philippians* 1:6. "Being confident of this, that he who began a
good work in you will carry it on to completion until the day of Christ
Jesus." This verse teaches that when it comes to our salvation, God fin-
ishes what he starts. This is true of all God's plans: he never begins a
work that he does not fully intend to complete. But this is true specifically of the gracious, sanctifying work of his Spirit in the minds and
hearts of his elect people. Since God never abandons his plans or purposes for our eternal destiny, he will not leave this work unfinished.
He refuses to give up on us until he makes us like Jesus Christ.

2. *John 10:27-30.* "My sheep listen to my voice; I know them, and
they follow me. I give them eternal life, and they shall never perish;
no one can snatch them out of my hand. My Father, who has given
them to me, is greater than all; no one can snatch them out of my
Father's hand. I and the Father are one." These verses are significant
for our purposes because they touch on nearly all five points of

Calvinism. Jesus identifies his sheep as having been given to him by the Father. In other words, they are the gift of God's electing love. However, these are the same sheep for whom Christ died (see v. 15), and thus they are the special objects of his atonement. Christ died exclusively for them, bearing the penalty for their sins in particular. Furthermore, by the efficacious work of the Holy Spirit, these sheep respond to God's irresistible grace. They are said not only to listen to Jesus' voice, but also to follow him.

What these verses emphasize, however, is God's persevering grace. The sheep are in some danger. There is the apparent threat that someone might try to snatch them away from salvation. Yet Jesus asserts their absolute security, emphatically promising their perseverance in three different ways. First, he gives his sheep eternal life. But of course this life can only be termed "eternal" if it lasts forever, which depends on the perseverance of God's grace. Second, Jesus says that his sheep will never perish. Once again, for this promise to have any validity, it requires the perseverance of God's grace. Finally, Jesus says "no one can snatch them out of my hand." This would seem secure enough. However, lest we think that somehow it is not secure enough, Jesus wraps his Father's hand around his own: "No one can snatch them out of my Father's hand." Thus we are doubly secure, clutched by both the Father and the Son. And if we still feel insecure, we should realize that even when we are held in this manner, both the Father and the Son have a hand free to defend us!

3. *Romans 8:35-39.* "Who shall separate us from the love of Christ? Shall trouble or hardship or persecution or famine or nakedness or danger or sword? As it is written: 'For your sake we face death all day long; we are considered as sheep to be slaughtered.' No, in all these things we are more than conquerors through him who loved us. For I am convinced that neither death nor life, neither angels nor demons, neither the present nor the future, nor any powers, neither height nor depth, nor anything else in all creation, will be able to separate us from the love of God that is in Christ Jesus our Lord." It is difficult to think of any words that could be more comprehensive than these, which prove that once we come to Christ, nothing can ever separate us from God's love.

In these verses the apostle Paul lists no fewer than seventeen obstacles to salvation. Yet none of them poses even the slightest threat to the believer's eternal security. Having considered all the contenders, Paul remains convinced that none of them could ever detach us from Christ. The point, of course, is not simply that these particular obstacles can be overcome but that *nothing* in time or eternity can ever threaten the security of God's elect, who must therefore persevere to the very end.

ANOTHER PERSEVERANCE PROMISE

These verses prove the power of God's persevering grace, yet they are not the only verses in the Bible that teach this doctrine, and it is to another that we turn now, because of its use of the word *grace:* 1 Peter 5:10. This verse says, "And the God of all grace, who called you to his eternal glory in Christ, after you have suffered a little while, will himself restore you and make you strong, firm and steadfast." Here are a few things to know before we examine the verse in detail:

1. *Peter was writing to Christians scattered throughout certain parts of Asia Minor, which we call Turkey.* Peter calls these people "God's elect, strangers in the world" (1 Peter 1:1).

2. *These believers in Christ had been suffering many kinds of trials.* There are four passages in the letter that deal with their trials: 1 Peter 1:6-7; 3:13-17; 4:12-19; and 5:9. These passages indicate that the suffering these Christians were experiencing included malicious slander from unbelievers, possible persecution from government authorities, and spiritual assaults from Satan—the very kind of sufferings believers face today.

3. *Peter wanted to encourage them by the certainty of a glory yet to come.* He does this throughout the letter. In chapter 1 he speaks of the believers' "living hope" (v. 3) and of "an inheritance that can never perish, spoil or fade—kept in heaven for you" (v. 4). He says that their trials have come so that their "faith—of greater worth than gold, which perishes even though refined by fire—may be proved genuine and may

result in praise, glory and honor when Jesus Christ is revealed" (v. 7). In chapter 3 he reminds them that "Christ died for sins once for all, the righteous for the unrighteous, to bring you to God" (v. 18). In chapter 4 he says, "Rejoice that you participate in the sufferings of Christ, so that you may be overjoyed when his glory is revealed" (v. 13).

The text we are focusing on (5:10) does this as well. It encourages the Christians of Asia Minor by reminding them of the glory that is to be theirs when they complete their earthly course and are with the Lord Jesus Christ in heaven, and it assures them that in the meantime God will strengthen them and keep them for the work they have to do here.

The text functions as a benediction, or a word of blessing, since it comes almost at the end of the letter. But it is important to note that the verbs in the verse are in the future indicative rather than the optative mood. That is, they express a promise, not a wish. If it were the latter, the verse would say something like: "May the God of all grace . . . restore you and make you strong." Benedictions are often like that, and this is the way the King James Version actually translates Peter's words: "The God of all grace . . . make you perfect, stablish, strengthen, settle you." But the verse is actually a promise in the future tense, not a wish, which means that it is a promise that "the God of all grace, who called you to his eternal glory in Christ, after you have suffered a little while, will himself restore you and make you strong, firm and steadfast." It is this future tense that makes 1 Peter 5:10 an important verse about persevering grace, a strong statement of the truth of eternal security.

No Escape from Suffering

When we look at 1 Peter 5:10 the first thing we see is that perseverance does not mean that believers in Christ are automatically delivered from all suffering. In fact, the verse teaches the opposite. It teaches that we will experience suffering, though it will be of relatively short duration (for this life, rather than for eternity), and that suffering will be replaced in time by an eternal glory.

Where did Peter get this understanding of suffering in the Christian life? It is no great mystery. He learned it from Jesus Christ.

This was one of the themes of the last discourses of Jesus before his crucifixion, recorded in chapters 14–16 of John's Gospel. In chapter 15 Jesus spoke of the world's hatred, which would lead to persecutions: "If the world hates you, keep in mind that it hated me first. If you belonged to the world, it would love you as its own. As it is, you do not belong to the world, but I have chosen you out of the world. That is why the world hates you. . . . If they persecuted me, they will persecute you also" (vv. 18-20). In the next chapter he tells of religious persecutions: "They will put you out of the synagogue; in fact, a time is coming when anyone who kills you will think he is offering a service to God. They will do such things because they have not known the Father or me" (16:2-3). His final words were: "In this world you will have trouble. But take heart! I have overcome the world" (v. 33).

Obviously, Peter had learned from this. Besides his own experiences as a Christian, his observations of the life and hardships of the early Christian community assured him that Jesus was not being hypothetical when he forecast suffering and persecution for his followers. Peter knew, and is reminding us, that suffering is both real and expected.

We notice something else that is important if we glance back one or two verses in 1 Peter 5 and place verse 10 in that context. In verses 8 and 9 Peter is writing about Satan, the devil, and he is saying that the suffering he is concerned about here is the suffering Satan causes. He calls Satan the Christian's enemy: "Your enemy the devil prowls around like a roaring lion looking for someone to devour. Resist him, standing firm in the faith, because you know that your brothers throughout the world are undergoing the same kind of sufferings."

But how can we do that, if Satan is really as powerful as the Bible says he is? The answer is that in ourselves we cannot resist the devil even for a moment. We can only resist him by the grace and power of God, which is where our text comes in. It assures us that in spite of Satan's threats, "the God of all grace, who called you to his eternal glory in Christ . . . will himself restore you and make you strong, firm and steadfast."

Peter had learned this from Jesus, too. Recall how Jesus told Peter at the Last Supper that "Satan has asked to sift you as wheat" (Luke 22:31). The devil must have meant something like this: "I know you are placing a lot of hope in these twelve disciples that you will be leaving behind when you return to heaven. But it is a hopeless gamble, and I will show you how hopeless it really is. If you will just let me get at Peter, your leading apostle, I will shake him so badly that all his faith will come tumbling out like chaff at threshing time, and he will be utterly ruined."

Satan is a liar, of course, but he was not lying at this point. He must have remembered how easy it had been for him to ruin our first parents in Eden long ago, and he concluded that if he had brought Adam and Eve to ruin, when they were then in their unfallen and pristine glory, it would be easy to knock down Peter, who was (unlike Adam) already sinful, ignorant, brash, and foolishly self-confident. And he was right. Peter had boasted that he would never deny Jesus. He thought that he was stronger than the other disciples, saying, "Even if all fall away on account of you, I never will" (Matt. 26:33). He told the Lord, "I am ready to go with you to prison and to death" (Luke 22:33). But when Satan blew upon Peter, he fell. In fact, it took only a little servant girl to say of Peter, "This man was with him [Jesus]" (v. 56), and at once Peter denied that he even knew the Lord.

What Satan had not counted on was what Jesus also told Peter in the Upper Room. He warned him that Satan would indeed attack him and that he would fall, but he added, "I have prayed for you, Simon, that your faith may not fail. And when you have turned back, strengthen your brothers" (v. 32).

If Peter could explain that statement, he would probably say something like this: "When Jesus told me he had prayed for me so that my faith would not fail, he was telling me that I could not stand against Satan alone. And neither can you! Satan is much too powerful for us. So do not make the mistake I made, assuming that because I loved Jesus I could never deny him. Satan can bend us any way he wishes. But if we are joined to Jesus, we will find that he is able to keep us from falling or, if he allows us to fall, he is able to keep us from falling the whole way, and will forgive us, bring us back to himself, and give us useful work to do."

Years ago at a Reformed theology conference, John Gerstner reflected on this story, suggesting (in jest) that before his fall Peter had written a hymn that goes, "Lord, we are able. . . ." But what Peter learned is that we are *not* able, not in ourselves, and that if we are to stand against Satan, it must be by the preserving grace of God. The doctrine of perseverance thus provides a stimulus to prayer. Reverend Al Martin, who serves as pastor of Trinity Baptist Church in Montville, New Jersey, has written a helpful booklet on *The Practical Implications of Calvinism*, in which he writes,

> If I believe the confession that God saves sinners, that he not only regenerates them, bringing them to repentance and faith, but that he keeps them and ultimately brings them into his presence—if that is his work then it will produce a consistent prayerfulness, not only a holy watchfulness and distrust of myself, but a constant application to him that he would perform in me that which he has promised. For what is prayer in the last analysis? It is a conscious spreading out of my helplessness before God. The true Calvinist is the man who confesses with his lips that grace must not only awaken him, and regenerate him, but that grace must preserve him.[3]

FOUR THINGS GOD WILL DO

In one respect, the King James translation of 1 Peter 5:10 is not as accurate as the New International Version, because it turns the promise "God . . . will . . . restore you" into a wish: "The God of all grace . . . make you perfect, stablish, strengthen, settle you." However, there is one way in which the King James Version is closer to the Greek text than the New International Version, and this is in the way it lists the four things Peter says God will do for believers. For some reason the NIV breaks them up, saying that God "will himself restore you and make you strong, firm and steadfast." But in the original text these are four powerful verbs, each in the future tense: "will perfect," "will establish," "will strengthen" and "will settle." In other words, the verse simply lists four things that God will do for all believers.

1. *God will perfect you.* The word that the King James Version renders "perfect" means "to make fully ready" or "to complete." It was used of making fishing nets ready by mending them, which is probably where

the New International Version translators got the idea of restoration. But this is not what Peter is thinking of. He has spoken of suffering, and the idea is not that we are restored from suffering but rather that suffering is used by God to complete or perfect what he is doing with us. The same idea emerges if we think of grace. The verse begins "and the God of all grace," which means that God is the source of every grace and will supply what we need to go on to spiritual wholeness or perfection.

2. *God will establish you.* The idea conveyed by this verb is to be established in a firm, defensive position so that the attacks of the devil will not dislodge the Christian from it. If we have any understanding of ourselves, we must worry at times about being dislodged from where God has placed us. What if Satan should attack our home? Our children? Our marriage? Suppose I lose my job? Or my health? Suppose the people I work with ostracize me because of my Christian faith, exclude me from office confidences, or pass over me for promotions? Will I be able to stand firm under such pressures? Or will I be ashamed of Jesus and disgrace him by refusing to speak up for him or by compromising what I stand for? What if I should even deny him, as Peter did?

Those fears are not groundless, because Christian homes sometimes are broken up, Christians often do fail to stand for Christ, and others at times deny him. In the midst of our fears, this text comes as a tremendous promise: "God will establish you." He will keep you in just such pressured situations. And if, in accord with his own wise counsel, he should allow you to stumble for a time and fall, you can know that Jesus nevertheless has prayed for you and that your fall will not be permanent. In fact, when it is past, you will be stronger than you were before and you will be able to use your experience of God's grace to help others.

3. *God will strengthen you.* The previous promise, that "God will establish you," had to do with holding one's ground. That is, it concerned a defensive stand. This promise goes further. It concerns an offensive action. It says that God will "strengthen" us to resist Satan, which is exactly what Peter told us to do in the previous verse: "Resist him, standing firm in the faith, because you know that your brothers throughout

the world are undergoing the same kind of sufferings" (v. 9). We cannot resist Satan in our own strength, but we can if God strengthens us.

4. *God will settle you.* The last of these promises is that God will "settle" us. The word means "to be made to rest securely," like a strong building on a sure foundation. It is important for this reason: The purpose of Satan's attacks is to dislodge us from our foundation, which is Jesus Christ. He will do that if he can. God's purpose is to settle us on Jesus, and God has arranged things so that the attacks of Satan, rather than unsettling us, actually serve to bond us to that foundation even more firmly than before. That is why Paul told the Romans, "We also rejoice in our sufferings, because we know that suffering produces perseverance; perseverance, character; and character, hope" (Rom. 5:3-4).

That happened to Peter himself, of course. Before he was tempted by Satan, Peter thought he was secure; but he was not secure, because he was trusting in himself. After he had been tempted, he knew that he could never prevail against Satan in his own strength and therefore stayed close to Jesus. It was from that proximity to Jesus and by resting on that foundation that Peter was able to strengthen his brethren in similar situations, which is what Jesus said he would do and what he is actually doing here.

We have a natural tendency to rely on ourselves. But God has arranged even the assaults of Satan so that we will be weaned away from self-reliance to trust God instead. Few experiences in life are more useful in settling us on the only sure foundation than the temptations and sufferings that come to us from Satan.

The Problem Passages

It is not possible to present the doctrine of perseverance without dealing with some of the passages that seem to contradict it. This is because these passages trouble people and are often in their minds when they hear the security of the believer mentioned.

What about Hebrews 6:4-6, which says, "It is impossible for those who have once been enlightened, who have tasted the heavenly gift, who have shared in the Holy Spirit, who have tasted the goodness of the word of God and the powers of the coming age, if they fall away, to be brought back to repentance. . . ."? Doesn't that imply that those who are saved can be lost?

Or 2 Peter 2:1-2: "But there were also false prophets among the people, just as there will be false teachers among you. They will secretly introduce destructive heresies, even denying the sovereign Lord who bought them—bringing swift destruction on themselves." Doesn't that suggest that people who have been redeemed by Christ can later deny him and thus fall away and perish?

Or what about Paul's words in 1 Corinthians 9:27, where he says, "I beat my body and make it my slave so that after I have preached to others, I myself will not be disqualified for the prize"?

Or what about the four kinds of soil in Jesus' parable in Matthew 13? Some of the seed springs up quickly, but is later scorched by the sun or choked by weeds. It perishes.

Or what about the five foolish virgins of Matthew 25? They were waiting for the bridegroom's coming, but because they went away to get oil and were not actually there when he came, they were excluded from the wedding banquet.

It is important to wrestle with these texts, of course, and not merely to dismiss them with some glib statement of "once saved, always saved." Otherwise, we will indeed be presumptuous, and we will miss the very important warnings these texts convey. However, a careful examination of these passages will show that although they can be said to put a proper hedge around perseverance, lest we presume upon it or take it lightly, they do not contradict it.

THREE CATEGORIES

How do we approach these difficulties? Martyn Lloyd-Jones does it at great length in more than one hundred pages of careful argument in the second of two volumes on Romans 8. Those who want to examine the matter in greater detail can consult the Welsh preacher's work.[4] However, Lloyd-Jones is helpful for us in that he puts the problem texts into a few manageable categories and treats them in that way. In a much briefer scope, we will follow that procedure here.

Category 1: Passages suggesting that we can "fall away" from grace.
This category contains the most difficult and most frequently cited passages. Therefore, it is the one we need to explore at greatest length. The first passage is the one in which the phrase "fallen away from grace" occurs, Galatians 5:4. An examination of the context shows that Paul is addressing the problem of false teaching that had been introduced into the Galatian churches by a party of legalistic Jews. They were insisting that circumcision and other Jewish practices had to be followed if the believers in Galatia were truly to be saved. Here the contrast with grace is law, and Paul is saying that if the believers allow themselves to be seduced by this false teaching, they will be led away from grace into legalism. This is not the same thing as saying that they will lose their salvation, though the doctrine of the legalists was indeed a false doctrine by which nobody could be saved. Paul's argument is that the Galatian Christians should "stand firm" in the liberty Christ had given them and not become "burdened again by a yoke of slavery" (Gal. 5:1).

The parable of the four kinds of soil also falls into this category of problem texts. Does it teach that it is possible for a person to be genuinely born again and then fall away and be lost, because of either the world's scorching persecutions or its materialistic entanglements? The image we have of young plants suggests this, since the plants in the story obviously do have life. But if we examine Jesus' own explanation of the story, we will see that he makes a distinction between a person who "hears" the word only and a person who "hears the word and understands it" (Matt. 13:19, 23). The one who merely hears may receive "with joy" the word he does not actually understand, and thus seem to be saved. But "he has no root" in him, which he proves by lasting only a short time. Those who understand and thus have the root of genuine life in them show it by their endurance and fruit. Jesus' point, since the parable concerns the preaching of the gospel in this age, is that not all preaching of the Word will be blessed by God to the saving of those who hear it. Only some will be converted.

Another passage that falls into this category of problem texts is the story of the five wise and five foolish virgins. This is a disturbing parable because it teaches that there will be people within the visible church who have been invited to the marriage supper, profess Jesus as their

Lord and Savior, and actually seem to be waiting for his promised return, but who are nevertheless lost at the end. It is meant to be disturbing. But if we compare it with the other parables in the same chapter—the parable of the talents and the parable of the sheep and the goats—it is clear that Jesus is saying only that in the church many who are not genuinely born again will pass for believers, until the end. It is only at the final judgment, when the Lord returns, that those who are truly saved and those who merely say they are saved will be distinguished.

The most difficult of the passages that seem to suggest that believers can fall away from grace is 2 Peter 2:1-2, which refers to people "denying the sovereign Lord who bought them." This sounds like people having been redeemed by Jesus and having believed in him later denying him and falling away.

We should be warned against this misunderstanding by the way the chapter continues, for it speaks of people who have learned about Jesus Christ and have even escaped a considerable amount of the external pollution of the world by having the high standards of the Christian life taught to them, but who have repudiated this teaching in order to return to the world's corruption, which they actually love. Peter rather crudely compares them to "a dog" returning to its vomit and "a sow that is washed" but which nevertheless goes back to "her wallowing in the mud" (v. 22). The reason they do this is because their inner nature is unchanged. They may have been cleaned up externally, but like the Pharisees, their insides are still full of corruption. These unbelievers are the ones who deny the Lord who bought them.

But how can Peter say that Jesus "bought" them? This is a difficult text and has proved so for many commentators. We began to address its difficulties near the end of chapter 5. In addition to what was stated there, it should be noted that Peter seems to be thinking of an external purchase or deliverance. Since he begins by speaking of those who were false prophets among the people of Israel, what he seems to be saying is that just as these false prophets were beneficiaries of the deliverance of the nation from Egypt but nevertheless were not true followers of God, so there will be people like this within the Christian church. They will seem to have been purchased by Christ and will show outward signs of such deliverance, but they will still be false prophets and professors.

None of these passages teaches that salvation can be lost. Some refer to something else, such as falling from grace into legalism. Others teach that those who are mere professors, however orthodox or holy they may seem, will fall away. As John writes in his first letter, "They went out from us, but they did not really belong to us. For if they had belonged to us, they would have remained with us; but their going showed that none of them belonged to us" (1 John 2:19).

Category 2: Passages suggesting that our salvation is uncertain. There are a large number of verses in this category, but they are much alike and therefore do not each require separate treatment. Examples include Philippians 2:12, which says, "Continue to work out your salvation with fear and trembling"; 2 Peter 1:10, "Therefore, my brothers, be all the more eager to make your calling and election sure. For if you do these things, you will never fail"; and Hebrews 6:4-6, "It is impossible for those who have once been enlightened, who have tasted the heavenly gift, who have shared in the Holy Spirit, who have tasted the goodness of the word of God and the powers of the coming age, if they fall away, to be brought back to repentance."

This last passage is particularly troubling to many, so it is a good place to begin. One observation is that even if the text indirectly teaches that a Christian can fall away and be lost, its specific teaching would be that such a person could thereafter never be saved a second time "because [they would be] crucifying the Son of God all over again" (v. 6). Few would want to accept such a denial of any second chance. So even those who do not believe in eternal security need to find another, better interpretation.

In this case, as we saw in chapter 5, the answer lies in the entire thrust of Hebrews, which was written to encourage Jews—who had been exposed to Christianity and had even seemed to accept it somewhat—to go on to full faith and not to fall back again into Judaism. Everything in the book points in this direction. So in this "problem" passage the writer is warning his readers against denying the faith. Speaking somewhat hypothetically, he points out the very real danger in being part of the church without ever actually becoming a true Christian. People may "taste" some of God's spiritual benefits in the church yet fail to partake of Christ himself. If this has happened, they will not come back, because in a certain sense they have been inoculated against Christianity.

However, the real situation emerges in verse 9, where the author of the book writes, "Even though we speak like this, dear friends, we are confident of better things in your case—things that accompany salvation." In other words, the author considered his readers to be genuine believers, which meant that, in his opinion, they would not commit apostasy but would go on to embrace the fullness of the doctrines of the faith, as he is urging them to do.

The other verses—Philippians 2:12 and 2 Peter 1:10—are not nearly so difficult. They merely remind us of what we saw earlier, namely, that the fact of God's perseverance with us does not suggest that somehow we do not have to persevere, too. We *do* have to persevere. In fact, it is because God is persevering with us that we will persevere. Remember that Philippians 2:12, which tells us to "work out" our salvation, is immediately followed by verse 13, which says, "for it is God who works in you to will and to act according to his good purpose." God gives us the desire and then enables us to achieve what he desires.

Category 3: Warning passages. The final category of problem passages contains warnings, like Romans 11:20-21, "Do not be arrogant, but be afraid. For if God did not spare the natural branches, he will not spare you either"; or Hebrews 2:3, "How shall we escape if we ignore such a great salvation"; or 1 Corinthians 9:27, where Paul issues a warning to himself, "so that after I have preached to others, I myself will not be disqualified."

The reason for these passages is that we need warnings from God in order to persevere. Or, to put it in other language, it is by means of such warnings that God ensures our perseverance. The proof of this is seen in the different ways in which unbelievers and believers react to such warnings. Do the verses I have been studying in this chapter trouble unbelievers? Not at all. Either they regard them as mere foolishness, something hardly to be considered, or they take them in a straightforward manner but assume that their lives are all right and that the verses therefore do not concern them. It is only believers who are troubled, because they are concerned about their relationship with God and do not want to presume that all is well with their souls when it may not be.

These passages provoke us to higher levels of commitment and greater godliness, which is what they were given to accomplish. And even this should encourage us. As Lloyd-Jones says, "To be concerned and troubled about the state of our soul when we read passages such as these is in and of itself evidence that we are sensitive to God's Word and to his Spirit, that we have spiritual life in us."[5]

GRACE AND GLORY

A few pages ago, in our discussion of 1 Peter 5:10, we called attention to the glory that is the Christian's ultimate destiny and hope: "God . . . who called you to his eternal glory in Christ . . ." We return to that theme now, because glory is the obvious place to end a study of the subject of the persevering grace of God. Grace perseveres with us precisely so that we might be brought to glory.

But glory is a difficult term to define. The Hebrew language has two words for it: *kabod*, which has the idea of "weight," and therefore of that which has value; and *shekinah*, which refers to the unapproachable light that surrounds and represents the Deity. In the New Testament the word for glory is *doxa*, which is used to translate both Hebrew words and embraces both of the Hebrew ideas. All three words are chiefly used of God, as in Psalm 24, which describes God as the King of glory:

Lift up your heads, O you gates;
  lift them up, you ancient doors,
  that the King of glory may come in.
Who is he, this King of glory?
  The LORD Almighty—
  he is the King of glory (vv. 9-10).

The psalm is teaching that God alone is of ultimate weight, worth, or value, and therefore that he alone is worthy of our highest praise. We are to give glory to God and to him only.

But here is where a problem arises: the word "glory" is also used of our destiny, as in 1 Peter 5, where Peter speaks of believers being "called to his eternal glory." What does that mean? It could mean being called to God himself, that is, to God's presence. But when we look at other relevant Bible passages we see that it means more than this. It means that we shall also share in God's glory, that in fact we shall be glorified. In other words, it does not refer only to where we will end up as Christians but also to what we will be and how we will be received when we get there.

Some of the most stimulating words that have ever been written on this subject are by C. S. Lewis in his essay "The Weight of Glory." Lewis began by admitting that for many years the idea of glory seemed unattractive to him because he associated it only with fame or luminosity. The first idea seemed wicked. Why should we want to be famous? Isn't that un-Christian? And as for the second idea, well, who wants to go around like a high-powered electric lightbulb?

However, as he looked into the matter, Lewis discovered that wanting to receive God's approval was not at all wicked. He remembered how Jesus said that no one can enter heaven except as a child, and he reflected on how natural and proper it is for a child to be pleased with praise. There is a wrong way of desiring praise, of course. It occurs when we want praise to come to us rather than to go to someone else. Moreover, it is always easy for a right desire for praise to lapse into a warped, evil, harmful desire. The pursuit of praise can take us over and consume us. But pursued in the right way, pleasure at being praised is the exact opposite of the pride Lewis had at first thought it signified. It is actually humility of a childlike sort. Since God is our Father, it is right that we should want to please him and be pleased at having pleased him.

This is not due to anything in ourselves. Salvation is God's work from start to finish. But what Lewis is saying is that for Christians the day will come when we will stand before God, who has persevered with us until the end, and who will look upon us and be pleased with what he sees. He will say, "It has all been worthwhile. It was good for me to have sent my Son to die on that cross, suffering the pain, agony, and torment of the crucifixion to save this sinner from his sins. He is what I wanted to make him. He is like my Son. I am satisfied. I am well pleased." When we hear that, we will be well pleased too. And far from taking glory to ourselves for what has happened, we will glorify the God who has glorified us.

Lewis says that the opposite of glory is to be ignored by God, to be rejected, exiled, and estranged. To be glorified is to be noticed, welcomed, acknowledged, and received. To be ignored by God is to be humiliated, turned aside, and shut out. He expresses the positive side like this:

> If we take the imagery of Scripture seriously, if we believe that God will one day give us the Morning Star and cause us to *put on* the splendor of the sun, then we may surmise that both the ancient myths and the modern poetry, so false as history, may be very near the truth as prophecy. At present we are on the outside of the world, the wrong side of the door. We discern the freshness and purity of the morning, but they do not make us fresh and pure. We cannot mingle with the splendors we see. But all the leaves of the New Testament are rustling with the rumor that it will not always be so. Some day, God willing, we shall get in. When human souls have become as perfect in voluntary obedience as the inanimate creation is in its lifeless obedience, then they will put on its glory, or rather that greater glory of which Nature is only the first sketch.[6]

Lewis was a professor of literature, not a theologian, and he freely admits that much of what he has written about glory in his essay is merely human speculation. But he has captured something of the wonder of what is in store for those who have become the objects of the electing, sanctifying, and persevering grace of God. Isn't it splendid? And shouldn't it transform how we look at the experiences we are passing through now?

The English hymn writer William H. Burleigh thought so, and thus he wrote:

> Let us press on, in patient self-denial,
> Accept the hardship, shrink not from the loss;
> Our portion lies beyond the hour of trial,
>   Our crown beyond the cross.[7]

Part Three

REDISCOVERING GOD'S GRACE

EIGHT

The True Calvinist

Since grace is the source of the life that is mine—
And faith is a gift from on high—
I'll boast in my Savior, all merit decline,
And glorify God 'til I die.

Sinclair B. Ferguson is the pastor of St. George's Tron Church in Glasgow, Scotland. Before he returned to Scotland he was Professor of Systematic Theology at Westminster Theological Seminary in Philadelphia. His students well remember how he would begin his course on the Holy Spirit. He would say, "The goal of theology is the worship of God. The posture of theology is on one's knees. The mode of theology is repentance."

That is a good set of guidelines to remember as we begin this chapter because so many of those who have discovered the beauty of Reformed theology, as described in this book, are anything but beautiful themselves. People sometimes speak of "TRs," meaning those who are "Truly Reformed." But what this term brings to mind usually is not very nice (some people have the same instinctive response to the term "Calvinist"). The "Truly Reformed" are considered narrow in their thinking, parochial in their outlook, and uncharitable in their attitude toward those who disagree. They have a bad reputation, and sadly, perhaps some of it is deserved.

There is a combative streak in Calvinism, and whenever the doctrines of grace are divorced from warm Christian piety, people tend to get ornery. Some Christians who identify themselves as Calvinists seem to be in a perpetual state of discontent with their pastors, often making uninvited suggestions for their personal improvement. Others seem overly concerned with converting people to their ecclesiastical denomination. Still others have memorized TULIP but somehow seem to be missing the heart of the gospel. Thus we have sympathy for the man who wrote: "Nothing will deaden a church or put a young man out of the ministry any more than an adherence to Calvinism. Nothing will foster pride and indifference as will an affection for Calvinism. Nothing will destroy holiness and spirituality as an attachment to Calvinism. . . . The doctrines of Calvinism will deaden and kill anything: prayer, faith, zeal, holiness."[1]

This ought not to be. In fact, it *cannot* be, provided that Calvinism is rightly understood. The doctrines of grace help to preserve all that is right and good in the Christian life: humility, holiness, and thankfulness, with a passion for prayer and evangelism. The true Calvinist ought to be the most outstanding Christian—not narrow and unkind, but grounded in God's grace and therefore generous of spirit. Toward that end, this chapter is a practical introduction to Reformed spirituality. In the next chapter we will explore the implications of Calvinism for public life. Here we consider what the doctrines of grace mean for personal growth in godliness, seeking to answer the question, What should a true Calvinist be like?

A God-centered Mind

Calvinism has implications for the whole person, but we begin with the mind because that is where the Scripture begins: "Do not conform any longer to the pattern of this world, but be transformed by the renewing of your mind" (Rom. 12:2a). While Calvinism is much more than a mindset, it nevertheless begins with a mind that is enlightened by the truth of the gospel.

What is most on the Calvinist's mind is the glory of God. This book began with B. B. Warfield's claim that "Evangelicalism stands or falls with Calvinism" (or, as we explained, that the gospel of grace stands or falls with the doctrines of grace). What Warfield himself meant by Calvinism is "that sight of the majesty of God that pervades all of life and all of experience." Or, to quote him at greater length, it is

> a profound apprehension of God in His majesty, with the poignant realization which inevitably accompanies this apprehension, of the relation sustained to God by the creature as such, and particularly by the sinful creature. The Calvinist is the man who has seen God, and who, having seen God in His glory, is filled on the one hand with a sense of his own unworthiness to stand in God's sight as a creature, and much more as a sinner, and on the other hand, with adoring wonder that nevertheless this God is a God who receives sinners. He who believes in God without reserve and is determined that God shall be God to him in all his thinking, feeling and willing—in the entire compass of his life activities, intellectual, moral and spiritual—throughout all his individual social and religious relations, is, by force of that strictest of all logic which presides over the outworking of principles into thought and life, by the very necessity of the case, a Calvinist.[2]

If the true Calvinist is a sinner who has received God's grace and seeks to live for God's glory, then the prophet Isaiah is the perfect example. In *The Practical Implications of Calvinism*, Al Martin claims that Isaiah 6 is the historical account of how God "makes a Calvinist."[3] To some this may seem a surprising connection to make. However, if the essence of Calvinism is a passion for God's glory, then one could hardly come up with a better example than the prophet Isaiah:

> In the year that King Uzziah died, I saw the Lord seated on a throne, high and exalted, and the train of his robe filled the temple. Above him were seraphs, each with six wings: With two wings they covered their faces, with two they covered their feet, and with two they were flying. And they were calling to one another:
>
> > "Holy, holy, holy is the LORD Almighty;
> > the whole earth is full of his glory."

At the sound of their voices the doorposts and thresholds shook and the temple was filled with smoke.

"Woe to me!" I cried. "I am ruined! For I am a man of unclean lips, and I live among a people of unclean lips, and my eyes have seen the King, the LORD Almighty."

Then one of the seraphs flew to me with a live coal in his hand, which he had taken with tongs from the altar. With it he touched my mouth and said, "See, this has touched your lips; your guilt is taken away and your sin atoned for."

Then I heard the voice of the Lord saying, "Whom shall I send? And who will go for us?"

And I said, "Here am I. Send me!" (Isa. 6:1-8).

This vision—in which God revealed his glory, majesty, holiness, and grace—changed Isaiah's entire life and ministry. The prophet was taken up into heaven, where everything conveys a sense of God's transcendence. Heaven is the place where God is most highly exalted. There his robe fills the temple and there he is surrounded by seraphim—literally "the burning ones"—who, despite their own glory, modestly avert their gaze and cover their feet so as to shield themselves from the greater glory of God. These angels offer a crescendo of praise, worshiping God in the beauty of his holiness. Their voices thunder, shaking the doorposts of the heavenly temple. To add to the sense of transcendence, the whole place is filled with smoke, shrouding glory with mystery.

What is perhaps most significant is what God is doing. God is seated on his kingly throne, reigning from the place of supreme royal authority over heaven and earth. As a further demonstration of his divine authority, the throne itself is exalted—it is high and lifted up. What Isaiah saw, therefore, was a vision of God's sovereignty. The God enthroned in heaven is the God who rules. From his throne he issues his royal decrees, including his sovereign decree of election, and also executes his plan of salvation, drawing sinners to himself by his efficacious, persevering grace. It is not without reason that God's throne is styled "the throne of grace" (Heb. 4:16), for all the grace defined by the doctrines of grace flows from his heavenly throne.

Isaiah's vision is not simply a dream of the past; it is a present reality. To this day, the Lord of glory sits at the center of heaven and receives the praise of countless angels. The book of Revelation confirms this, for when the apostle John visited God's throne room, he saw the same thing that Isaiah had seen hundreds of years before. He saw the Lord exalted on his heavenly throne, and he heard the six living creatures around the throne saying, "Holy, holy, holy is the Lord God Almighty, who was, and is, and is to come" (Rev. 4:8). The only difference is that in John's vision the Lord who reigns is explicitly identified as Christ: "Then I saw a Lamb, looking as if it had been slain, standing in the center of the throne" (Rev. 5:6; cf. Heb. 1:3). Not only is Christ at the center of the throne, but the throne itself is at the center of heaven, encircled by men and angels who offer perpetual praise.

The way that God "makes a Calvinist" is by bringing a person into this throne room, there to bow before his supreme majesty. As it was once said of the typical Puritan, "His God is his center." God *is* the center, ruling in sovereign might. The true Calvinist has seen this, and thus keeps God at the center of everything he does. God is the center of his worship, for in true worship attention is drawn away from earthly things and reverently fixed upon God and his glory. God is also the center of the true Calvinist's thinking. His goal is to "take captive every thought to make it obedient to Christ" (2 Cor. 10:5b), and to that end his reasoning begins and ends with God. His vision of sovereign majesty shapes his entire mindset, filling his mind with thoughts of God and his glory, and in this way the God of grace becomes the center of his whole life. What the American Puritan John Winthrop experienced after his conversion is the testimony of every true Calvinist: "I was now grown familiar with the Lord Jesus Christ. . . . If I went abroad, he went with me, when I returned, he came home with me. I talked with him upon the way, he lay down with me, and usually I did awake with him: and so sweet was his love to me, as I desired nothing but him in heaven or earth."[4]

A PENITENT SPIRIT

Although true Calvinism begins in the mind, it does not end there. This point needs to be emphasized, because although people who identify themselves as Calvinists are usually strong-minded, they are not always large-hearted. Thus it is especially important to understand that Calvinism is not a set of doctrines but a whole way of life. God has revealed the doctrines of grace not simply for the instruction of our minds but ultimately for the transformation of our lives.

Here again the prophet Isaiah is the perfect example, for when he saw the Lord high and lifted up, his own self-righteousness was utterly destroyed and he received true righteousness as a gift of God's grace. Humanly speaking, he was a righteous man even before he entered God's throne room. As a prophet, he had dedicated his life to God's service. Yet something was missing. There were depths of his own depravity that he had yet to confront, and thus he still needed a shattering experience of having God's grace applied to his guilt. To put it anachronistically, although Isaiah was a dedicated Christian, he had not yet become a thorough Calvinist.

Many terrifying thoughts must have run through Isaiah's mind when he saw God on his holy throne. Frankly, he thought he was a dead man, for he knew that it was impossible for anyone to see God . . . and live (see Ex. 33:20). "Woe to me!" he said, "For . . . my eyes have *seen* the King, the LORD Almighty" (Isa. 6:5, emphasis added). Isaiah also remembered what had happened to King Uzziah, who had died earlier that same year. Uzziah had been one of Judah's more successful monarchs. He was a good king, a man who "sought God" and "did what was right in the eyes of the LORD" (2 Chron. 26:4-5). However, Uzziah became proud of his accomplishments, and in his pride he entered the Holy Place to burn incense on God's altar. This was strictly forbidden, so the priests tried to bar the king's entrance. While they argued back and forth, Uzziah was struck with leprosy. This made him ceremonially unclean, and he was thus forced to leave the temple and never return. The king lived in seclusion until his dying day. This was the consequence of his unlawful entrance into God's holy sanctuary (2 Chron. 26:16-23).

With all of this somewhere in the back of his mind, Isaiah was terrified by his vision of God's majesty, and understandably so. He cried, "Woe to me! . . . I am ruined!" The word "woe" is significant. In the previous chapter, Isaiah had pronounced six woes against the people of Jerusalem, condemning them for everything from drunkenness to unethical real estate development. However, according to the conventions of Hebrew literature (in which things ordinarily come in sevens), one would expect one more woe. By pronouncing only six woes, Isaiah seemed to have left things hanging.

Then the prophet saw the sovereign Lord, seated in majesty, and his woe was made complete. "Woe is me!" he cried, pronouncing the seventh and final woe. Isaiah knew that he was finished. There was no way that he would ever survive this encounter, let alone join the angels in praising God's holiness. All he could do was say, "I am ruined." In other words, "It's over. I am undone. I am devastated and dismantled. I'm all in pieces. I cease to exist." What so completely overwhelmed Isaiah was a clear view of his own depravity. He now had what Martin calls "a deep experimental acquaintance with his own sinfulness."[5] This is what always happens when we see God on his throne: by seeing him as *he* really is, we see ourselves as *we* really are. We stop comparing ourselves to others and start comparing ourselves to God. Thus a true vision of God's sovereign majesty always includes a painful awareness of our own radical depravity. The more we see of God's glory, the more we recognize our need for his grace. Martin writes: "God never makes Calvinists by displaying to them his glory and his majesty without bringing with it this commensurate exposure of sin in the light of his sovereignty and his holiness."[6]

What is particularly striking in Isaiah's case is the specific sin that he confessed: foul language. He discovered that he was a sinner in the one area of life where he was most committed to doing God's will. Isaiah was a prophet, and as a prophet it was his job to speak God's Word. In the course of his work, he often had occasion to pronounce judgment against the sins of others. Yet he had not fully understood the depth of his own depravity, and it was not until he saw God's glory that he realized that he himself was a foul-mouthed sinner. When he was confronted with God's sovereign holiness, he was forced to admit that he, too, was a man of unclean lips—a sinner like everyone else.

Furthermore, Isaiah recognized that he lived "among a people of unclean lips" (Isa. 6:5). In other words, he had a heightened sensitiv-

ity to the depravity of his entire generation. This is the very opposite
of the kind of worldliness that now plagues the evangelical church.
Rather than going with the crowd, and bowing to the pressure of public opinion, Isaiah realized that his contemporaries were in violation
of God's holiness. This realization was necessary for him to fulfill his
calling as a prophet. However, it also had the danger of tempting him
to become proud of his own spiritual accomplishments. What preserved him was his unforgettable encounter with God's transcendent
glory, which produced a forthright confession of his own personal sin.
Subsequently, when Isaiah confronted the sins of others, he did so in
a spirit of humble contrition.

A penitent spirit is one of the hallmarks of Calvinism. The true
Calvinist is the man or woman who wakes up in the morning saying,
"God, have mercy on me, a sinner" (Luke 18:13). This daily confession
brings with it a healthy mistrust of one's own capacity for godliness and
a corresponding dependence on God for his grace. It also enables a
Christian to promote God's holiness with all humility and gentleness.

A GRATEFUL HEART

God did not leave Isaiah in his sins. Isaiah knew that he was a sinner—
that he was too unholy to stand in the presence of the thrice-holy God.
But once Isaiah confessed his sins, he received abundant grace and
mercy: "Then one of the seraphs flew to me with a live coal in his
hand, which he had taken with tongs from the altar. With it he
touched my mouth and said, 'See, this has touched your lips; your
guilt is taken away and your sin atoned for'" (Isa. 6:6-7).

It was a powerful demonstration of saving grace. The angel took
the coal from the altar. In other words—and this is the important
thing—the coal came from the place of sacrifice, the altar where a
lamb had been offered to atone for sin. Therefore, Isaiah was reconciled to God on the basis of a blood sacrifice. This is fundamental, for
without the shedding of blood there is no remission of sin (Heb. 9:22).

Next, the sacrifice was applied directly to the place of Isaiah's
guilt. Sssss! The burning coal made contact with the prophet's lips. It
must have been excruciatingly painful. It was necessary, however,

because Isaiah had used his lips to utter sinful speech. The angel said, "See, this has touched your lips; your guilt is taken away and your sin atoned for" (Isa. 6:7). The touching of the hot coal symbolized two things. First, it represented the removal of the prophet's guilt. The sacrifice on the altar had removed the general guilt of Isaiah's sinful nature, which he had inherited from Adam. The burning coal also symbolized the atonement. The sacrifice had paid the price for the particular sins that Isaiah had committed, thereby reconciling him to God. Both his sin and his sins had to be dealt with, and God did away with them both. Isaiah did nothing to remove his own guilt or to pay for his own sins. He was the object of sovereign grace, for God both accomplished and applied his redemption.

It does not require much imagination to see how all of this points to the grace that God has given in Jesus Christ. Christ's death on the Cross was a guilt-removing, sin-atoning sacrifice. As we saw back in chapter 5, his crucifixion served actually to accomplish our redemption. The Holy Spirit's work is to apply that redemption to the individual sinner. He does this by his irresistible grace, touching (as it were) the live coal of Christ's atonement directly to the unclean lips of our sin. In this way, the ruined sinner is reconciled to the God who reigns.

The only proper response to such amazing grace is profound gratitude. If God has touched us with his mercy, thereby infallibly securing our salvation, then we must thank him with grateful hearts. Back in chapter 2 we had occasion to mention the life and ministry of Abraham Kuyper, the great Dutch Calvinist. Kuyper's knowledge of the doctrines of grace caused him to recognize the necessary connection between grace and gratitude. The true Calvinist, Kuyper observed, is someone "who in his own soul, personally, has been struck by the Majesty of the Almighty, and yielding to the overpowering might of his eternal Love, has dared to proclaim this majestic love over against Satan and the world, and the worldliness of his own heart, in the personal conviction of being chosen by God Himself, and therefore of having to thank Him and Him alone, for every grace everlasting."[7]

The apostle Paul was thinking like a true Calvinist when he wrote, "by the grace of God I am what I am" (1 Cor. 15:10). Paul's sense of personal identity was determined by his grasp of the doctrines of grace. He was so painfully aware of his own depravity that on occasion he described himself as the very worst of sinners (1 Tim. 1:15). Whatever he attained in the Christian life, therefore, he owed entirely to God's grace in election and redemption. He was what he was by the sheer grace of God. The English Reformer John Bradford echoed Paul's statement when he spied a drunk lying in the gutter and said, "There but for the grace of God lies John Bradford." Spoken like a true Calvinist! Bradford knew his own heart well enough to realize that he was as depraved as anyone, and that the only thing that prevented him from a life of dissolution and despair was sovereign grace.

It is the knowledge of such redeeming grace that makes the Calvinist sing,

> Creation, life, salvation too,
> And all things else both good and true,
> Come from and through our God always,
> And fill our hearts with grateful praise.
> Come, lift your voice to heaven's high throne,
> And glory give to God alone![8]

A SUBMISSIVE WILL

As overwhelmed as he was by God's majesty, and as grateful as he was to have his sins forgiven, Isaiah did not stay in the throne room of heaven for long. God had work for him to do: "Then I heard the voice of the Lord saying, 'Whom shall I send? And who will go for us?' And I said, 'Here am I. Send me!'" (Isa. 6:8).

There was no hesitation, no negotiation, no discussion or argument. Isaiah was ready to go. Sovereign grace constrained him to surrender his will to God's will, and thus to commit his whole life to the service of God. Nor did Isaiah reconsider his calling when he found out what God actually wanted him to do. It was not an easy mission. God was sending him to preach judgment to people who would neither listen nor repent:

He said, "Go and tell this people:

> "'Be ever hearing, but never understanding;
>   be ever seeing, but never perceiving.'
> Make the heart of this people calloused;
>   make their ears dull
>   and close their eyes.
> Otherwise they might see with their eyes,
>   hear with their ears,
>   understand with their hearts,
> and turn and be healed" (Isa. 6:9-10).

By conventional standards, Isaiah was destined to become a failed prophet, a spectacularly unsuccessful evangelist. But he did not try to bargain for a better job offer. All he said was, "For how long, O Lord?" (Isa. 6:11). It promised to be such a difficult mission that Isaiah wanted to know how long it would last, but there was no question as to whether or not he would go. Such submission is the mark of someone who has embraced the doctrines of grace. Martin writes: "This is how God makes a man a Calvinist. In one way or another he gives him such a sight of his own majesty and sovereignty and holiness as the high and the lofty One, that it brings with it a deep, experimental acquaintance with human sinfulness personally and in terms of our own generation. It brings experimental acquaintance with the grace of God, an intimate acquaintance with the voice of God, an utter resignation to the will and the ways of God."[9]

The doctrines of grace teach that, in salvation, God does for us what we cannot do for ourselves. This is true at every step of the way. Long before we could choose for God, the Father chose us in Christ. When we were unable to remove our guilt, the Son died for our sins. And when we would not come to God in faith, the Spirit drew us by his irresistible grace. The doctrines of grace thus require the sinner to accept God's sovereignty in salvation.

This submission also comes to characterize the Christian's entire experience, beginning with conversion. A wonderful example comes from the life of Archibald Alexander, who was one of the founding professors of Princeton Seminary. This is how Alexander described the spiritual crisis that led him to faith in Christ:

I prayed, and then read in the Bible, prayed and read, prayed and read, until my strength was exhausted. . . . But the more I strove the harder my heart became, and the more barren was my mind of every serious or tender feeling. . . . I was about to desist from the endeavor, when the thought occurred to me, that though I was helpless, and my case was nearly desperate, yet it would be well to cry to God to help me in this extremity. I knelt upon the ground, and had poured out perhaps a single petition . . . when, in a moment, I had such a view of a crucified Savior, as is without parallel in my experience. The whole plan of grace appeared as clear as day. I was persuaded that God was willing to accept me, just as I was, and convinced that I had never before understood the freeness of salvation, but had always been striving to bring some price in my hand, or to prepare myself for receiving Christ. Now I discovered that I could receive him in all his offices at that very moment. . . . I felt truly a joy which was unspeakable and full of glory.[10]

It was not until he admitted his spiritual impotence and threw himself entirely on God's mercy that Alexander entered the joy of salvation. Yet for those who grasp the doctrines of grace, the whole Christian life is lived with the same spirit of trusting dependence. What is a true Calvinist? B. B. Warfield insisted that true Calvinists are "humble souls, who, in the quiet of retired lives, have caught a vision of God in His glory and are cherishing in their hearts that vital flame of complete dependence on Him which is the very essence of Calvinism."[11]

One way true Calvinists demonstrate the complete dependence of a submissive will is by making a commitment to the life of prayer. It is sometimes thought that God's sovereignty inhibits prayer. If God has already decided what he is going to do, the argument goes, and there is nothing that we can do to change what he has planned from all eternity, then why should we pray? It won't make any difference anyway, so why bother?

The flaw in this argument should immediately be evident to anyone who knows the Lord's Prayer, for Jesus taught us to pray, "Your will be done" (Matt. 6:10). In prayer we surrender our will to God's will. Prayer is not a way of getting God to do what we want him to do; rather, it is a way of submitting to God's will in all things. Furthermore, the sovereignty of God proves to be absolutely essential to the efficacy of prayer, for only a sovereign God has the power to answer! This is why it is sometimes said that when they are on their knees, all Christians are Calvinists. True prayer is prostration before the sovereignty of God, and Calvinism simply maintains this posture all through life. As J. I. Packer observed, "The Calvinist is the Christian who confesses before men in his theology just what he believes in his heart before God when he prays."[12] Or to quote again from B. B. Warfield, "The Calvinist is the man who is determined to preserve the attitude he takes in prayer in all his thinking, in all his feeling, in all his doing. . . . Other men are Calvinists on their knees; the Calvinist is the man who is determined that his intellect, and heart, and will shall remain on their knees continually, and only from this attitude think, and feel and act."[13]

One way to test the claim that every Christian is a Calvinist at prayer is to consider how believers pray for the unconverted. Imagine for a moment that God is not sovereign in grace, that salvation ultimately depends on the sinner's own choice. How then should we pray? Do we say: "Dear Lord, I realize that there may not be much that you can do about this, but if there is, please help my friend somehow to become a Christian"? Of course no one actually prays this way; the very idea is absurd. But what makes it so absurd is that, deep down, every Christian believes in the sovereignty of God's grace. When we pray for sinners to be converted, therefore, we ask God to do something for them that we know they are utterly incapable of doing for themselves. We ask God to invade their minds, change their hearts, and bend their wills so that they will come to him in faith and repentance. In short, in our intercession we depend on God to *save* them.

This attitude of dependence ought to characterize the Christian's entire approach to evangelism. More will be said about proclaiming the gospel in the chapter that follows. Here it is sufficient to note that true evangelism is entirely dependent on God for its success. The regeneration of the sinner's mind and heart is the work of God's Spirit. It does not depend on saying the right words or using the most effective technique. The true Calvinist surrenders to God's will in sharing the gospel, because God's sovereignty in grace gives the only hope of success. Packer writes:

> In evangelism . . . we are impotent; we depend wholly upon God to make our witness effective; only because He is able to give men new hearts can we hope that through our preaching of the gospel sinners will be born again. These facts ought to drive us to prayer. It is God's intention that they should drive us to prayer. God means us, in this as in other things, to recognize and confess our impotence, and to tell Him that we rely on Him alone, and to plead with Him to glorify His name. . . . God will make us pray before He blesses our labours in order that we may constantly learn afresh that we depend on God for everything. And then, when God permits us to see conversions, we shall not be tempted to ascribe them to our own gifts, or skill, or wisdom, or persuasiveness, but to His work alone, and so we shall know whom we ought to thank for them.[14]

A good example of an evangelist who submitted to God's will is the apostle Paul. No one was more committed to the doctrines of grace than Paul, whose writings we quoted frequently in our exposition of the Five Points of Calvinism. At the same time, no one was more committed to prayer and evangelism. To the Thessalonians he wrote, "Brothers, pray for us that the message of the Lord may spread rapidly" (2 Thess. 3:1). Paul did not assume that because God is sovereign in grace, therefore prayer is unnecessary. On the contrary, he understood that since salvation is entirely due to God's grace, for that very reason prayer is absolutely essential. Prayer is the heart's surrender to the will of God. Those who believe most strongly in the sovereignty of grace ought to be most persistent in asking God to do what only he *can* do, and that is to save sinners.

A HOLY LIFE

Absolute dependence on God, with a complete resignation to his will, does not diminish the need for active spiritual growth. On the contrary, the true Calvinist practices the pursuit of holiness.

To be sure, Calvinism recognizes that God is sovereign in sanctification. Paul prayed, "May God himself, the God of peace, sanctify you through and through. May your whole spirit, soul and body be kept blameless at the coming of our Lord Jesus Christ. The one who calls you is faithful and he will do it" (1 Thess. 5:23-24). Similarly, the writer to the Hebrews asked God to "work in us what is pleasing to him, through Jesus Christ" (Heb. 13:21). Christianity is not a performance-based religion. Those who are saved by grace also live by grace, and their growth in grace is due to the gracious work of God's Spirit. This is what preserves Calvinism from legalism. If someone who claims to be a Calvinist turns out to be a legalist, he must not understand the doctrines of grace very well after all, because the true Calvinist is overwhelmed by God's mercy for sinners. A graceless Calvinism is thoroughly repugnant to the gospel, for unless the pursuit of holiness is motivated by an ever deepening love for God and his grace, it quickly becomes joyless and fruitless.

One way to see the vital connection between God's sovereign grace and our spiritual growth is to consider what each of the doctrines of grace has to say about holiness. Back in chapter 1 we stated that the Five Points of Calvinism establish what is really only one point, namely, that every aspect of salvation is the gracious work of the sovereign God. However, there is another great truth that unifies the doctrines of grace, which is that each of them promotes personal holiness.

Radical depravity exposes our lack of holiness. The reason that we need God's grace in the first place is because we are sinners. If ever we are to enter into a relationship with God, something will have to be done about our sin, for "without holiness no one will see the Lord" (Heb. 12:14b). When the Bible describes the totality of our depravity, it is generally in the context of our need to find holiness by grace. Romans 3 is a good example. Here Paul quotes from the Psalms in order to prove the universality of sin:

> There is no one righteous, not even one;
>   there is no one who understands,
>   no one who seeks God.

194 THE DOCTRINES OF GRACE

All have turned away,
   they have together become worthless;
there is no one who does good,
   not even one (Rom. 3:10-12).

The Bible never stops at sin, however. It always moves on to salvation, and so Paul proceeds to explain that holiness is available through faith: "But now a righteousness from God, apart from law, has been made known, to which the Law and the Prophets testify. This righteousness from God comes through faith in Jesus Christ to all who believe" (Rom. 3:21-22). The point here is the rather obvious one that by exposing our sin, the doctrine of total depravity convinces us to seek the holiness of God.

What is the connection between holiness and unconditional election? If election is an eternal decree that God issued before the beginning of time, what is its practical relevance for personal godliness? The answer is that God chose us for the very purpose of making us holy. This point is made quite simply in Ephesians 1, Paul's encomium on election: "Praise be to the God and Father of our Lord Jesus Christ, who has blessed us in the heavenly realms with every spiritual blessing in Christ. For he chose us in him before the creation of the world *to be holy and blameless in his sight*" (Eph. 1:3-4, emphasis added). This is perhaps the clearest statement of God's design for election. We were chosen in Christ for the explicit purpose of being made holy in Christ. As Paul explained to the Romans, we were predestined to be conformed to the likeness of God's Son (Rom. 8:29). Or to put all this another way, God's intention for election is our sanctification.

When it comes to *particular redemption,* the connection between grace and holiness is easy to see. One of the primary purposes of the Cross is the sanctification of those for whom Christ died. Consider the following Scriptures:

2 Corinthians 5:21. "God made him who had no sin to be sin for us, so that in him we might become the righteousness of God."

Ephesians 5:25-27. "Christ loved the church and gave himself up for her to make her holy, cleansing her by the washing with water through the word, and to present her to himself as a radiant church, without stain or wrinkle or any other blemish, but holy and blameless."

Colossians 1:22. "But now he has reconciled you by Christ's physical body through death to present you holy in his sight, without blemish and free from accusation."

Titus 2:13b-14. "Our great God and Savior, Jesus Christ, . . . gave himself for us to redeem us from all wickedness and to purify for himself a people that are his very own, eager to do what is good."

Christ was doing more than one thing on the Cross, of course, and his atonement results in many saving benefits. But one of the primary purposes of the crucifixion was to make God's people holy. The death of Christ means death to our sin.

Since Christ accomplished redemption with the goal of making us holy, the Spirit also applies redemption with the same end in view. His irresistible work of *efficacious grace* in calling sinners to Christ has as its purpose the sanctification of the elect. Again, there are many Scriptures to support this point. Paul addressed the Corinthians as "those sanctified in Christ Jesus and called to be holy" (1 Cor. 1:2). Similarly, he reminded Timothy that God "has saved us and called us to a holy life—not because of anything we have done but because of his own purpose and grace" (2 Tim. 1:9a). The apostle Peter taught the same thing: "But just as he who called you is holy, so be holy in all you do; for it is written: 'Be holy, because I am holy'" (1 Pet. 1:15-16). The calling of the Holy Spirit—the effectual call that leads to salvation—is a call to holiness.

This brings us, finally, to *perseverance*. Perseverance is not simply a matter of surviving to the end of the Christian life, and then somehow making it to heaven. Rather, to persevere is to lead a holy and productive Christian life. Here the Calvinist takes particular comfort in Paul's encouragement to the Philippians, "that he who began a good work in you will carry it on to completion until the day of Christ Jesus" (Phil. 1:6). Persevering grace is also sanctifying grace, and all through life the Holy Spirit is at work to make the Christian holy.

It is for just this reason that the true Calvinist aspires to become ever more holy. Although sanctification is by faith, it is not by faith alone. We are called to do good works. These works do not win our salvation. They do not even preserve our salvation, as if God's grace were unable to persevere without our help. But they are works nonetheless! So the Scripture tells us to "make every effort . . . to be holy" (Heb. 12:14). It also gives this command: "Continue to work out your salvation with fear and trembling, for it is God who works in you to will and to act according to his good purpose" (Phil. 2:12-13). When it comes to sanctification, the true Calvinist is busy working out what God has worked in. As Calvin himself wrote, "Holiness is not a merit by which we can attain communion with God, but a gift of Christ, which enables us to cling to him, and to follow him."[15]

It is sometimes thought that Calvinism leads to quietism—a passive approach to life that is not vigorous in the pursuit of godliness. But the Scriptures teach exactly the opposite. The doctrines of grace themselves point to the necessity of holiness. Each of the Five Points of Calvinism promotes holy Christian living. The true Calvinist, then, is one who recognizes Christ's call to holiness: "For the grace of God that brings salvation has appeared to all men. It teaches us to say 'No' to ungodliness and worldly passions, and to live self-controlled, upright and godly lives in this present age" (Titus 2:11-12). The mention of "worldly passions" is especially significant. Back in chapter 1 we identified worldliness as a fundamental failing of the evangelical church. Here we discover that what teaches us to say "No" to worldliness is the doctrines of God's sovereign, saving grace.

This is an important confirmation of our thesis, which is that Calvinism is vital to the spiritual health of evangelicalism. Worldliness is a preoccupation with the world's standards for significance and success. Those who say "Yes" to worldly passions seek power, prestige, pleasure, and possessions. The way to be delivered from the pursuit of these sinful passions is to be captivated by God and his sovereign grace in salvation. Hence the church's great need to recover the doctrines of grace, that not only preserve the grace of the gospel but also teach us the art of gracious living.

A GLORIOUS PURPOSE

Holiness is not an end in itself, but serves the greater glory of God. Earlier we noted from Ephesians 1 that election promotes sanctification. In that same passage, the apostle Paul goes on to say that "we were also chosen . . . in order that we, who were the first to hope in Christ, might be for the praise of his glory" (Eph. 1:11-12). The final goal of our election, and thus of our sanctification, is the glory of God. The Puritan Thomas Brooks wrote: "The end of that obedience that accompanies salvation is, *divine glory.* The aim of the obedient soul, in prayer and praises, in talking and walking, in giving and receiving, in living and doing, is divine glory. . . . In all actions, the obedient soul intends to promote the divine glory." [16]

One way that God accomplishes his glory in the life of the Christian is through suffering. The Christian life is difficult, and God never promised otherwise. Jesus frankly told his disciples, "In this world you will have trouble" (John 16:33). In addition to all the hardships of living in a fallen world—disease, disaster, and death—the Christian is always at risk of persecution. Calvinism is committed to realism, and Calvin himself observed that "all whom the Lord has chosen and received into the society of his saints, ought to prepare themselves for a life that is hard, difficult, laborious, and full of countless griefs."[17] This is because the Christian life is patterned after the life of Christ. As it was for Christ, so it is for the Christian: through suffering into glory. First humiliation, then exaltation—the cross before the crown.

This is not the place for a complete discussion of suffering in the Christian life. It should be noted, however, that Calvinism brings a unique perspective. The fact that God is sovereign means that all things (including our sufferings) serve to fulfill his ultimate purpose in bringing glory to himself. When trouble comes, the true Calvinist assumes from the outset that God is still in control and that he will accomplish his good purpose in the end. Therefore, every affliction is an opportunity for submission to God's good and perfect will.

The most famous statement of God's sovereignty over suffering comes near the end of Romans 8: "And we know that in all things God works for the good of those who love him, who have been called according to his purpose" (Rom. 8:28). Perhaps because it is so familiar, this statement has become something of a Christian cliché. In fact, it is sometimes suggested that the verse is too trite to share with those who are suffering. Certainly it is possible to use this or any other Bible verse in an uncaring or unfeeling way. However, it would be a mistake to think that what Romans 8:28 teaches would ever be inappropriate to share, for this verse presents the true Christian perspective on adversity.

This perspective is founded squarely on the doctrines of grace. If Paul had stopped halfway through, the verse would offer little comfort at all, for in that case it would read: "And we know that in all things God works for the good of those who love him" (Rom. 8:28a). In that case, God's good work would depend on our ability to kindle love for him within our own cold hearts. Thankfully, the apostle went on to explain that those who love God are those "who have been called according to his purpose. For those God foreknew he also predestined to be conformed to the likeness of his Son, that he might be the first-born among many brothers. And those he predestined, he also called; those he called, he also justified; those he justified, he also glorified" (Rom. 8:28b-30). Therefore, our certainty that God is working out his good purpose does not depend upon our own uncertain affections, but on the election, calling, and redemption of the triune God, who has predestined us to glory.

The chief end of God is to glorify himself. He is directing and disposing all things (including our sufferings) for his glory. And if God's purpose is to pursue his glory, then it only makes sense that this is also *our* purpose. The true Calvinist embraces the eternal purpose of the sovereign God by living for his glory. To summarize everything we have said thus far, the true Calvinist has a mind that is centered on God's majesty, a spirit that is sorry for sin, a heart that is full of gratitude for God's grace, and a will that submits to his holy purpose. In other words, the true Calvinist is a person whose whole person and entire life are dedicated to the glory of God.

The true Calvinist not only recognizes God's glory but is also jealous to promote it. Indeed, that is part of the motivation for this book, which was written out of a longing for the evangelical church to rediscover a theology of grace. Reformed theology is the system of doctrine that seeks to give God all the glory for his grace in the gospel. Thus its recovery furthers the greatest of all goals and the highest of all purposes: the glory of God.

It is impossible to be jealous for God's glory without having an equal passion for correct doctrine, because correct doctrine is what preserves the graciousness of the gospel. It was said of George Whitefield that, "He knew errors in the great truths of the Gospel are not indifferent, but dreadful and fatal; he knew it was not candour and charity to say that errors in judgment are not hurtful, but the greatest unmercifulness and cruelty; therefore he often reproved such sharply."[18] Whitefield knew all this because he knew the New Testament, in which there is a constant concern for sound doctrine. From the time of the apostles, the church has been in constant danger of succumbing to the counterfeit grace of a false gospel. Thus it has always been necessary to teach sovereign grace, as well as to refute all those who oppose it. As Whitefield rightly understood, defending the doctrines of grace is not simply a matter of duty but also a matter of charity. The New Testament that preaches the good news about Jesus Christ is the same New Testament that teaches how to defend his gospel against error. And it does both of these things—preaching the gospel of grace and teaching the doctrines of grace—out of a love for the lost souls of humanity.

Those who are jealous for God's glory must promote sound doctrine with all humility, for as we have seen, humility is one of the cardinal virtues of Calvinism. A good example of what it means to be jealous for God's glory comes from the life of Henry Martyn, the Cambridge scholar and early nineteenth-century Anglican missionary to India. On one occasion, as Martyn was traveling through an Islamic nation, he was shown a picture of Jesus bowing down and clinging to the robes of Mohammed. Martyn broke down in tears, and when one of his colleagues asked what was the matter, he said, "I could not endure existence if Jesus were not to be glorified. It would be hell to me, if He were always thus to be dishonored."[19] Martyn was a true Calvinist—tenderhearted and evangelistically minded, with a holy jealousy for God's glory.

Calvinism at Work

Yet now I am living with work to be done
For I am God's workmanship too,
Created in Christ with a race to be run,
Which God has ordained me to do.

Christianity is not a private religion. The grace that draws sinners into a personal, saving relationship with Jesus Christ has implications for all of life. This is one of the strengths of Calvinism—its comprehensive vision for bringing every aspect of human existence under divine authority and thereby directing every human endeavor to the glory of God. Abraham Kuyper identified as "the special trait of Calvinism" its ability to place "the believer *before the face of God,* not only in His church, but also in his personal, family, social, and political life. The majesty of God, and the authority of God press upon the Calvinist in the whole of his human existence."[1]

This cosmic vision of Reformed theology obviously encompasses much more than the Five Points of Calvinism. It thus serves as a helpful reminder that the heart of Reformed theology is a passion for God's glory, not simply in redemption but in all of creation. The doctrines of grace teach that God is sovereign in the salvation of an individual sinner, but this is only one implication of the all-encompassing truth that God rules over everything. The God who is sovereign in grace is sovereign over all. This chapter thus moves beyond Reformed spirituality to a Reformed society, showing Calvinism at work in church and culture.

HAVE MERCY!

God is sovereign in the church—the community of his grace. He exercises this sovereignty through Jesus Christ, who alone is the supreme Lord of the church: "God placed all things under his feet and appointed him to be head over everything for the church" (Eph. 1:22); "He is the head of the body, the church . . . so that in everything he might have the supremacy" (Col. 1:18).

The grace of the Lord Jesus Christ shapes the mind and heart of the church. A congregation that embraces the doctrines of grace displays all the attitudes and attributes mentioned in the previous chapter. Its worship is God-centered, as its praise and proclamation are joyfully and reverently directed toward the glory of God. Its members pursue the practice of holiness, penitently and gratefully seeking to lead lives that are pleasing to God. All of their spiritual efforts are suffused with an attitude of absolute submission to God. The doctrines of grace foster dependence on "the means of grace," which for most Calvinists refers to the Word, the sacraments, and prayer. These are means of grace because ordinarily God uses them to save and to sanctify his people. This does not mean that those who read their Bibles, get baptized, and say their prayers will be saved automatically. If that were so, then spiritual growth would become another method of self-improvement rather than a transforming work of divine grace. So in order for the means of grace to be effectual, they must be received by faith. As a church studies the Bible, receives the Lord's Supper, and kneels in prayer, it must at the same time trust God's Spirit to bring enlightenment, nourishment, and spiritual refreshment. Having been gathered by grace, the church continues to depend on sovereign grace for its progress in the faith.

Two aspects of the church's work deserve to be explored at greater length: mercy and evangelism. What implications do the doctrines of grace have for the church's ministry in word and deed?

The church saved by sovereign grace is a merciful church (or at least it ought to be). Its commitment to outreach is based on the mercy it has received from God. In his letter to the Romans, the apostle Paul takes eleven full chapters to explain the theology of salvation. Then in chapter 12 he applies his doctrine, beginning with these words: "Therefore, I urge you, brothers, in view of God's mercy, to offer your bodies as living sacrifices, holy and pleasing to God—this is your spiritual act of worship. Do not conform any longer to the pattern of this world" (Rom. 12:1-2a). The alternative to worldliness—to being squeezed into the world's pattern like the evangelical church sometimes is—is sacrificial living. This sacrifice is motivated by mercy, for Paul makes his exhortation "in view of God's mercy." Given the wider context of Romans, the mercy he has in mind is entailed in the doctrines of grace: election, redemption, calling, and perseverance (see Romans 8–9). It is the kind of mercy that can only come from God, "For from him and through him and to him are all things. To him be the glory forever!" (Rom. 11:36). And it is only on the basis of such mercy that a church is empowered to live by sacrificial love. Sinners who have been liberated from the deadly clutches of sin by the irresistible, choosing, redeeming grace of God are compelled to share the love of Christ. They are made merciful by God's mercy.

To apply this at the congregational level, a church that embraces the doctrines of grace must be active in outreach. This can be illustrated from the recent history of Tenth Presbyterian Church in Center City Philadelphia. Especially since the 1980s, the church has demonstrated a strong commitment to meeting the needs of the city, providing practical assistance and spiritual instruction to international students, drug addicts, AIDS victims, pregnant teens, homosexuals, the disabled, the homeless, and others suffering from acute personal need.

Tenth is located not far from the heart of Philadelphia's homosexual community, so it is not uncommon for male prostitutes to operate on street corners near the church, and sometimes in front of the church itself. In 1984 Tenth members who had received God's grace, including some who had experienced his transforming work in their sexual orientation, began to pray for Philadelphia's gay community. Out of their efforts grew Harvest USA, an evangelistic and counseling ministry providing information, services, and programs to those desiring freedom from homosexuality, and to their families. As Harvest has grown, the ministry has expanded to include those struggling with other forms of sexual brokenness and addiction. A growing concern for the gay community naturally prompted greater compassion for those dying from AIDS. In 1988 a ministry called HOPE was established to provide friendship and practical assistance for patients suffering from AIDS and HIV-related disease. Especially at the end of life, victims of the disease find themselves abandoned by their families and friends. Yet the church is there, offering love and support in the name of Christ.

The church is also there for teens struggling with problem pregnancies. In 1980 a group of Tenth members began to seek positive Christian alternatives to abortion. This was partly in response to the work of one of the church's elders, former United States Surgeon General Dr. C. Everett Koop, who along with Dr. Francis Schaeffer had produced the pro-life film series *Whatever Happened to the Human Race?* The group sought to oppose infanticide in a way that would demonstrate the power of God's grace. Rather than staging a political protest, they decided to open a crisis pregnancy center. ALPHA Pregnancy Services provides free medical testing, counseling, education, friendship, clothing, and other forms of practical care to mothers and their newborn children.

Another significant urban need is education. Cities like Philadelphia struggle to meet the goal of helping every child achieve even basic competency in reading and writing, which is why in 1984 James and Linda Boice founded City Center Academy, a college-preparatory high school for urban students. City Center Academy is a Christian school that seeks to teach Christ across the curriculum. It is not an elite school for wealthy families but a quality low-cost high school for families with limited means; nevertheless, nearly all its graduates go on to higher education.

Then there are the needs of the urban poor. Once a month Tenth sponsors a Community Dinner at which one hundred or more homeless guests receive hospitality in the name of Christ. After a worship service, the guests are invited to a sit-down dinner, hosted and served by members of the church and other Christians. Visitors who are interested in receiving further instruction are invited to attend the weekly Fellowship Bible Study, which meets on Sunday afternoons. There have been other ministries as well: a divorce recovery workshop; a support group for single parents; an ongoing racial reconciliation seminar; tutoring for children in a nearby housing project; and worship services at nursing homes, homeless shelters, and the local AIDS community center. All of these programs are under the oversight of ACTS—Active Compassion Through Service—a mercy ministry founded in 1982. Each of them developed "in view of God's mercy," as the church sought to work out the implications of sovereign grace in the context of the city.

Other ministries of the church could be mentioned. Philadelphia is a major center for international education, and under the ministry of Donald Grey Barnhouse in the early 1950s, Tenth began welcoming international students for monthly dinners. This ministry expanded in the 1980s to include tutoring in English as a second language, Bible studies, and a weekly worship service. Tenth International Fellowship now functions as a church within a church, enjoying the spiritual oversight of its own pastor, elder, and deacon.

Two new ministries began in the 1990s. One is the Summer Medical Institute, sponsored by the Medical Campus Outreach of Tenth Presbyterian Church. Beginning in 1992, teams of medical students spent six weeks or more on the streets of Philadelphia every summer, providing basic medical screening, immunizations, and AIDS testing in the Hispanic neighborhoods of North Philadelphia—all in the name of Jesus Christ. Around the same time there was a growing concern for the needs of the disabled and the people who care for them. GRACE is a support ministry of people with special needs as a result of handicap or chronic illness. In addition to launching a deaf ministry, GRACE has sponsored classes, seminars, and conferences to help some of the 50 million Americans who struggle with chronic illness and disability, as well as those who care for them. The goal of the ministry is not simply to raise awareness but to integrate the disabled into the body of Christ by equipping them to exercise their spiritual gifts.

More recently, a new Federal Detention Center opened in Center City Philadelphia. In the months prior to its opening, Tenth leaders and members prayed that God would enable the church to fulfill Christ's command to visit those who are in prison (Matt. 25:36). By the time the facility was ready to receive volunteers, two dozen Bible study leaders had been trained, and inmates on each floor began to receive sound instruction in the Scriptures.

The point of mentioning these examples is not to suggest that Tenth's ministry is extraordinary, or even exemplary. The church's overall impact on the City of Philadelphia is small, and if anything, our history shows how long it can take for mercy to mature in the life of a congregation. Yet these ministries illustrate what God is able to do in and through the lives of ordinary Christians when he is honored for his sovereign mercy, which always demands a life of sacrificial service to the poor, the weak, and the needy. For all our faults, we have seen God's blessing on the doctrines of grace, for where grace is preached in all its power, grace is demonstrated in and through the lives of those who are saved by it.

THE GOSPEL-SPREADING CHURCH

In order to have a saving effect, the love of Christ must be demonstrated not only in deed but also in word. This is why all the ministries of Tenth Church include evangelistic Bible teaching. Although acts of mercy can display the love of Christ, they cannot by themselves produce faith and repentance. In order for conversion to occur, such acts of mercy must be coupled with the preaching of the gospel.

The theme of evangelism has come up throughout this book, and with good reason. Evangelism has always been one of the hallmarks of evangelicalism. If the case for Calvinism is to be successful, therefore, it must show that the doctrines of grace promote the proclamation of the gospel. Yet this is precisely the point at which Calvinism so often comes under attack. If God has already decided who will be saved, the argument goes, then why bother to evangelize? And if Christ died only for the elect, then how can the gospel be offered to everyone? Although we have already attempted to answer these questions (see chapters 4 and 5), this is a good place to summarize the vital and necessary connection between Calvinism and evangelism. A church that is truly Reformed is a gospel-spreading church.

In the previous chapter we presented the prophet Isaiah as an

example of how God "makes a Calvinist." One further point should
be noted: Isaiah was called to be an evangelist. God told him to preach
a message of judgment and grace to Israel, saying,

"Go and tell this people:

"'Be ever hearing, but never understanding;
    be ever seeing, but never perceiving.'
Make the heart of this people calloused;
    make their ears dull
    and close their eyes.
Otherwise they might see with their eyes,
    hear with their ears,
    understand with their hearts,
and turn and be healed" (Isa. 6:9-10).

What is striking about this commission is that it is so thoroughly
"Calvinistic." From the very beginning, God asserted his sovereignty
over Isaiah's preaching. Would the prophet win thousands of converts? Hardly. The primary effect of his ministry was not to save but
to condemn. Did that make Isaiah any less an evangelist? Not at all.
His responsibility was to get the message right and get the message
out. How people would respond was God's business, because he alone
is sovereign over the mind, the heart, and the will of the sinner. And
apparently God did not consider his sovereignty a hindrance to Isaiah's
motivation for evangelism. The argument is often made, of course,
that the reason we share the gospel is because the salvation of the lost
depends on us. On this view, a strong doctrine of divine sovereignty
would seem to inhibit the missionary impulse. If God saves whom
God chooses, then why not leave it all up to God?

There are many motives for evangelism. Certainly one of them is
a love for lost souls. But fundamentally, evangelism is a matter of obedience to the will of Jesus Christ, who commands: "All authority in
heaven and on earth has been given to me. Therefore go and make disciples of all nations, baptizing them in the name of the Father and of
the Son and of the Holy Spirit, and teaching them to obey everything
I have commanded you. And surely I am with you always, to the very

end of the age" (Matt. 28:18-20). Having received this Great Commission, what further motivation is needed? Like all Christians, Calvinists recognize Christ's call to evangelism.

What we are not called to do, however, is actually to convert anyone. Our job is simply to proclaim the gospel, and it is God's job to save—or not—as he pleases. The results of our evangelistic endeavors do not depend on our intentions, but on God's sovereign will. As J. I. Packer correctly observes:

> If we regarded it as our job, not simply to present Christ, but actually to produce converts—to evangelize, not only faithfully, but also successfully—our approach to evangelism would become pragmatic and calculating. . . . This shows the danger of forgetting the practical implications of God's sovereignty. It is right to recognize our responsibility to engage in aggressive evangelism. It is right to desire the conversion of unbelievers. . . . But it is not right when we take it on us to do more than God has given us to do. It is not right when we regard ourselves as responsible for securing converts, and look to our own enterprise and techniques to accomplish what only God can accomplish. To do that is to intrude ourselves into the office of the Holy Ghost, and to exalt ourselves as the agents of the new birth. And the point that we must see is this: *only by letting our knowledge of God's sovereignty control the way in which we plan, and pray, and work in His service, can we avoid becoming guilty of this fault.* For where we are not consciously relying on God, there we shall inevitably be found relying on ourselves.[2]

One way to see how the sovereignty of God controls the manner in which we evangelize is to consider the relationship that each of the doctrines of grace bears to the task of preaching the gospel. Radical depravity, of course, points to the need for evangelism. It is because human beings are desperately lost in their sins, and thus vulnerable to the wrath of God and the pains of hell, that they need to hear the good news of salvation through the Cross and the empty tomb. Unconditional election is the choice of God unto salvation. However, as we saw in chapter 4, this choice includes both the end result (making it to heaven) and the means to that end (hearing the gospel). Therefore, rather than making evangelism unnecessary, the doctrine of election actually *requires* it as the appointed means of salvation.

Next comes the doctrine of *particular redemption,* which guarantees that Christ saved sinners when he died on the Cross. He did not make their salvation merely possible but actually accomplished it. Here we must address the issue of the free offer of the gospel. Does the extent of the atonement limit the free offer of the gospel? Not at all. For one thing, the evangelist never knows who is among the elect. This is a secret known only to God, who has chosen to accomplish his saving purpose through the general proclamation of the gospel. So the preacher simply obeys the plain teaching of Scripture, and declares, "Whoever is thirsty, let him come; and whoever wishes, let him take the free gift of the water of life" (Rev. 22:17b).

Remember also that the New Testament nowhere invites people to believe in Christ on the basis that he died specifically and particularly for them. Rather, sinners are informed that they are in need of a Savior; further, they are told that he is offered to them, if only they will repent of their sin and believe in him. The same gospel offer characterized the evangelistic preaching of great Calvinists like George Whitefield and Charles Spurgeon, and even the preaching of Arminians like John Wesley. What these preachers offered to sinners was not a doctrine of the atonement, but Christ himself—crucified and risen—with power to save. Here it is important to understand what the gospel is (and is not). The gospel does not say, "Believe that Christ died for everybody's sins, yours included." Nor, for that matter, does the gospel say, "Believe that Christ died for your sins, even though he did not die for others." Rather, the gospel says, "Believe on the Lord Jesus Christ, who died for sinners, and who now offers himself to you as Savior and Lord" (see John 3:14-16; 6:40; Acts 10:43; etc.). The faith that God requires is not faith in the extent of the atonement but faith in the living Christ, who is not dead but risen.

Not only are sinners invited to come to Christ; they are actually *commanded* to do so. This brings us to the gospel's *efficacious grace* in its call to salvation, which for the elect is irresistible. The effectual call comes through the preaching of the gospel: "'Everyone who calls on the

name of the Lord will be saved.' How, then, can they call on the one they
have not believed in? And how can they believe in the one of whom they
have not heard? And how can they hear without someone preaching to
them?" (Rom. 10:13-14). The answer, of course, is that sinners cannot
call on the Lord until they hear God's special call through the general
call of a minister; hence the need for gospel preaching.

The fact that God is sovereign in grace does not diminish the per-
suasiveness of the gospel message in any way, but actually establishes
it. In *Evangelism and the Sovereignty of God,* Packer shows how the
doctrines of grace preserve the necessity, urgency, and genuineness of
the gospel offer, while still maintaining the sinner's personal responsibility for receiving or rejecting it.[3] Evangelism is still *necessary,*
because no one can possibly be saved without the proclamation of the
gospel. Evangelism is still *urgent,* because whatever we may happen to
believe about election, the fact remains that without Christ, sinners
are lost. Frankly, God's purpose in election is none of our business.
What *is* our business is a passionate commitment to proclaiming the
good news about Jesus Christ to those who need to hear it. Nor do the
doctrines of grace diminish the *genuineness* of the gospel invitation.
The offer of the gospel is well-meant, for in it God really does offer
Jesus Christ to anyone who will receive him, with the promise of eternal life for those who believe. Finally, the sovereignty of grace does not
in any way undermine the responsibility of individual sinners for their
response to the gospel. Whatever we may believe about predestination, the fact remains that anyone who rejects Christ is the cause of
his own condemnation, and ultimately of his own damnation. Packer
writes, "The Bible never says that sinners miss heaven because they
are not elect, but because they 'neglect the great salvation', and
because they will not repent and believe."[4]

The final thing to say on this subject is that only the sovereignty
of grace can give evangelism the slightest possibility of success. If the
doctrines of grace are false, then preaching the gospel is a complete
waste of time, for without sovereign grace sinners cannot possibly be
delivered from their lost and deadly condition. The problem with most
contemporary approaches to evangelism is their assumption that sinners have the ability to receive Christ. But we must take passages such

as 1 Corinthians 2:14 with the utmost seriousness: "The man without the Spirit does not accept the things that come from the Spirit of God, for they are foolishness to him, and he cannot understand them, because they are spiritually discerned." The difficulty is not simply that he *will not* understand the good news about Jesus Christ but that he *cannot*—his natural depravity renders him impervious to the gospel. Humanly speaking, therefore, effective evangelism is impossible. But because God is sovereign in grace, he is able to do for sinners what they cannot do for themselves. Thus the doctrines of grace provide the strongest certainty that evangelism will be effective.

Far from being a weakness of Calvinist theology, therefore, evangelism is one of its areas of greatest strength. The doctrines of grace preserve the great gospel truth that *God saves sinners.*[5] Yes, *God* saves them, for they cannot save themselves. The ones who are saved really are *sinners,* depraved human beings who are utterly lost apart from God's saving grace. And God really does *save* them, having accomplished their total redemption through the death and resurrection of Jesus Christ. *God saves sinners.* This is the gospel that Calvinists preach because it is the biblical gospel.

God's sovereignty in grace has many salutary effects on the church's proclamation of the gospel. Calvinistic evangelism is patient and persistent, knowing that by his grace, God is able to transform the most hardened sinner. It is also prayerful. Packer writes that the Great Commission "is a commission not only to preach, but also to pray; not only to talk to men about God, but also to talk to God about men. . . . We are to preach, because without knowledge of the gospel no man can be saved. We are to pray, because only the sovereign Holy Spirit in us and in men's hearts can make our preaching effective to men's salvation, and God will not send His Spirit where there is no prayer."[6] In our praying and our preaching, we are called simply to be faithful. And if we are faithful, then by God's grace our evangelism may also be successful.

THE BODY POLITIC

While evangelicalism has rightly emphasized the importance of evangelism (and, perhaps to a lesser extent, mercy ministry), it has gener-

ally neglected its duty to cultivate the Christian mind.[7] This neglect
has dire consequences, not only for the church but also for the wider
culture. Nearly a century ago, J. Gresham Machen warned that "We
may preach with all the fervor of a reformer and yet succeed only in
winning a straggler here and there, if we permit the whole collective
thought of the nation or of the world to be controlled by ideas which,
by the relentless force of logic, prevent Christianity from being
regarded as anything more than a harmless delusion."[8] Of course this
is precisely what has happened. The collective thought of America has
become progressively more humanistic, naturalistic, and relativistic,
with the inevitable consequence that, for all its numerical strength,
evangelical Christianity is regarded as intellectually suspect and culturally irrelevant. As Mark Noll has observed, "The scandal of the
evangelical mind is that there is not much of an evangelical mind."[9]

Evangelism is not enough. What is needed is a total world and life
view, in which the fundamental principles of biblical Christianity are
applied to every area of human life and thought. This has been a characteristic strength of Calvinism—its ability to articulate the importance of Christianity for culture. This strength flows ultimately from
the doctrines of grace, for it is in the sovereignty of grace that the
human heart discovers "its high and holy calling to consecrate every
department of life and every energy at its disposal to the glory of God."
These words come from Abraham Kuyper, who went on to say:
"Wherever man may stand, whatever he may do, to whatever he may
apply his hand, in agriculture, in commerce, and in industry, or his
mind, in the world of art, and science, he is, in whatsoever it may be,
constantly standing before the face of his God, he is employed in the
service of his God, he has strictly to obey his God, and above all, he
has to aim at the glory of his God."[10]

While Reformed theology has implications for each of the areas
that Kuyper mentions, we can do no more here than outline some
basic principles in three representative disciplines: politics, science,
and the arts. Our goal is not to present a full-orbed theology of culture, but to highlight a few of the ways that Calvinism can make a distinctive contribution.

The most fundamental principle in Calvinist political thought is that God is sovereign over the secular state. The God who rules in grace for the church also rules over the state. This is the plain teaching of the New Testament, which demands that "Everyone must submit himself to the governing authorities, for there is no authority except that which God has established. The authorities that exist have been established by God" (Rom. 13:1; cf. Titus 3:1). This divine establishment is true even for a democracy. Here the Puritan theory of government may be taken as representative of Calvinist political thought in general:

> Basic in Puritan political thought is the doctrine of divine sovereignty. It was the sovereign God who created the state and gave to it its powers and functions. The earthly magistrate held his position and exercised his power by a divine decree. He was a minister of God under common grace for the execution of the laws of God among the people at large, for the maintenance of law and order, and for so ruling the state that it would provide an atmosphere favorable for the preaching of the Gospel. He was to so rule that the people of God, the elect, could live individually and collectively a life that is truly Christian. In Puritan political theory the magistrate derived his powers from God and not from the people. Human government was divinely ordained for the realization of the purposes of God in history. His powers did not come from the people, nor was he primarily responsible to them for the stewardship of his office. . . . The rulers and the people were thus subject to the revealed will of God, and the will of the people could never take precedence over the divinely ordained powers and functions of human government.[11]

The state, then, does not derive its mandate from military superiority, hereditary succession, or even the democratic voice of the people, but ultimately from the will and pleasure of God. As Romans teaches, God has given the state "authority" (*exousia*), meaning "delegated power." This power is temporal, granted to the state in order to preserve peace, promote justice, punish crime, and protect its citizens. It should be noted that each of these functions is necessitated by human depravity. Here Calvinism introduces a healthy dose of realism.

Because secular government cannot remove sin, its role is non-redemptive; nevertheless, its purpose is to restrain the corrupting effects of iniquity. As it fulfills this role, the state is an instrument of divine government in the world, bearing the sword as the servant of God (see Rom. 13:4).

God has also given authority to the church. This authority—which is not temporal, but spiritual—is exercised through the ordained ministry of Word, sacrament, and discipline. The question is, given the fact that God is sovereign over both the church and the state, what is the proper relationship between them? History shows that various arrangements have been attempted. In the days when the Roman Empire persecuted the first Christians, the state obviously was against the church. However, when Constantine converted to Christianity early in the fourth century, he laid the foundations of Christendom and brought the church under the aegis of the state. The situation was nearly reversed by the popes of the high Middle Ages, who sought to bring the state under ecclesiastical control.

The Calvinist view, which bears some similarity to Martin Luther's doctrine of the two kingdoms, insists that the church and the state stand side by side, each exercising divine authority within its respective realm of responsibility. The state rules by law; its authority is temporal and coercive. The church trains by the gospel; its authority is spiritual and non-coercive. The church cannot perform the duties of the state; nor should the state claim the rights of the church. And neither has the right to usurp the powers and prerogatives of the other. Kuyper called this principle "sovereignty in the spheres of life," by which he meant that each area of human life has its own God-given responsibilities and divinely ordained limitations. Political leaders have a divine right to govern, but only within the sphere that God has designated for them. Likewise, pastors and elders have a right to spiritual government within the community of God's people—a right not granted by the state but divinely ordained, and therefore inviolable.

The Reformed theory of government has a noble history. It exercised a formative role in the development of constitutional law and representative democracy in the United States of America. By insisting on the freedom of the church (and on the right of resistance when that freedom was restricted), it also contributed the rise of religious liberty. But what might Calvinism contribute to evangelical politics today?

First, the Calvinist theory of government demands a high degree of respect for political office. Calvin himself wrote: "The first duty of subjects towards magistrates is to think most honorably of their office";[12] and "We must be very careful not to despise or violate that authority of magistrates, full of venerable majesty, which God has established by the weightiest decrees, even though it may reside with the most unworthy men."[13] In other words, honor should be given to political office even when the one who holds it is personally disreputable. This perspective, which in recent decades has been noticeably absent from American political discourse, stems from the Reformed belief that God is sovereign over the state.

Calvinism also helps to remind the church of the spirituality of its mission. On questions of moral or spiritual concern, the church may seek to persuade politicians to recognize their God-given duties. Individual Christians also have the right to participate in the political process, and even to hold political office, albeit not as representatives of the church. However, any quest for political power is beyond the scope of the church's God-given authority. Calvinism thus reminds evangelicalism that only God—not the church—is sovereign over secular government. The church is called to prayer and patient longing for the day when it will finally be acknowledged that, in the words of the Puritan Richard Barnard, "The ultimate and supreme ends of government are the same with the last end of all creatures, and all their actions: that God in all things may be glorified."[14]

SCIENCE

If any area of contemporary culture has become as thoroughly secularized as political government, it is the study of science. Science—not simply as a method, but as a worldview—has become a dominant perspective in Western civilization. Its reigning philosophy has been identified as naturalism, but it could also be termed *scientism*. It is the view that all of reality can be reduced to merely scientific explanations, that nature is "all there is."[15] The universe is made up of molecules in motion, and nothing more. One common manifestation of this perspective is evolutionism (again, not simply as a theory of biological change but as a comprehensive worldview), with its belief that "the human species was not designed, has no purpose, and is the product of mere mechanical mechanisms."[16]

Because it leaves God out of the equation, naturalism has proven thoroughly unequipped to deal with the ethical dilemmas scientists now face: euthanasia, cloning, stem cell research, partial-birth abortion, gene therapy, global warming—the list goes on and on. Although scientists are able to make new discoveries and develop new techniques, they are unable to provide guidance for the moral questions their work continually raises. Our collective difficulty in coming to a consensus on these conundrums reflects not only deep spiritual confusion but also a fundamental misunderstanding of the nature of science, which is not an autonomous enterprise but is governed by the mind and will of God

The proper study of science begins with God's sovereignty, specifically with his rule over creation: "In the beginning God created the heavens and the earth" (Gen. 1:1). "In the beginning was the Word, and the Word was with God, and the Word was God. He was with God in the beginning. Through him all things were made; without him nothing was made that has been made" (John 1:1-3). The universe is the product of intelligent, personal design, and thus the first principle for a properly Calvinist approach to science is the most basic of all natural principles: God made all things, and thus there is an absolute distinction between the Creator and his creation.

Science can never be divorced from theology, because creation itself is an expression of God's sovereign will. As the Belgic Confession (1561) states, nature is "before our eyes as a most beautiful book in which all created things, whether great or small, are as letters showing the invisible things of God to us." Similarly, Calvin viewed the created order as a "theater of the glory of God." He wrote:

> In order that no one might be excluded from the means of obtaining happiness, God has been pleased, not only to place

in our minds the seeds of religion of which we have already spoken, but to make known his perfection in the whole structure of the universe, and daily place himself in our view, in such a manner that we cannot open our eyes without being compelled to observe him. . . . To prove his remarkable wisdom, both the heavens and the earth present us with countless proofs—not just those more advanced proofs which astronomy, medicine and all the other natural sciences are designed to illustrate, but proofs which force themselves on the attention of the most illiterate peasant, who cannot open his eyes without seeing them.[17]

These proofs can be suppressed, of course, but inevitably they impress themselves upon the conscience. "For since the creation of the world God's invisible qualities—his eternal power and divine nature—have been clearly seen, being understood from what has been made, so that men are without excuse" (Rom. 1:20). To know creation is to know God, and to know God is to know that everything in his creation is open to investigation. The Christian dedication to science is grounded in the knowledge that we are living in our Father's world. This world is neither divine (as some Eastern religions would have it) nor despicable (as the pagans thought), but derives its worth from its display of God's handiwork. If nature were divine, science would be sacrilege; if it were despicable, science could be dismissed. But the Christian believes that nature is created by God, and therefore knows that scientific investigation can give glory to the Creator.

Having begun with the doctrine of creation, the Calvinist approach to science then moves on to the doctrine of providence. God did not create the world only to let it run down; he also continues to sustain it. This, too, is a manifestation of his divine sovereignty. By his almighty power, and by the wisdom of his rule, God constantly superintends his vast universe, "sustaining all things by his powerful word" (Heb. 1:3). Thus, as R. C. Sproul has observed, there is not so much as "one maverick molecule" in the entire cosmos.[18] All of creation remains under God's governance. In his providence, and by his design, everything in the cosmos continues to obey the fundamental laws of creation.

It is the orderliness of the cosmos that makes scientific investigation possible. Here there is a close connection between the doctrines of grace and a Reformed theology of culture. In his famous lectures on Calvinism, Abraham Kuyper identified "the Calvinistic dogma of predestination as the strongest motive . . . for the cultivation of science." The reason is that predestination affirms a universal principle of governance, without which scientific investigation is rendered impossible. The decrees of God, Kuyper proceeded to argue, provide "the certainty that the existence and course of all things, *i.e.*, of the entire cosmos, instead of being a plaything of caprice and chance, obeys law and order, and that there exists a firm will which carries out its designs both in nature and in history." The whole development of science requires stability and regularity. It presupposes that the cosmos is not subject to the vagaries of chance, but "exists and develops from one principle, according to a firm order, aiming at one fixed plan." Science also presupposes the intelligibility of the cosmos, that humans are rational beings who are able to understand the things that God has made. Kuyper thus concluded that "Faith in such an *unity, stability* and *order* of things, personally, as predestination, cosmically, as the counsel of God's decree, could not but awaken as with a loud voice, and vigorously foster love for science."[19]

To an extent, Kuyper's claim that Calvinism provides the logical basis for scientific investigation can be supported from history. The brilliant achievements of the seventeenth century were encouraged by the Reformed belief in an orderly creation. Among the scientists who took their cue from Calvinism was Francis Bacon, the father of the scientific method. Bacon simply took the inductive approach that Calvin used in his investigation of Scripture and applied it to the facts of nature. The point here is not that Bacon or other leading scientists were Christians, although as we saw in chapter 2, many of them were. Rather, the point is that the Reformed worldview opened up the possibility of scientific advance.

There is one further doctrine that has implications for the study of science, and that is the doctrine of common grace. On the one hand, Calvinism has a healthy respect for human depravity, which includes recognizing that sin has a corrupting influence on the human intellect. There is a difference—even an antithesis—between regenerate and unregenerate thought that extends across the entire domain of the sciences. Depending on the science, this difference is more or less obvious—more obvious in social sciences like psychology and anthropology, less obvious in pure sciences like physics or mathematics. But in every scientific discipline, there is a common body of knowledge that is shared by believers and nonbelievers alike. This is the product of common grace, which includes both the restraint that God exercises on the corrupting influence of sin and the favor he shows to humanity in general. Even the secular mind is capable of grasping and expressing part of the truth. The doctrine of God's common grace is a uniquely Calvinist contribution to theology, a contribution that arises from the belief that God is sovereign over all of human life and thought. It contributes to scientific investigation by preventing creation from being overthrown by depravity. Culture is not inherently evil; it is a perverted good. The Fall notwithstanding, the creation is still under God's sovereign rule, and by his common grace the pursuit of knowledge—including scientific knowledge—is preserved.

Common grace is not saving grace. Nevertheless, it has a gracious role to play in the consummation of salvation by preserving creation until the coming of redemption. God has intervened in human history with a view to the reclamation of the cosmos, and now "the creation waits in eager expectation for the sons of God to be revealed. For the creation was subjected to frustration, not by its own choice, but by the will of the one who subjected it, in hope that the creation itself will be liberated from its bondage to decay and brought into the glorious freedom of the children of God" (Rom. 8:19-21). Part of the dignity and value of creation—and thus part of the legitimacy for the study of science—lies in this promise of redemption. At the same time that it looks back to creation, Calvinistic science also looks forward to redemption, seeking to reclaim natural investigation for the glory of God. Francis Bacon wrote, "Man by the Fall fell at the same time from his state of innocence and from his dominion over nature. Both of these losses, however, can even in this life be in some part repaired; the former by religion and faith, the latter by the arts and sciences."[20]

THE ARTS

For our last area of investigation we move from the world of fact to
the realm of the imagination, where, as Francis Schaeffer said, the
Christian "should fly beyond the stars." Sadly, this has not always been
the case. Schaeffer himself admitted that, "As evangelical Christians
we have tended to relegate art to the very fringe of life."[21]

Calvinism can help to rectify this unfortunate situation, but it
must be admitted from the outset that Reformed theology has not
always been congenial to the arts. There are several reasons for this.
One is that Calvinism is iconoclastic; that is, it opposes the use of art
as an object of religious worship. Since most Catholic art was iconic
in its tendency, the Reformers not only removed most sacred art from
the church but were also suspicious of its secular use outside the
church. They rightly resisted the tendency of artistry to become idol-
atry. In principle, however, the Reformation was not opposed to the
use of art but only to its abuse. Thus there are some notable exceptions to the apparent prejudice against the arts. The music of Johann
Sebastian Bach is an obvious example, as are the poetry of John
Milton and many of the landscapes painted by the Dutch Masters.

Scripture teaches that although it is wrong to worship art, it is not
wrong to make art. The Bible itself is full of artistry. Rather obviously,
it contains all kinds of literature: history, poetry, prophecy, allegory,
tragedy, psalmody . . . even comedy. There is also visual art in the Bible.
The tabernacle and the temple were filled with *objets d'art*—works that
fell into all three major categories of visual art: abstraction, symbolism,
and representation. Although many of these objects had a sacred
function, their decorations were non-utilitarian. For example, in
2 Chronicles 3:6 we read that Solomon "garnished the house with precious stones *for beauty*" (KJV, emphasis added). Then there is all the
music and the dancing, from the Song of Moses and Miriam (Exodus
15) to David's triumphant dance in Jerusalem (2 Sam. 6:14-16). "Speak
to one another with psalms, hymns and spiritual songs," the Scripture
says. "Sing and make music in your heart to the Lord" (Eph. 5:19).

Beyond providing some notable examples of artistic expression,
the Bible contains the requisite theological principles for constructing

a Christian philosophy of art. The Calvinist aesthetic begins with the doctrine of creation. God is the Creator—that is to say, the Artist. In creating the world, he performed the essentially artistic task of giving form to what was formless. And when God saw what he had formed, he rendered the world's first aesthetic judgment, declaring that everything he had made was very good. There is an essential goodness to creation, which is not only functional but also beautiful—an echo of the transcendent beauty of God. All art finds its standards within the structure of this created reality. Specifically Christian art also finds its joy in this structure. The apostle Paul wrote, "Whatever is true, whatever is noble, whatever is right, whatever is pure, whatever is lovely, whatever is admirable—if anything is excellent or praiseworthy—think about such things" (Phil. 4:8). Although this verse has much wider implications, at the very least it outlines a set of ethical and aesthetic norms for art and the artist. Paul's list assumes that these things—truth, nobility, purity, and loveliness—are present in the world that God has made. Knowing that such things are present, and believing in the essential goodness of creation, Christian art is doxological: it presents beauty to the praise and celebration of God.

The doctrine of creation includes the truth that human beings are made in the image of God (Gen. 1:27). This has at least two significant implications for Christian art. One is that it legitimizes human creativity. If God is our Maker, and if we ourselves are made in his image, then we must also be makers. As Calvin said, "All the arts come from God and are to be respected as divine inventions."[22] We create because God is the Creator; we are artists because he is the Artist. And since we bear the image of God, we are capable not only of making something beautiful but also of delighting in it. Abraham Kuyper claimed that, "The world of sounds, the world of forms, the world of tints, and the world of poetic ideas, can have no other source than God; and it is our privilege as bearers of His image, to have a perception of this beautiful world, artistically to reproduce, and humanly to enjoy it."[23]

A second implication of the divine image is that the artist can celebrate the beauty and dignity of humanity, not as an end in itself but for the glory of God. Human beings have value because they are made in the image of God, and thus their experiences and aspirations are important subjects for Christian art. Here Kuyper sees a connection with the doctrines of grace, specifically with the doctrine of election:

> If a common man, to whom the world pays no special attention, is valued and even chosen by God as one of his elect, this must lead the artist also to find a motive for his artistic studies in what is common and of every-day occurrence, to pay attention to the emotions and the issues of the human heart in it. . . . Thus far the artist had only traced upon his canvas the idealized figures of prophets and apostles, of saints and priests; now, however, when he saw how God had chosen the porter and the wage-earner for Himself, he found interest not only in the head, the figure and the entire personality of the man of the people, but began to reproduce the human expression of every rank and station.[24]

Of course, human beings are also fallen, and this, too, has important implications for art and the artist. The totality of our depravity makes sin an important subject for art. At the same time, it perverts the arts from their original purpose, and this prevents us from embracing them uncritically. The doctrine of creation teaches that by God's common grace, even non-Christian artists can represent virtue, beauty, and truth. Yet their work also contains much that is immoral, ugly, and dishonest. This is especially the case with postmodern art, which if it is true at all, is true only to the unhappiness, alienation, and absurdity of life without God.

The Calvinist approach to human depravity is more hopeful and thus ultimately more truthful. The doctrines of grace explain life's ugliness—it is the result of sin—and also show that there is a way out. This enables the artist to present evil as evil while at the same time believing that beauty is truly beautiful. When truly Christian art portrays fallen humanity, it always does so with a tragic sensibility, as in the paintings of Rembrandt. There is an acknowledgment not only of what we are in our sin but also of what we were when God made us: creatures fashioned in God's image. Better still, there is a sense of what we can become: "God's workmanship, created in Christ Jesus" (Eph. 2:10). The Calvinist aesthetic is redemptive, and this is the highest purpose of art. According to Hans Rookmaaker, Reformed teaching about grace resolves

> the very practical problem of how we are to live in a world that is full of sin and ungodliness. Where things are loving, good, right and true, where things are according to God's law and His will for creation, there is no problem. The Christian will appreciate and actively enjoy and enter into all the good things God has made. But where they have been spoilt or warped by sin, then the Christian must show by his life, his words, his action, his creativity what God really intended them to be. He has been made new in Christ, been given a new quality of life which is in harmony with God's original intention for man. He has been given the power of God Himself by the Holy Spirit, who will help him to work out his new life into the world around him.[25]

Rookmaaker does not mean that art should be used simply as a vehicle for evangelism. Still less does he mean that Christian art ought to be sentimental (as so much evangelical art has been), for sentimentality is dishonest to the tragic implications of sin. What he does mean is that Christian art stands against meaningless despair. Art is always an interpretation of reality, and the Christian should interpret reality in its total aspect, including the hope of redemption in Christ. Thus art has the dual function of reminding us of the lost beauties of paradise and awakening our desire for the glory of the new heavens and the new earth.

In his wonderful little book on *Art and the Bible,* Francis Schaeffer describes a mural in the art museum at Neuchatel, painted by the Swiss artist Paul Robert. Schaeffer writes:

> In the background of this mural he pictured Neuchatel, the lake on which it is situated and even the art museum which contains the mural. In the foreground near the bottom is a great dragon wounded to the death. Underneath the dragon is the vile and the ugly—the pornographic and the rebellious. Near the top Jesus is seen coming in the sky with his endless hosts. On the left side is a beautiful stairway, and on the stairway are young

and beautiful men and women carrying the symbols of the various forms of art—architecture, music and so forth. And as they are carrying them up and away from the dragon to present them to Christ, Christ is coming down to accept them.[26]

The mural represents the redemption of the arts, including the triumph of beauty over ugliness. Schaeffer went on to observe that this future reality should shape the present, for "if these things are to be carried up to the praise of God and the Lordship of Christ at the Second Coming, then we should be offering them to God now."[27] Where Calvinism is at work, the arts are to flourish, not for art's sake but for God's sake. Then the gift will fully achieve the purpose of the Giver. Jonathan Edwards wrote: "For as God is infinitely the greatest Being, so he is allowed to be infinitely the most beautiful and excellent: and all the beauty to be found throughout the whole creation, is but the reflection of the diffused beams of that Being who hath an infinite fullness of brightness and glory; God . . . is the foundation and fountain of all being and all beauty."[28]

A GLORIOUS FUTURE?

When Abraham Kuyper addressed the faculty and students of Princeton Seminary on the subject of Calvinism, he closed on an optimistic note. The year was 1898. While not denying the many godless forces then at work in Western culture, and while admitting that God's sovereignty was routinely flouted, Kuyper nevertheless believed that for Reformed theology, the future was bright. It is time, he said, to "broaden our spiritual horizon and recognize that Jesus as King has sovereignty over the totality of human culture. Once that is realized, it becomes inevitable that both our spiritual development unto eternal life and our general cultural development, that has led to such an amazing increase in our knowledge and control over nature, are placed under his rule." Calvinism, he went on to claim, has still "a blessing to bring and a bright hope to unveil for the future."[29]

One suspects that by the time of his death in 1920, Kuyper was somewhat less sanguine, for by then the world had witnessed the horrors of global warfare. Nor is there much reason for optimism at present. The twentieth century brought a dark and deadly close to the millennium. Near the century's end another Dutch Calvinist, Hans Rookmaaker, proclaimed the death of a culture. "If any confirmation is needed," he suggested, "go to the films, read the books of today, walk round a modern art gallery, listen to the music of our times—and hear, see, open your eyes and ears to the cries of despair, the cursing, the collapse of this world . . . and see your Lord coming with judgment."[30] In the areas of culture we have mentioned in this chapter (politics, science, and art), there is now a prevailing spirit of hopelessness and godlessness that is thoroughly at odds with the world-affirming, God-glorifying theology of Calvinism.

What, then, of the future? What will it hold for Calvinism, and thus also for evangelicalism, if our thesis is correct that the latter cannot stand without the former? In America, orthodox Christianity is becoming increasingly "counter-cultural." This is especially true of Calvinism, with its inherent suspicion of human autonomy and supreme confidence in divine sovereignty. All indications are that the church—including the Reformed churches—will continue to decline in its integrity and influence. While this trend is discouraging in itself, the coming darkness may give the church an unprecedented opportunity to shine with the light of Jesus Christ, who has promised that against his church the gates of hell cannot prevail (Matt. 16:18). This is the promise of the sovereign God, whose purpose will stand (Isa. 46:10), and who has called us to live for his glory in the church and the culture.

Our ability to fulfill this glorious calling will depend in large measure on our response to the doctrines of grace. Perhaps the best way to end this book, then, is with the question that the apostle Paul posed at the end of Romans 8: "What, then, shall we say in response to this?" (v. 31). What Paul meant by "this" was the doctrines of grace: election, calling, redemption, and perseverance unto glorification. These gracious doctrines always demand a response, so Paul posed the question, "How shall we respond?"

Paul phrased his question in the plural ("What shall *we* say?"), but it can also be posed in the singular: "What do *you* say in response to this? What is *your* response?" This question separates faith from unbelief. Ask it of a person who is not a Christian, and there will be one of two responses. Either the person will be utterly indifferent to the question and to the doctrines that lie behind it, or the person will be hostile: "Who are you to think that God has shown such special favor to you? Why would he send his Son to die for you and then promise to preserve you through all the problems of this life and take you to heaven? What amazing arrogance!" Sooner or later, anyone who tries to share the gospel of grace with unbelievers will meet similar responses.

But what about Christians? Their response is very different. They rejoice in what God has done for them. Admittedly, some may be confused by the doctrines of grace, or intimidated by them. Some may be afraid to speak very strongly about unconditional election, particular redemption, efficacious grace, or eternal security. "Won't these doctrines cause people to grow careless in their faith?" they wonder. Yet despite these apprehensions, the hearts of believers warm to the grace that these truths express because they know that God's love is a great love. They know that his love is the very foundation of our salvation and that, because his love is divine, all who are Christians can know that his love will never shake, weaken, vary, fluctuate, or change. On the contrary, believers know that the love of God in Christ is the greatest reality in the universe—the strongest, steadiest, and firmest, the most unbending, solid, constant, and dependable thing of all.

So the question remains: "What do you say to these things?" Do they strike a harmonious note in your soul? If so, it is proof that God has been at work in your life, bringing you out of darkness and into his marvelous light. However, if these doctrines do not seem appealing to you—if they do not seem true, or if you can regard them with indifference—it is worth asking whether you know the Lord Jesus Christ in a saving way. For the doctrines of grace present the gospel of the fixed love of God in Jesus Christ, affirming that "While we were still sinners, Christ died for us" (Rom. 5:8). The person who believes this great truth, and who seeks to live by it, has been captivated by the sovereignty of grace. Like the Calvinist described by B. B. Warfield, "He has caught sight of the ineffable Vision, and he will not let it fade for a moment from his eyes—God in nature, God in history, God in grace. Everywhere he sees God in His mighty stepping, everywhere he feels the working of his mighty arm, the throbbing of His mighty heart."[31]

Notes

Chapter 1: Why Evangelicalism Needs Calvinism

1. B. B. Warfield, quoted in Arthur C. Custance, *The Sovereignty of Grace* (Phillipsburg, N.J.: Presbyterian and Reformed, 1979), 83-84.

2. James Montgomery Boice, *Whatever Happened to the Gospel of Grace? Recovering the Doctrines That Shook the World* (Wheaton, Ill.: Crossway, 2001).

3. Larry Eskridge and Mark A. Noll, eds., *More Money, More Ministry: Money and Evangelicalism in Recent North American History* (Grand Rapids, Mich.: Eerdmans, 2000).

4. The complete text of "The Cambridge Declaration" is published in *Here We Stand: A Call from Confessing Evangelicals*, edited by James Montgomery Boice and Benjamin E. Sasse (Grand Rapids, Mich.: Baker, 1996), 14-20. It is also available from the Alliance of Confessing Evangelicals at www.AllianceNet.org.

5. J. I. Packer, *Evangelism and the Sovereignty of God* (Downers Grove, Ill.: InterVarsity, 1961), 40.

6. Charles H. Spurgeon, quoted by J. I. Packer in his "Introductory Essay" to John Owen, *The Death of Death in the Death of Christ* (London: Banner of Truth, 1959), 10.

7. "The Five Arminian Articles," in *The Creeds of Christendom*, 3 vols., 6th edn., ed. Philip Schaff, rev. David S. Schaff (1931; repr. Grand Rapids, Mich.: Baker, 1983), 3:545-59.

8. Roger Nicole, "Arminianism," *Baker's Dictionary of Theology*, ed. Everett F. Harrison (Grand Rapids, Mich.: Baker, 1960), 64.

9. David N. Steele and Curtis C. Thomas, *The Five Points of Calvinism Defined, Defended, Documented* (Phillipsburg, N.J.: Presbyterian and Reformed, 1963), 19.

10. B. B. Warfield, "A Review of Studies in Theology," in *Selected Shorter Writings of Benjamin B. Warfield, II*, ed. John E. Meeter (Nutley, N.J.: Presbyterian and Reformed, 1973), 316.

11. James Boice had hoped to help remedy this deficiency by writing a book on the attributes of God entitled *Whatever Happened to the God of Grace?* Two of the best books on this subject are Herman Bavinck's *The Doctrine of God*, trans. William Hendricksen (Edinburgh: Banner of Truth, 1977), and Arthur W. Pink's *The Attributes of God* (Grand Rapids, Mich.: Baker, 1961). For a popular-level introduction to the subject, see Philip Graham Ryken, *Discovering God in Stories from the Bible* (Wheaton, Ill.: Crossway, 1999).

12. Thomas R. Schreiner and Bruce A. Ware, eds., *Still Sovereign: Contemporary Perspectives on Election, Foreknowledge, and Grace* (Grand Rapids, Mich.: Baker, 2000), 11.

13. This argument is carefully worked out by Packer in his "Introductory Essay" to Owen's *Death of Death*, 4-5.

14. Charles Simeon, Preface to *Horae Homileticae*, quoted in Packer, *Evangelism and the Sovereignty of God*, 13-14.

15. Arthur C. Custance, *The Sovereignty of Grace* (Phillipsburg, N.J.: Presbyterian and Reformed, 1979), 363, 364.

Chapter 2: What Calvinism Does in History

1. John Calvin, *Institutes of the Christian Religion*, ed. John T. McNeill, trans. Ford Lewis Battles, 2 vols., Library of Christian Classics, 20-21 (Philadelphia: Westminster, 1960), III.XXI.vii.

2. Alister E. McGrath, *Reformation Thought: An Introduction*, 2nd edn. (Oxford: Blackwell, 1993), 217.

3. Marcellus Kik, *Church and State: The Story of Two Kingdoms* (New York: Thomas Nelson,

1963), 83. See also W. Fred Graham, *Constructive Revolutionary: John Calvin and His Socio-Economic Impact* (East Lansing: Michigan State University Press, 1989).

4. John Knox, quoted in Hans J. Hillerbrand, *The World of the Reformation* (1973; repr. Grand Rapids, Mich.: Baker, 1981), 75.

5. Richard Baxter, *Reliquiae Baxterianae* (London, 1696), 154.

6. Quoted in Horton Davies, *The Worship of the English Puritans* (1948; repr. Morgan, Pa.: Soli Deo Gloria, 1997), 9-10.

7. Cotton Mather, quoted in Leland Ryken, *Worldly Saints: The Puritans as They Really Were* (Grand Rapids, Mich.: Zondervan, 1986), 25.

8. Benjamin Wadsworth, *The Well-Ordered Family*, quoted in ibid., 74.

9. Thomas Becon, *Book of Matrimony*, quoted in ibid., 49.

10. Thomas Shepard, quoted in ibid., 168.

11. Quoted in ibid., 161.

12. Cotton Mather, *Christian Calling*, quoted in ibid., 26.

13. W. K. Jordan, *Philanthropy in England, 1480–1660* (London: Allen and Unwin, 1959), 151.

14. Paul Seaver, *The Puritan Lectureships: The Politics of Religious Dissent, 1560–1662* (Stanford, Calif.: Stanford University Press, 1970), 44.

15. C. S. Lewis, *Studies in Medieval and Renaissance Literature* (Cambridge: Cambridge University Press, 1966), 121.

16. John Cotton, *Christian Calling*, quoted in Ryken, *Worldly Saints*, 208.

17. Jonathan Edwards, *A History of the Work of Redemption* (1774), quoted in *The Great Awakening*, ed. Alan Heimert and Perry Miller (Indianapolis: Bobbs-Merrill, 1967), 21.

18. Samuel Davies, *Sermons on Important Subjects*, vol. 4 (London, 1824), 49-50.

19. Jonathan Edwards, "On the Great Religious Revival," in *The Annals of America; Volume 1, 1493–1754: Discovering a New World* (Chicago: Encyclopaedia Britannica, 1976), 458-463.

20. Richard Hofstadter, *America at 1750: A Social Portrait* (New York: Random House, 1973).

21. Abraham Kuyper, *Near unto God*, quoted in James Edward McGoldrick, *God's Renaissance Man: The Life and Work of Abraham Kuyper* (Darlington, UK: Evangelical Press, 2000), 158.

22. It should be noted that other Calvinists—J. Gresham Machen is a notable example— would consider Kuyper's quest for the Reformation of a political nation to be a threat to the true spirituality of the church.

23. Abraham Kuyper, *Confidentie* (Amsterdam: Hoveker and Zoon, 1873).

24. Abraham Kuyper, *Calvinism: Six Stone Foundation Lectures* (Grand Rapids, Mich.: Eerdmans, 1943), 24, 46.

25. Abraham Kuyper, "Calvinism and Confessional Revision," *Presbyterian and Reformed Review*, vol. 2 (1891), 378-379.

26. Abraham Kuyper, *Sovereiniteit in Eigen Kring* (Amsterdam: J. H. Kruyt, 1880), 35.

27. Richard Greenham, *Of the Good Education of Children*, quoted in Ryken, *Worldly Saints*, 180.

28. John T. McNeill, *The History and Character of Calvinism* (Oxford: Oxford University Press, 1954), 383-385.

29. William Rogers, quoted in Iain H. Murray, *Revival and Revivalism: The Making and Marring of American Evangelicalism, 1750–1858* (Edinburgh: Banner of Truth, 1994), 129.

30. This history has been traced by Iain H. Murray in *Revival and Revivalism*. But see also Mark A. Noll's critique in "How We Remember Revivals," *Christianity Today* (April 24, 1995), 31, 34.

31. Gardiner Spring, *Personal Reminiscences of the Life and Times of Gardiner Spring*, vol. 1 (New York, 1866), 218.

32. Also note the title of Edwards's account of the revivals at Northampton: *A Faithful Narrative of the Surprising Work of God* (1737).

33. Charles Grandison Finney, *Memoirs of Rev. Charles G. Finney, Written by Himself*, ed. J. H. Fairchild (New York: Revell, 1903), 46 (cf. 177ff.).

34. Ibid., 189.
35. See George M. Marsden, *Reforming Fundamentalism: Fuller Seminary and the New Evangelicalism* (Grand Rapids, Mich.: Eerdmans, 1987).
36. This issue is explored at somewhat greater length in Philip Graham Ryken, *Is Jesus the Only Way?* (Wheaton, Ill.: Crossway, 1999).
37. See Clark Pinnock, *A Wideness in God's Mercy: The Finality of Jesus Christ in a World of Religions* (Grand Rapids, Mich.: Zondervan, 1992).
38. For a useful critique of the new perspective on Paul, see Richard B. Gaffin, Jr., "Paul the Theologian," *Westminster Theological Journal*, vol. 62, no. 1 (Spring 2000), 121-141. See also Mark A. Seifrid, *Christ Our Righteousness: Paul's Theology of Justification,* New Studies in Biblical Theology (Downers Grove, Ill.: InterVarsity, 2000).
39. For a thorough discussion of Evangelical-Catholic rapprochement, see R. C. Sproul, *Faith Alone: The Evangelical Doctrine of Justification* (Grand Rapids, Mich.: Baker, 1995), and *Getting the Gospel Right: The Tie That Binds Evangelicals Together* (Grand Rapids, Mich.: Baker, 1999).
40. Gregory A. Boyd, *God of the Possible: A Biblical Introduction to the Open View of God* (Grand Rapids, Mich.: Baker, 2000), 8, 94. See also Clark Pinnock, *The Openness of God* (Downers Grove, Ill.: InterVarsity, 1994).
41. The doctrinal errors of open theism are exposed in John M. Frame, *No Other God: A Response to Open Theism* (Phillipsburg, N.J.: Presbyterian and Reformed, 2001), and Bruce A. Ware, *God's Lesser Glory: The Diminished God of Open Theism* (Wheaton, Ill.: Crossway, 2000).

Chapter 3: Radical Depravity

1. Arthur C. Custance, *The Sovereignty of Grace* (Phillipsburg, N.J.: Presbyterian and Reformed, 1979), 91.
2. Karl Menninger, *Whatever Became of Sin?* (New York: Bantam, 1978). He argues: "There are no substitutes for words like 'sin' and 'grace'" (54).
3. Loraine Boettner, *The Reformed Doctrine of Predestination* (Philadelphia: Presbyterian and Reformed, 1963), 61.
4. Abraham Kuyper, *The Work of the Holy Spirit,* trans. Henri De Vries (1900; repr. Grand Rapids, Mich.: Eerdmans, 1979), 338.
5. Robert Brow, *Religion: Origins and Ideas* (Downers Grove, Ill.: InterVarsity, 1966).
6. The subsequent history of Augustine's thinking on this subject is traced in Philip Graham Ryken, *Thomas Boston as Preacher of the Fourfold State,* Rutherford Studies in Historical Theology (Carlisle, UK: Paternoster, 1999), 67-76.
7. Martin Luther, *The Bondage of the Will,* trans. J. I. Packer and O. R. Johnston (Westwood, N.J.: Revell, 1957), 319.
8. Ibid., 102.
9. Jonathan Edwards, "A Careful and Strict Inquiry into the Prevailing Notions of the Freedom of the Will," *The Works of Jonathan Edwards,* vol. 1, rev. Edward Hickman with a memoir by Sereno E. Dwight (Edinburgh: Banner of Truth, 1976), 3-93.
10. Boettner, *Reformed Doctrine of Predestination,* 62.
11. Benjamin Morgan Palmer, quoted in T. C. Johnson, *The Life and Letters of B. M. Palmer* (1906), quoted in Iain Murray, *Revival and Revivalism: The Making and Marring of American Evangelicalism, 1750–1858* (Edinburgh: Banner of Truth, 1994), 373-374.

Chapter 4: Unconditional Election

1. Loraine Boettner, *The Reformed Doctrine of Predestination* (Philadelphia: Presbyterian and Reformed, 1963), 71.
2. Ibid., 90.
3. John Calvin, *Sermons on Election and Reprobation* (Audubon, N.J.: Old Paths, 1996), 39. Original edition 1579.
4. Boettner, *Reformed Doctrine of Predestination,* 99.
5. On the other hand, *The Living Bible* betrays its Arminian bias by the unjustified paraphrase: "For from the very beginning God decided that those who came to him—and all

along he knew who would—should become like his Son." Happily, the *New Living Translation* has improved this to read, "For God knew his people in advance, and he chose them to become like his Son."

6. Abraham Kuyper, *The Biblical Doctrine of Election,* trans. G. M. Pernis (Grand Rapids, Mich.: Zondervan, 1934), 5.

7. Martin Luther, *The Bondage of the Will,* trans. J. I. Packer and O. R. Johnston (Westwood, N.J.: Revell, 1957), 78.

Chapter 5: Particular Redemption

1. Loraine Boettner, *The Reformed Doctrine of Predestination* (Grand Rapids, Mich.: Eerdmans, 1948), 153.

2. Charles H. Spurgeon, quoted by J. I. Packer in his "Introductory Essay" to John Owen, *The Death of Death in the Death of Christ* (London: Banner of Truth, 1959), 14, note 1.

3. This is what Lewis Sperry Chafer taught. He wrote, "Christ's death does not save either actually or potentially; rather it makes all men saveable" ("For Whom Did Christ Die?" reprinted in *Bibliotheca Sacra,* [October–December 1980], 325).

4. John Murray, *Redemption Accomplished and Applied* (Grand Rapids, Mich.: Eerdmans, 1955), 63-64.

5. John Owen, "The Death of Death in the Death of Christ: A Treatise of the Redemption and Reconciliation That Is in the Blood of Christ," *The Works of John Owen,* vol. 10, ed. William H. Goold, (London: Banner of Truth, 1967), 173-174.

6. John Owen, "The Death of Death in the Death of Christ," 348.

7. J. I. Packer, *Evangelism and the Sovereignty of God* (Leicester, UK: InterVarsity, 1961), 68-69.

Chapter 6: Efficacious Grace

1. Martin Luther, *The Bondage of the Will,* trans. and ed. J. I. Packer and O. R. Johnston (Westwood, N.J.: Revell, 1957), 103.

2. John Murray, *Redemption Accomplished and Applied* (Grand Rapids, Mich.: Eerdmans, 1970), 96.

3. Ibid., 88.

4. Donald Grey Barnhouse, *God's Heirs: Exposition of Bible Doctrines, Taking the Epistle to the Romans as a Point of Departure,* vol. 7, *Romans 8:1-39* (Grand Rapids, Mich.: Eerdmans, 1963), 171-172.

5. For a fuller discussion of the order of these steps see Murray, *Redemption Accomplished and Applied,* 79-87. A more popular version of the *ordo salutis* is presented in Philip Graham Ryken, *The Message of Salvation,* The Bible Speaks Today (Leicester, UK: InterVarsity, 2001).

6. John Murray, *The Epistle to the Romans* (Grand Rapids, Mich.: Eerdmans, 1968), 316.

7. Ibid., 318.

8. John Calvin, *Institutes of the Christian Religion,* ed. John T. McNeil, trans. Ford Lewis Battles, 2 vols., Library of Christian Classics, 20-21 (Philadelphia: Westminster, 1960), III.iii.2.

9. Robert L. Dabney, *Lectures in Systematic Theology* (Grand Rapids, Mich.: Zondervan, 1972).

10. Murray, *Redemption Accomplished and Applied,* 148-149.

11. The story is told by Ray C. Stedman, *From Guilt to Glory,* vol. 1, *Hope for the Helpless* (Portland, Ore.: Multnomah, 1978), 302.

Chapter 7: Persevering Grace

1. Loraine Boettner, *The Reformed Doctrine of Predestination* (Philadelphia: Presbyterian and Reformed, 1963), 189.

2. John Calvin, *The Commentaries of John Calvin on the Prophet Hosea,* Calvin's Commentaries, vol. 13 (Grand Rapids, Mich.: Baker, 1999), 83.

3. A. N. Martin, *The Practical Implications of Calvinism* (Edinburgh: Banner of Truth, 1979), 20-21.

4. D. Martyn Lloyd-Jones, *Romans, An Exposition of Chapter 8:17-39, The Final Perseverance of the Saints* (Grand Rapids, Mich.: Zondervan, 1976), 263-366.
5. Ibid., 332.
6. C. S. Lewis, *The Weight of Glory and Other Addresses* (1949; repr. Grand Rapids, Mich.: Eerdmans, 1969), 13.
7. William H. Burleigh, "Trust" (1868).

Chapter 8: The True Calvinist

1. Laurence M. Vance, *The Other Side of Calvinism* (Vance Publications, 1991), viii, 15.
2. B. B. Warfield, *Calvin as a Theologian and Calvinism Today*, quoted in A. N. Martin, *The Practical Implications of Calvinism* (Edinburgh: Banner of Truth, 1979), 4.
3. Martin, *Practical Implications of Calvinism,* 9.
4. John Winthrop, quoted in Leland Ryken, *Worldly Saints: The Puritans as They Really Were* (Grand Rapids, Mich.: Zondervan, 1986), 206-207.
5. Martin, *Practical Implications of Calvinism,* 7.
6. Ibid.
7. Abraham Kuyper, *Calvinism: Six Stone Foundation Lectures* (Grand Rapids, Mich.: Eerdmans, 1943), 69.
8. James Montgomery Boice, "Give Praise to God," in *Hymns for a Modern Reformation* (Philadelphia: Tenth Presbyterian Church, 2000), 9.
9. Martin, *Practical Implications of Calvinism,* 9.
10. Archibald Alexander, quoted in J. W. Alexander, *The Life of Archibald Alexander* (New York: Charles Scribner, 1854), 4.
11. B. B. Warfield, *Calvin and Augustine* (Philadelphia: Presbyterian and Reformed, 1956), 496.
12. J. I. Packer, "Introductory Essay," in John Owen, *The Death of Death in the Death of Christ* (London: Banner of Truth, 1959), 10.
13. B. B. Warfield, *Shorter Writings,* 1:390, quoted in Terry Johnson, *When Grace Comes Home: The Practical Difference That Calvinism Makes* (Fearn, Ross-Shire, UK: Christian Focus, 2000), 170.
14. J. I. Packer, *Evangelism and the Sovereignty of God* (Downers Grove, Ill.: InterVarsity, 1961), 122-123.
15. John Calvin, *The Golden Booklet of the True Christian Life,* trans. Henry J. Van Andel (Grand Rapids, Mich.: Baker, 1952), 13.
16. Thomas Brooks, *Heaven on Earth: A Treatise on Christian Assurance* (1654; repr. Edinburgh: Banner of Truth, 1961), 234.
17. Calvin, *Golden Booklet,* 45.
18. Cited in Iain Murray, *Evangelicalism Divided: The Record of Crucial Change, 1950–2000* (Edinburgh: Banner of Truth, 2000), 262.
19. Henry Martyn, quoted in Eric J. Alexander, "Plea for Revival," *Tenth* (October 1982), 24-32 (30).

Chapter 9: Calvinism at Work

1. Abraham Kuyper, *Calvinism: Six Stone Foundation Lectures* (Grand Rapids, Mich.: Eerdmans, 1943), 69.
2. J. I. Packer, *Evangelism and the Sovereignty of God* (Downers Grove, Ill.: InterVarsity, 1961), 27-29.
3. Ibid., 96-106.
4. Ibid., 105.
5. J. I. Packer develops this argument in his "Introductory Essay" to John Owen, *The Death of Death in the Death of Christ* (London: Banner of Truth, 1959).
6. Packer, *Evangelism and the Sovereignty of God,* 124.
7. See especially Mark A. Noll, *The Scandal of the Evangelical Mind* (Grand Rapids, Mich.: Eerdmans, 1994).

8. J. Gresham Machen, "The Scientific Preparation of the Minister" (address given at Princeton Theological Seminary, September 20, 1912).
9. Noll, *Scandal of the Evangelical Mind*, 3.
10. Kuyper, *Calvinism*, 24, 53.
11. C. Gregg Singer, *A Theological Interpretation of American History* (Phillipsburg, N.J.: Presbyterian and Reformed, 1964), 13-14.
12. John Calvin, *Institutes of the Christian Religion*, ed. John T. McNeill, trans. Ford Lewis Battles, 2 vols., Library of Christian Classics, 20-21 (Philadelphia: Westminster, 1960), IV.xx.xxii.
13. John Calvin, quoted in Keith Randell, *John Calvin and the Later Reformation* (London: Hodder and Stoughton, 1990), 63.
14. Richard Barnard, quoted in Leland Ryken, *Worldly Saints: The Puritans as They Really Were* (Grand Rapids, Mich.: Zondervan, 1986), 174.
15. See the writings of Berkeley law professor Phillip Johnson, especially his *Reason in the Balance: The Case Against Naturalism in Science, Law and Education* (Downers Grove, Ill.: InterVarsity, 1995).
16. Douglas Futuyma, quoted in ibid., 8-9.
17. John Calvin, quoted in Alister E. McGrath, *Reformation Thought: An Introduction*, 2nd edn. (Oxford: Blackwell, 1993), 231.
18. R. C. Sproul, *Chosen by God* (Carol Stream, Ill.: Tyndale, 1994), 27.
19. Kuyper, *Calvinism*, 112-115.
20. Francis Bacon, quoted in Francis A. Schaeffer, *Art and the Bible* (Downers Grove, Ill.: InterVarsity, 1973), 10.
21. Ibid., 5, 7.
22. John Calvin, quoted in Kuyper, *Calvinism*, 153.
23. Ibid., 156-157.
24. Ibid., 166.
25. H. R. Rookmaaker, *Modern Art and the Death of a Culture* (Wheaton, Ill.: Crossway, 1994), 38.
26. Schaeffer, *Art and the Bible*, 30.
27. Ibid., 31.
28. Jonathan Edwards, *The Nature of True Virtue*, quoted in Leland Ryken, *The Liberated Imagination: Thinking Christianly About the Arts*, Wheaton Literary Series (Wheaton, Ill.: Harold Shaw, 1989), 70.
29. Abraham Kuyper, *You Can Do Greater Things than Christ*, trans. Jan H. Boer (Jos, Nigeria: Institute of Church and Society, 1991), 38, 40.
30. Rookmaaker, *Modern Art and the Death of a Culture*, 220.
31. B. B. Warfield, *Calvin and Augustine* (Philadelphia: Presbyterian and Reformed, 1956), 503.

General Index

synergism, 36-38, 158
Synod of Carthage, 82
Synod of Dort, 18, 27, 41, 45

Taylor, N. W., 59
temple, 184, 220
temptation, 168
Tennent, Gilbert, 50
Tennent, William, 50
Tenth International Fellowship, 205
Tenth Presbyterian Church, 141, 203-206
Terah, 95
theodicy, 93, 107-108, 110
theology, 48, 91, 179, 191, 198-199, 216, 219
  of culture, 55-56, 212, 217
Thirty-Nine Articles, 86
Thomas, Curtis, 28
tolerance, 63
total depravity (see also radical depravity), 18
total inability, 59, 71, 85, 87-89, 210
Trinity, 34, 135, 198
"Truly Reformed," 179
truth, 222
TULIP, 18, 31, 113, 135, 180
tutoring, 205
twentieth century, 225
two kingdoms, 214
Tyndale, William, 19

ugliness, 222, 224
unbelief, 103-104, 124, 146, 171-173, 219, 225-226
universal call (see general call)
universal redemption, 115
universalism, 118-119, 121, 124, 130-131
University of Leiden, 54
urban renewal, 57, 203-206
Uriah, 156
Uzziah (king), 181, 184

virgin birth, 55, 61

Wadsworth, Benjamin, 46
Ware, Bruce, 33-34
warfare, 224
Warfield, Benjamin B., 17-18, 24, 32, 61, 180-181, 190-191, 226
wealth, 48
"Weight of Glory, The," 175
Wells, H. G., 69
Wesley, John, 35-36, 52, 209
Westminster Assembly, 45
Westminster Confession of Faith, 31-32, 45, 87, 103, 136, 158
Westminster Larger Catechism, 87
Westminster Shorter Catechism, 44
Westminster Theological Seminary, 179
"Whatever became of sin?" 69
Whatever Happened to the Gospel of Grace? 20-21
Whatever Happened to the Human Race? 204
Whitefield, George, 19, 50, 139, 199, 209
will, 111, 136, 190-192, 198, 207
  bondage of, 60, 79-87, 91
Winthrop, John, 183
wisdom, 77
woe, 185
Word, the, 202, 214
work, 47
World War I, 69
worldliness, 21-22, 186, 196, 203
worldview, 212, 215, 218
worship, 21, 42, 44, 111, 176, 179, 182-183, 202, 204
wrath, 116, 118, 122, 124
Wright, N. T., 63

Yale, 49, 59

zombie, 74
Zwingli, Ulrich, 19

Scripture Index